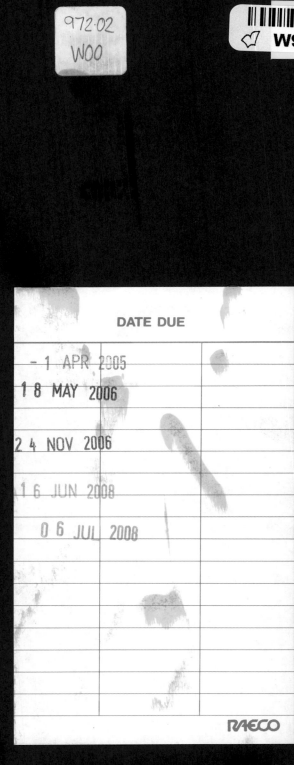

CONQUISTADORS

CONQUISTADORS

MICHAEL WOOD

The age will come in the ripeness of time
When Ocean will loosen the chain of things
And bare new worlds to the storms.
Then a huge country will be revealed
and Thule will no longer be the last land.

SENECA'S *Medea*,
quoted by AUGUSTINE DE ZARATE in
The History of the Discovery and Conquest of Peru, 1555

Illustrations
Page 1: The Spanish fleet disembarks in Mexico; from a sixteenth-century
History of the Conquest of Mexico.
Frontispiece: *The Indian Hunter*, an idealized painting of the New World
by Alexandre-François Desportes (1661–1743).
Page 6: Alvarado and companions besieged by Aztec warriors; from the sixteenth-century Duran Codex.
Page 7: Bust of Cortes in the Hospital of Jesus, Mexico City.
Page 8: Detail of a painting of Francisco Pizarro by Daniel Diaz Vazquez, 1948.
Page 9: Spaniards shipping gold back to Spain; engraving by Théodor de Bry (1528–98).

This book is published to accompany the television series
Conquistadors
produced by MayaVision and first broadcast on BBC2 in 2000
Producer: Rebecca Dobbs • Director: David Wallace

First published in 2000
Reprinted 2000, 2001
© Michael Wood 2000
The moral right of the author has been asserted

ISBN 0 563 55116 X

Published by BBC Worldwide Limited, 80 Wood Lane, London W12 0TT

Commissioning editors: Sheila Ableman and Shirley Patton
Project editor: Martha Caute • Text editor: Barbara Nash
Designer: Linda Blakemore • Picture researcher: Deirdre O'Day
Cartographer: Olive Pearson

Set in Simoncini Garamond by BBC Worldwide
Printed and bound in France by Imprimerie Pollina s.a. - n° L 83313

To
Joaquín García Sánchez
and
David Wallace

CONTENTS

PROLOGUE: 'THE LORD OF THE SNOW STAR'

UP JUST BEFORE 3 A.M., we gulp down several cups of hot coca tea and then each of us carefully packs a ball of coca leaves in the cheek. Outside the ground is white with frost. It is bitterly cold, and we cram on every available layer of clothing. A deep breath, then on with the rucksack. Hieronymo, the jolly horse-handler, has four helpers to carry the heavy gear, the tripod and boxes, though we have cut the shooting kit down to the minimum. I take the rucksack for my cameras, and soon regret it. Any extra weight becomes a struggle.

We start off at 15,000 feet, going up to nearly 17,000 on a steep rocky climb over a treacherous scree of boulders intersected by streams. The first few hundred yards from the camp are lung-bursting: you gasp in the freezing night air every few seconds and never seem to get enough, almost drowning in air. The night is cloudy, but a full moon, just on the wane, watery behind a thin curtain of cloud, helps to light our way. We stop every ten minutes for a rest, and in about an hour reach the foot of the glacier, the sacred ice that the pilgrims call in Quechua, the Inca language, Quoyllur Riti, 'The Lord of the Snow Star'.

Coming up from below the glacier, the huge white mass of ice suddenly looms up under the deep blue night, framed between black crags like a still, pale monster. We stumble the last few yards down a rocky step to the very edge of the ice. Glistening, gently dripping, it almost feels alive. Rows of wax candles have been left under its lip, and little knots of people sit in silence, some praying, some just holding hands. Two women in traditional country dress with round fringed hats and *huipils* (tunics) sit by their candles, murmuring quietly.

Our guide immediately goes down into the trough by the ice edge, touches the ice with his forehead, salutes and embraces it, scattering coca leaves across its surface. Then he gestures with his feathered walking stick, and strokes the ice once more, mouthing a little prayer in Quechua to the *apu*, the spirit of the mountain. It is

Everything that has happened since the marvellous discovery of the Americas has been so extraordinary that the whole story remains quite incredible to anyone who has not experienced it at first hand. Indeed, it seems to overshadow all the deeds of famous people in the past, no matter how heroic, and to silence all talk of other wonders of the world.

•

BARTOLOME DE LAS CASAS *A Short Account of the Destruction of the Indies*, 1542

◀◀ The procession of pilgrims on the glacier Quoyllur Riti, 'The Lord of the Snow Star'.

a magical moment, made all the more poignant by the plaintive sound of pipe, accordion and drum somewhere out in the darkness.

Higher up on the glacier, there is a magnificent view in the pre-dawn light: black jagged peaks, streamers of snow lifting off their tops, while the first hints of dawn soften the deep blue of the night sky. Up the snow slopes, groups of dancers perform their rituals with the bear men in their animal skins and whips. This is the most ancient kind of worship here, pre-Spanish, pre-Inca even.

The light grows, the peaks are touched golden; shining streaks of light spread across the snow in the high ravines. There are scenes of great jollity – brass bands and lilting songs. There is a snow slide on a steep part of the glacier and crowds have gathered, taking turns to whoosh down accompanied by loud whoops and cheers, one man cradling his euphonium. The sky is now an intense dazzling blue and around eight o'clock the sun flashes over the top to roars from the crowd.

Up the glacier, hundreds of tiny dots are visible, people bringing back the most important souvenir: ice hacked out of the ice floe. To one side, lone pilgrims are loading blocks of ice on their backs just as they are depicted on the old Andean drinking cups, and in the pages of the sixteenth-century Andean chronicler Waman Poma. One of them stops and, with a gesture to the surrounding peaks, speaks to us:

These mountains are our apus, our spirits. We are a community from Paucartambo in the Sacred Valley. We come here every year. After we have been up on the ice, we head off on foot to Tayankani along that path up there, to a huaca, a holy rock, up to the west of the valley. We walk till midday tomorrow. This is what our ancestors have always done. These ceremonies are not to do with the Church.

More people had joined us now, and an old man butted in, speaking in Spanish: 'Ours is a true worship, though it is not to do with the Church.' A third man, more educated, spoke:

We are told that when Inca Manco fought the Spanish at the time of the coming of the whites, he said this to the indigenous people: 'Don't forget the rituals of your ancestors…do what you have to in public, but in private keep our old customs and ceremonies close to your hearts.' And this we still do.

It was a theme we would encounter again and again in our journeys through the Americas in the footsteps of the conquistadors.

This book is about events which took place nearly 500 years ago. The Spanish conquest was one of the most cataclysmic events in history, events which, in a couple of generations, overthrew the last high civilizations which had arisen independently on earth; which saw Spanish expeditions endure the most unbelievable hardships to open up lands from Tierra del Fuego to the Carolinas. Few events, if any in history, match these for sheer drama, endurance, and the incredible distances covered. And the conquest is still within living history; its effects are still with us, working themselves out now across the globe.

Here in Peru, as they had done in Mexico, the Spanish conquistadors swept away the indigenous state, the Inca empire, and its state religion, but below the level of the rulers, as we were to discover, history works in mysterious ways, and many beliefs and customs were maintained tenaciously by the ordinary Andean people. And this ceremony on the wild and forbidding slopes of the sacred mountain was one of them.

After the pilgrims had begun their descent, I lingered on the ice, unwilling to let go of such a haunting, splendid scene. History leaves many wounds – some never heal; in time some do. The *Conquista* was at once one of the most significant events in history, and one of the most cruel and devastating. But in history there is no going back – and blame or regret are pointless. All we can do is try to understand. The Inca past was already being idealized in the immediate post-conquest generation, by Peruvian historians such as Waman Poma and Garcilaso Inca. And it still is today. But that past is irrecoverable now. What we see is as much the product of the conquest, and of what has happened in the nearly 500 years since, as it is of that deeper past.

Many times on these journeys I found myself feeling pessimistic about the fate of all these traditional cultures, fighting against the onset of global culture, their encoded identities, built up over millennia, being scrubbed away so rapidly in a generation or two. But events such as the Quoyllur Riti pilgrimage are galvanizing mixes of past and present, Inca and Spanish, and they show that out of the debris of history, new identities are shaped from what is at hand and, in some magical way, these carry on the encoded memories, in societies and civilizations, just as in people. Something gets handed down, almost in the manner of genetics. At the start of the third millennium, the past still lives on in us, forming new worlds out of the debris of the old, and the remorseless and destructive march of history.

As we prepared to go, sunlight flooded the valley, the sound of brass bands echoed around the peaks, and a spindrift of snow floated along the glacier above our heads, swirling coca leaves in the wind, and what looked like the finest sparkling shards of gold. Looking back now, it was a fitting beginning to a series of journeys which would lead us in the footsteps of the conquistadors from Miami Beach to Lake Titicaca, from the deserts of northern Mexico to the snowpeaks of the Andes, and from the forests of the Amazon to the heights of Machu Picchu.

Michael Wood, July 2000

1
CORTES AND MONTEZUMA

AT THE END OF THE HOT AUGUST of 1520 – Monday, the 27th, to be precise – the German artist Albrecht Dürer paid a visit to the royal residence of the Spanish king and Holy Roman emperor, Charles V, in Brussels. Dürer, now aged fifty, and a famous painter, wandered in the delightful garden behind the house, admiring the fountains, the labyrinth and the beast-garden, taking pleasure in the creations of the humanistic civilization of Europe. As it happened, that very day – indeed that very hour – far away in Mexico, Hernan Cortes, in the name of King Charles, was preparing to attack the Mexican town of Tepeaca, to massacre its warriors, to brand and enslave its women, to lance, burn and even feed human beings alive to dogs.

By now Cortes had been campaigning in Mexico for eighteen months. He had already sent the first news of Aztec wonders back to Europe: an account which included a map of the great capital city of Tenochtitlan, its myriad waterways and canals like a grander and more spectacular Venice (as Cortes said, 'the most beautiful thing in the world'). Cortes had also sent treasures and works of art back to Europe from this hitherto unknown civilization. These had now arrived in Brussels and come to the king's house. Dürer was taken inside to see the pieces laid out in several chambers. He recorded his reaction in his diary:

When we saw all those cities and villages built on water; and the other great towns on dry land, and that straight and level causeway leading to Mexico, we were astounded. These great towns and shrines and buildings rising from the water, all made of stone, seemed like an enchanted vision from the tale of Amadis. Indeed some of our soldiers asked whether it was not all a dream. It is not surprising therefore that I should write in this vein. It was all so wonderful that I do not know how to describe this first glimpse of things never heard of, never seen, and never dreamed of before.

•

BERNAL DIAZ DEL CASTILLO
The Conquest of New Spain, c. 1565

I saw the things which have been brought to the King from the new land of gold, a sun all of gold a whole fathom broad, and a moon all of silver of the same size, also two rooms of the armour of the people there, with all manner of wondrous weapons, harness, spears, wonderful shields, extraordinary clothing, beds and all manner of wonderful objects of human use, much better worth seeing than prodigies.

◄◄ An Aztec feather shield on a leather backing: one of the treasures sent by Cortes from Mexico to King Charles V.

These things are all so precious they are valued at 100,000 florins. All the days of my life I have seen nothing that touches my heart so much as these things, for I saw amongst them wonderful works of art, and I marvelled at the subtle ingenia of men in foreign lands. Indeed I cannot express my feelings about what I saw there...

The gold disc (an Aztec calendar?) and the other precious metals have long since been melted down. But a few pieces have survived from what Dürer saw that day: ornate ceremonial spear-throwers crusted with gold, a tiny jade frog, an obsidian blade. Most remarkable of all, the featherwork sent to King Charles can still be seen: shields, fans, standards and cloaks, a mosaic depicting the demon Ahuitzotl; and, even now, nearly 500 years after they were made, although their colour is somewhat faded, the green quetzal plumes and blue macaw feathers, when breathed on, or gently brushed, still fluff out. In their vivacity and strangeness, they conjure up the shock of the new felt by the many during that astonishing time when treasures of the Aztecs and the Maya, or the gold of the Incas, landed in Europe.

'It was a miracle,' said the conquistador Cieza de Leon, 'that these wonderful lands had remained unknown to the rest of the world through all of history, and were saved by God to be discovered in our time...'

The Shock of the New

THE DISCOVERY OF THE NEW WORLD has been called the greatest event in history. It had a profound impact on the imagination as well as on the economies and cultures of the world. The scene Dürer describes epitomizes this collision of worlds: an extraordinary moment when things from an unknown continent came into European Renaissance society.

The conquistadors brought back exotic foods which would change the diet that Europeans had followed since the Stone Age: potatoes, tomatoes, peppers, maize, sweet potatoes, avocados, guavas, pineapples, tobacco and chocolate (a good Aztec word) are just a few of them. They also brought back samples of New World flora and fauna – magnolias from Central America, lupins from the Andes, and dahlias whose quilled petals were hybridized in Aztec gardens. They brought back parrots, macaws and toucans to satisfy the curiosity of the rich.

There was also human freight. Columbus had already shipped bemused Carib Indians back to Europe; now Cortes transported Mexican ball-players and jugglers to perform before the king in Seville. Later, they went to Rome and 'juggled a log with their feet...before a delighted Pope'. In Paris, Amazonian Indians acted out their forest lives in circus shows; a Brazilian chief was presented to Henry VIII, and an Eskimo man and woman, from Baffin Island, impressed Londoners with their dignified bearing and modesty.

Artefacts made by these peoples were coveted by collectors, as they still are. Jade figures, turquoise masks, Aztec sacrificial knives – all found their places in antiquarians' cabinets alongside ancient Greek votive phalli and Roman coins. Elizabeth I's astrologer, John Dee, owned an Aztec obsidian disc and conjured spirits through his 'devil's looking glass'. Such things could thrill, inform, evoke a sense of wonder – and drive men mad. Images of New World Indians appear on Renaissance mausolea, and church pews, in sculptures by Bernini, and paintings by Velasquez. And the idea of the New World informs poems, plays and works of literature as various as Thomas More's *Utopia*, Montaigne's *Essays* and Shakespeare's *The Tempest*, with its problematical and ironical commentary on the 'Brave New World'.

Other aspects of what has been called the 'Columbian exchange' between the Old and New World, were almost inconceivably destructive. The *Conquista* unleashed violence, death and destruction on a scale unknown until then. Smallpox, malaria, measles and many sexually transmitted diseases were among the bequests of the Old World to the New. Syphilis, perhaps (although this is still controversial), came the other way – from the New to the Old.

The impact of disease, as we shall see, was shattering – a holocaust (it may be called) unparalleled in history. Several tens of millions of people died during the sixteenth century. An equally momentous consequence of the Conquest and its pandemics was the slave trade with Africa, which the European colonial powers used to replace the devastated workforce throughout the Americas. This is estimated at one million people in the first century, but increasing until, in the eighteenth century, it is thought there were as many as seven million slaves in the New World, with eleven million people transported from Africa by force over the whole period. It was the largest movement of population in history. In the light of these horrifying statistics, it is no wonder that it was in the sixteenth century, and in Spain, that the fight began to establish universal human rights and to globalize justice (see page 267) – a fight which still goes on.

At the root of this amazing expansion was the lure of gold. The Age of Discovery was also the first Age of Capital. The bankers of Europe helped to finance the expeditions of the conquistadors. When he first touched the New World, Columbus asked for gold, 'for with gold one may do what one wishes in the world'.

In Mexico, Cortes, with his finely tuned irony, told the Aztecs that he and his men 'suffered from a disease of the heart which is only cured by gold'. Cieza de Leon was inspired to sail to Peru after seeing the Inca gold unloaded in Seville: 'As long as I live I cannot get it out of my mind.' All of which perplexed – and, in the end, disgusted – the native peoples. The half-Inca historian Waman Poma

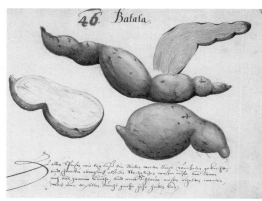

portrayed an Indian asking a Spaniard: 'Do you actually eat this gold?' And the Spaniard replies, 'Yes, we certainly do!' The last of the great Incas, Manco himself, bitterly remarked, 'Even if the snows of the Andes turned to gold still they would not be satisfied.'

The encounter of the two worlds, then, was both a physical collision and a collision of mindsets. And these are, therefore, not only stories of conquest and exploration, heroism and greed, but stories about changes in the way we see the world; changes in our view of history and civilization, and in the way we understand humanity and nature.

The conquest of the New World also had a tremendous effect on the economies of the world, with reverberations extending far beyond the frontiers of Europe and the Americas; it accelerated a shift in the centre of gravity of the old Eurasian landmass to the lands of the Atlantic seaboard; it outflanked the traditional civilizations of China, India, Persia and the Arab world. The conquest saw the appropriation by European countries of a whole continent with its people and natural resources: the beginning of the modern globalization of politics and economies, of information technology and culture. And, in this light, the story of the conquest gains a poignancy today as its consequences unfold across the world. That is why Karl Marx and others have called it 'the greatest event in the history of the world'.

What Cortes Didn't Know

EVENTS MOVED SO FAST AFTER COLUMBUS that it is easy for us to treat the conquest almost as a *fait accompli*: a continent simply waiting to be appropriated by the winners of the game of History. But that is by no means how it appeared to those who were living at the time – the Spaniards or the Native Americans.

The discovery of the New World, as we call it from a European perspective, took place over quite some time, centuries rather than years. It unfolded in people's minds as well as in physical space, and it would be a mistake to imagine that, in its early stages, the Europeans had any idea that a vast and populous continent was waiting to be discovered.

For all the high culture of the Renaissance, theirs was still a credulous age with undeveloped ideas of geography and comparative ethnology. Nothing in their past history had remotely prepared them for what was about to happen. Their understanding of Creation was

▲ The flora and fauna of the New World were objects of fascination and desire to rich Europeans. Parrots and other exotic birds were much sought after, and the potato, native to the Andes, became a staple of the European diet.

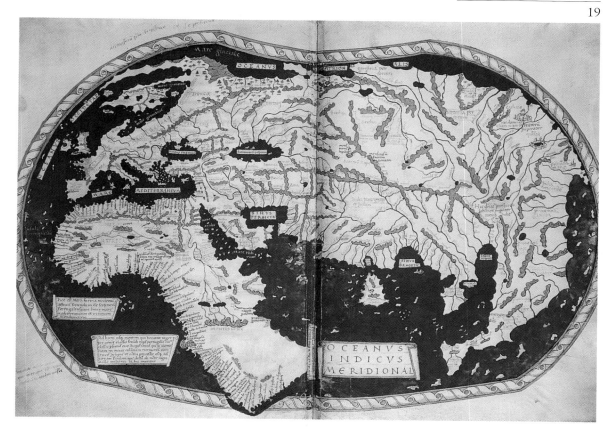

still underpinned by the Bible. And, as we can see from maps painted in the years leading up to Columbus's voyages (above) their conception of the physical world was still that of the classical geographers, for whom Europe,

▲ This map, printed in 1489, shows the world according to the classical Greeks, three years before Columbus's first voyage. It suggests that by sailing west one would come to China.

Africa and Asia constituted the 'tripartite world'. They had no good instruments or maps, and even twenty or thirty years after Columbus, the view still persisted that what had been found, including the Yucatan and Florida, were merely islands between Europe and Asia. So, when the Pope divided the New World between Spanish and Portuguese zones of influence at the Treaty of Tordesillas in 1494, he was really drawing an arbitrary line of longitude in a blank space, with no anchor in reality.

To descend into the world of Cortes and his contemporaries, then, we have to imagine the world at progressive stages of a slow gathering of knowledge; a world where the space now occupied by the Americas was largely open sea, in which a cluster of islands were inhabited by strange and primitive peoples, people not 'like us' – perhaps not even of the same creation described in the Bible.

To some, the Native Americans were untouched by the word of God and had been debased by the Devil; to others, they were a remnant from before the Fall, living in an innocence long lost by the corrupted West. Either way, it was almost impossible, throughout this whole period, for the indigenous peoples to be considered as humans in their own right. The Europeans brought with them the baggage of centuries of Eurocentrism, and Christian monotheism, which espoused one truth, one time and one version of reality.

Artists such as Dürer might have been impressed by primitive people's artistic works; activists, such as Las Casas, by their humanity; conquistadors, such as Cieza de Leon and Mansio Serra de Leguizamon, by their innate sense of justice, by the orderliness of their states, by the 'rationality' of their societies; but most treated them as inferior beings.

Europeans endlessly debated whether or not they had souls. Or were they people like them? Did their political organization constitute civilization in the sense understood by Christians? Was their religion the direct work of the Devil? Such arguments spawned a host of pronouncements: laws for Indians, rituals of submission, utopian texts, sermons, lectures, papal bulls; and, while the likes of Las Casas asserted that the Indians had full human rights, the humanist Juan Gines de Sepulveda saw them as a barbarous and inhumane people, whose beautiful art was 'no proof of higher intelligence, for do not bees and spiders make beautiful things human beings cannot entirely emulate?' How to see the Other is at the heart of our story.

What Cortes Knew

TIMING IS EVERYTHING IN HISTORY. The last of the four voyages of Columbus returned in 1504. By that time, the Portuguese had reached Brazil and, going the other way, had opened a trade route to India. In the Indian Ocean the Portuguese had made contact with Chinese navigators who had rounded the Cape of Good Hope in the early fifteenth century. The Chinese ships were four or five times longer than Columbus's vessels; huge ships using the technology later used by the West to dominate the globe: gunpowder, stern rudders, watertight compartments, compasses. Their sailing gazetteers mapped the staging posts from China to Madagascar; their fleets carried up to 27,000 men with shipboard gardens growing fresh vegetables. In the 1420s, a Chinese junk had sailed forty days into the South Atlantic; and Chinese sailors walked the streets of Jeddah on the Red Sea.

The story told in this book abounds with the 'what ifs' of history. It could so easily have been the Chinese in the New World. And what an interesting meeting that would have been if Ming navigators had walked into Inca Cuzco, meeting peoples who shared their ancient origins in Asia, and who still, in some aspects of

their culture, had preserved uncanny deep connections with their Asiatic roots. No doubt they would have understood each other better and perhaps in some distant sense would have recognized each other. Instead, it was the Spanish and Portuguese, and then the French and the English, who would appropriate the New World.

After Columbus's initial explorations, European geographical knowledge expanded rapidly. In January 1500, a Spanish navigator, Vicente Pinzon, struck the coast of Brazil near Pernambuco and reached the mouth of a river which they sailed for nearly a hundred miles into a maze of island channels. It was an immense river, which they named Santa Maria de la Mar Dulce (Saint Mary of the Sweet Sea). This was the Amazon.

A few months later, by accident, en route to India, but blown too far west, the Portuguese navigator Pedro Alvarez Cabral 'discovered' the southern part of Brazil. In the north, northern Europeans, Bretons and Bristoleans had long fished off the Grand Banks; the Scandinavian voyages to Newfoundland and Canada had not been entirely forgotten, but as the information had not been shared, the shape and extent of the continent, if such it was, was still unknown.

Although the Brazilian coast was seen in 1500, nothing more was heard for thirty years. In the early decades of the sixteenth century, further exploration of the Amazon coast of Brazil did not take place – perhaps because early reports were scathing about the harshness of the terrain and climate, and its unsuitability for colonizing. The real exploration was done from the Caribbean into Central America, and along the south-east coast of what is now the United States. The first maps (see page 110) show a cluster of islands in the Caribbean and a disarticulated length of shore beyond.

In 1508/9, the Spanish crossed to the Yucatan, which they thought was possibly another island; in 1510, they touched the shore of Florida. After Ponce de Leon's voyage of 1513, there was no doubt that a large landmass extended north of Cuba and west of the Bahamas. But how far was still unclear until the 1520s. The view was that these must all be islands off Asia, or peninsulas jutting out from it, and that it ought to be possible to sail through them and reach China. At this moment, a dramatic series of voyages transformed the picture.

In September 1513, the conquistador Vasco Nunez de Balboa hacked his way through the tropical forests of the isthmus of Panama and gazed on the Pacific (the 'South Sea'). The same year, the Portuguese reached the River Plate. With electrifying pace, knowledge opened up, culminating in the first circumnavigation of the globe by the Portuguese navigator Magellan. Then in 1517, the Spanish adventurer Grijalva explored the Yucatan and for the first time discovered not 'primitive' tribes, but an unknown civilization.

So, as we read this story, we have to remember that it was only after Cortes's conquest of Mexico that it became clear that a single landmass extended from Panama to Florida. Had they put that knowledge together with Columbus's last voyage and Cabral's exploits in Brazil, then they might have seen that this land extended far below the Equator. But how far north did it run, and was it the same landmass as that associated with the cod fisheries in the far north, which had been long known to Bretons, English and Scandinavians? Or was there open water at some point so one could sail through to Asia?

These questions began to be answered in the 1520s. In 1521, Spanish captains, sailing from Santo Domingo (Haiti), made land at the Santee river in today's South Carolina. Subsequently, they explored the coast from near Delaware Bay to Saint Simon's Sound, nowhere seeing evidence of a strait. Meanwhile, in 1523, another Spanish pilot had sailed from the north and travelled along the New England coast to Long Island and the Hudson river, gazing on the peninsula of Manhattan, but again finding no strait.

So, by the end of 1525, the Spaniards understood that a great landmass stood between Europe and Asia, and, with the evidence from Magellan's voyage now circulating, knew that beyond it was an ocean even wider than the Atlantic. Even though the Pacific coast of South America was still a blank, and the Incas' world still unknown, the globe was beginning to take its modern shape. 'The Indies', as the Spanish called them, truly were a New World.

First Contact: The Yucatan, 1517

SO THIS BRINGS US TO THE YEARS when Cortes was in Cuba, his mind still bounded by a narrow horizon. There were rumours that, 'other islands lay beyond', that is to the west. But the crucial moment came with two exploratory expeditions to the Yucatan.

In 1517, the Spanish captain Cordoba took 110 men in four ships and, at Cape Catoche, saw Mayan urban civilization for the first time. Indians paddled out in canoes to his ships, came aboard to exchange beads and clothes, and the Spanish were impressed by their high culture. By then, Mayan civilization had been in a long decline from its heyday in the ninth century. Even the great city states of the later period, such as Chichen Itza in the Yucatan, were abandoned and overgrown. But there were still organized city states which traded along the coast, and used writing.

Cordoba went ashore to be greeted by the natives of what he thought was an island. There he stayed for several days as guest of the Mayan chief of a town that his men, on account of its pyramids, called 'El Gran Cairo'. But news of the terrible events of the last twenty years in the Caribbean, when most of the population had died through Spanish violence and disease, must have got through to

the mainland. At another place on the coast, near Campeche, there was a sudden ferocious attack by a local chief who had decided that the Spaniards were not gods, but merely predatory barbarians who should be repelled forthwith.

▲ The coastal pyramids of Tulum, Yucatan, seen by Grijalva in 1518 and by Cortes the next year. Perhaps this was the major town 'as grand as the city of Seville'.

Over twenty of Cordoba's Spaniards were killed, and most of the force was wounded and only evacuated with difficulty. One ship had to be abandoned and Cordoba got back to Cuba with half his expedition dead. It was not an auspicious first encounter, but Cordoba had brought back gold pieces which the Maya had traded from a land to the north, a land called 'Mexico'. A chain reaction was about to start, which would reshape the history of the world.

The Spanish governor of Cuba, Diego Velasquez, immediately understood the importance of this discovery: 'Better lands have never been discovered,' he announced. A new expedition was organized under his nephew, Juan de Grijalva, and, in April 1518, Grijalva made his landfall at Swallow Island: Cozumel. Here the Spaniards saw unmistakable signs of a high civilization: 'a towered land' with pyramids and grand buildings. Coasting round the Yucatan, they saw more impressive towns, one of them with pillared buildings 'as grand as the city of Seville'.

Grijalva now stopped where Cordoba had landed the previous year, and suffered the same outcome. The Mayan Indians told the Spaniards that they did not wish to have them as guests and that they should leave or they would be attacked.

In the night, the Spaniards were unnerved by the terrifying noise of drums, and in a fierce skirmish many were wounded, thirteen of whom later died. Finally, after a sea journey of several hundred miles, Grijalva reached the coast of what is now Veracruz and landed at a little island inside a reef, where he saw grisly evidence of Aztec human sacrifice. He named the place the Isle of Sacrifices.

On the coast opposite, he communicated as best he could with the local people, who were Totonacs. (Two of his Mayan prisoners spoke a little Spanish and Totonac.) In no way shy, the Totonacs welcomed him and were keen to talk. They repeatedly mentioned a great city beyond the snowy range of mountains to the east. They told him that they lived under the empire of this city, and resented it. The empire had a political order, 'laws, ordinances and courts for the administration of justice'. Grijalva and his men now realized that, judging by the size of the rivers, the height of the distant snow-capped mountains, and the variety and richness of human cultures and languages, they were on part of a continent, not an island. The empire was called Mexico.

'A Gentlemanly Pirate'

THE NEWS OF GRIJALVA'S ENCOUNTERS AND DISCOVERIES made an electrifying impression on the Spanish colonists in Cuba. Among these was Hernan Cortes. Cortes's story has been told many times but, like all the great stories in history, it never wearies in the retelling.

Cortes had been out in the Indies since 1506. He was descended from a turbulent family in the little fortified town of Medellin, in Estremadura, the wildest part of Castile. Many of the conquistadors came from this region. It was a harsh land, which in summer can be a dustbowl, and in winter a bleak landscape of cork trees, oaks and drystone walls. The old towns – like Trujillo – still resemble medieval fortresses with their great ramparts and bastions.

Families such as the Cortes clan were inured to war: they were of a rough, hardy stock, lesser gentry who had fought their way south during the conquest of Muslim Spain. Within living memory, they had seen the end of Muslim culture in Spain, the expulsion of the Jews and, more recently, many had fought as mercenaries in the wars in Italy. Cortes's father, Martin, had been such a man, a small-time gentleman who had carried his sword on foreign fields.

Cortes was born in 1484, and was a sickly child. At the age of twelve, he spent two years with his father's family in the university town of Salamanca and while there seems to have had lessons in Latin and grammar as a preparation for a career in law. It is not certain that he went to the university itself, although he may have attended classes. His contemporary, Bartolome de Las Casas – the great Dominican human rights agitator and author of a history of the Indies – says he was a bachelor at law and a good Latinist who could converse in Latin, but this is still unproven.

When Cortes was seventeen, he returned to Medellin and, to the disappointment of his family, decided on a career not in the law but in arms. Like many young men, he seems to have had ambitions to fight in Italy, where fortunes were to be made, but for some reason he never set sail. For the next couple of years he wandered in Spain, and for a while we lose track of him between the royal city of Valladolid, his old haunts of Salamanca and the colourful markets of Granada in the south. Perhaps he paid his way by taking jobs as a notary. Of this time, his secretary, Gomara, later wrote disapprovingly that Cortes was 'a mere wanderer, on the loose'. Then, still looking for somewhere to make his mark, he turned to the Indies, where many of his contemporaries were heading to carve themselves estates and live in a style beyond their dreams in old Castile.

So Cortes grew up as a typical product of Renaissance Spain, hankering after arms and letters, a seeker of glory and fame, as such ideals were articulated in the famous works of literature of his day. A young man already adept at discourse, he was an individualist in an age of individualism, in a century which ends with *Hamlet* and *Don Quixote*. He left Spain for the Indies in the summer of 1506, aged twenty-two. He lived first in Hispaniola, where he rapidly gained a reputation for gambling and womanizing. Both can get a man into trouble, and one fight left him with a scar on his chin.

Hispaniola had been devastated by disease and greed – and the native population decimated by rapacious colonists. There were better pickings to be had in Cuba, and Cortes moved there in 1509. Cuba was the laboratory of the destruction of the New World: slavery, mining, forced conversions, extermination. 'The four months I was there seven thousand people died of starvation,' says Las Casas in one of the great journalistic tracts of the age. Such cruelties did not, it would appear, unduly trouble Cortes. He settled in Baracoa, a picturesque little town at the eastern end of Cuba. As the first notary there, he shipped livestock over, and became the first man on the island to own cattle. But his biggest interest was gold.

In about 1512, at Cuvanacan, he and his Indian slaves began to pan and mine gold and he started to make a fortune. He established a *hacienda* – a country house – at Duaban. ('It was the best *hacienda* in all the island,' he later said, with the boastfulness of a self-made man.) Like all Spanish colonists, he used Indian women for sex, and had a daughter by an Indian girl – the first of many children by many different women ('numberless mistresses', as was observed later). Around this time, he seduced Catalina Suarez, the sister of a fellow colonist. Pressure followed from her family, who enlisted the support of the governor, Diego Velasquez (perhaps a source of lasting enmity between the two men), and Cortes reluctantly married her. With someone who plays such a great role in history, we sift through evidence of their early life for a clue to their character that portends later events,

but with Cortes there is little to go on. At nearly thirty, he was known as a clever, tough-minded man who enjoyed being a big fish in a small pool. He was also resourceful, tenacious, and patient – a man who knew when to play a waiting game and when to move fast.

But perhaps there is a clue to his character in a remark that he made during his early days in the Caribbean: that he was a compulsive gambler and a man 'inordinately given to women'. While we need to be wary about applying modern psychology to people of the past, the 'qualities' of both these male types – gambler and seducer – shade into each other. A gambler is adept at weighing up situations, calculating odds, a man who is willing to take risks, but also adept at hiding his true intentions. A womanizer must seduce, persuade, charm, conceal his true feelings, make the other feel desired, respected – treasured even.

What both have in common is a need to control. Cortes we are told 'never lost his temper' – which suggests something almost icy in his make-up. But much about him is a mystery, still hidden before he steps onto the stage of history. There is a story from this period of his life, that he drew a wheel of fortune and told friends that he would 'either die to the sound of trumpets or die on the scaffold'. This suggests that he already had a myth of himself in which he believed, and which, given the chance, he hoped to act out.

The Expedition to Mexico

SO, DURING THOSE YEARS IN CUBA, Cortes kept a big house and worked hard. By 1517, he had moved to Santiago from Baracoa. Santiago was the centre of government on the island, and Cortes was now Chief Magistrate, his fortunes so high that he had been involved in getting backers for Grijalva's expedition to the Yucatan. Now with Grijalva's return, all the talk was of the Yucatan – and Mexico. It was 'the finest land under the sun... All of us wanted to go there...believing we would each take more than 1000 pesos in gold from it... We believe this land to be the richest in the world in terms of value of precious stones.'

Governor Velasquez now spoke to Cortes. The islands of the Yucatan were rich and their inhabitants were 'highly civilized people with law and order and public places devoted to the administration of justice'. The land would obviously yield great wealth. The failure of Grijalva had been due, many said unfairly, to his craven attitude. This is where Cortes came in as one of richest men in Cuba. A new expedition would make him a greater fortune, and make him famous. The governor would provide two or three ships if Cortes would find the rest of the money, and lead the army. Cortes saw his chance and agreed.

▸▸ An anonymous portrait of the older Hernan Cortes (above) shows him as a thinker and man of action – no longer in the prime of life, but retaining a hint of the steely will that won Mexico. The nineteenth-century painting (below) shows Cortes as a latter-day St James, freeing the Aztecs from human sacrifice. It was a myth that Cortes himself encouraged.

He would pay the larger share of the costs. On 23 October 1518, Velasquez appointed him captain-general of the new expedition.

Cortes was expected to act within the law. The expedition was supposed to be a journey of discovery and modest trading; any Indians encountered were to be fairly treated, the women not abused. His instructions contain no hint that they expected to encounter a great empire. But Cortes knew he was entering lands occupied by civilized peoples with organized polities, and we must assume that his instructions left much unsaid: that Cortes and the governor had agreed he might exceed their bounds, if and when the opportunity arose.

Governor Velasquez perhaps regarded the expedition as a holding operation, to stake a claim in the face of rival speculators. Cortes, though, may already have had a grander design. Perhaps he secretly planned a

more ambitious operation to find the route west. We know that he remained fascinated by the passage to Japan, even after his conquest of Mexico. In the end, we simply cannot guess his imaginings. But he surely must have talked about the mysterious empire of Mexico which seemed to lie inland from the Isle of Sacrifices. He may even have devised a plan to go there without sharing all the information with the governor, whom he tolerated but may have disliked and mistrusted. At any rate, he was careful to form his own team, among them the charismatic Pedro de Alvarado, who had already been to the Yucatan; he was a man who, although rash and cruel, Cortes knew he could trust.

This might explain why Cortes invested his all in the expedition. The stakes were high and he acted as if he felt Fortune was running with him. He organized the expedition swiftly, borrowed funds from friends, purchased ships, supplies, bought rations and hired footloose young soldiers on the basis of a cut of the profits. The atmosphere of those days was like a gold rush, and in hardly a fortnight Cortes had two ships, a brigantine and 300 men.

This rang alarm bells with Velasquez and his family and supporters, who became concerned about the scale and success of Cortes's preparations. As part-funders of the enterprise, they now regretted giving Cortes control. For his part, Cortes began to worry that Velasquez would not keep his side of the bargain on the sharing of profits. Eventually Velasquez decided to remove Cortes as captain-general and issued orders that he should not be allowed to buy any more food and provisions. Cortes ignored this, and Velasquez then sent orders to relieve him of his command, but Cortes's brother-in-law killed the messenger and took the governor's papers to Cortes himself.

Alerted to Velasquez's plans, Cortes now moved fast. Having seized all the meat supplies in Santiago, he decided to set sail at daybreak on 18 February 1519. At the last minute, Velasquez hurried down to the quayside where he had an almost comic last exchange with Cortes, who was pulling away in a small boat: 'Come, come, my dear fellow [compadre], why are you setting off in this fashion? Is this a good way to say goodbye to me?' Cortes shouted back: 'Forgive me, but these things have all been thought about for some time before they were ordered. What are your orders now?'

Velasquez was too stunned to reply; Cortes gave the orders to sail.

Cortes's Fleet Sets Sail

IT WAS A GAMBLER'S THROW. Cortes's story is not only a series of incredibly risky moves against Native American kingdoms, but also against the representatives of the king of Spain. From the very beginning, Cortes was technically in revolt against his own ruler. The story is told in an unrivalled series of documents and eye-witness accounts, including Cortes's

own letters from the New World, sent while these events were happening – though obviously these are partisan in the extreme.

Remarkably, we also have material from the Aztec side. The most detailed and fascinating is the account produced in the Nahuatl language by the Franciscan Bernardino de Sahagun, from interviews with Aztec eye-witnesses. But there are also several Aztec songs and poems, and a brief set of annals. Although most of these were written twenty or thirty years later, and were inevitably touched by the fact of defeat, they still constitute a remarkable insight into amazing events whose tragedy still has the power to move us.

The fleet that left Cuba comprised eleven ships, four of reasonable size (the biggest a hundred-tonner), the others smaller open boats, or brigantines. Cortes had 530 Europeans, thirty of them crossbowmen, and twelve with arquebuses, muzzle-loaded handguns – weapons that were to prove deadly and unnerving to the Aztecs. He also had fourteen small pieces of artillery and some portable breech-loading cannon on the ships.

Along with nearly a hundred sailors, there was also a doctor, several carpenters and at least eight women, one of whom would later proudly call herself a *conquistadora*. There were many non-Europeans, including several hundred Cuban Indians and some Africans, both freemen and slaves. Cortes also took a Mayan-speaking Indian fisherman, who had been captured in the Yucatan on an earlier expedition; his most pressing problem, of course, was how to talk to the natives.

His secret weapon was sixteen horses, which the Native Americans had never before seen. There were also many dogs, wolfhounds or mastiffs. In Europe, the use of dogs in war was common and they were deployed with horrible effect in the New World where, once again, the Indians had never seen such creatures. Like many of his contemporaries, Cortes had no qualms, when the necessity arose, about setting the dogs on defenceless human beings.

The crossing from Cuba to the Yucatan is only 120 miles, and Cortes coasted down to Cozumel, where, for the first time, he saw the Mayan pyramids, with their thatched sanctuaries on top. Almost immediately, he had an incredible stroke of luck. The people of the island told him that in the next-door land, known as the Yucatan, there were two Christians, who had been carried there a long time ago in a boat, and held as captives.

A message was sent and, some days later, a bearded sun-burned Spaniard, dressed as a native, arrived in a canoe. Geronimo de Aguilar had been on a ship in 1511, when the conquistador Valdivia had been shipwrecked near Jamaica. The crew had been washed ashore and, after many terrifying adventures, all had either been killed or sacrificed, save for two – Geronimo de Aguilar and Gonzalo Guerrero.

Thanks to Aguilar's survival, Cortes now had a translator who could speak the local Mayan tongue – the first necessary step if he wished to penetrate the interior. Aguilar was more than happy to go with him, but told him that his friend Guerrero had gone native. He now had a Mayan wife and children, and had been tattooed as a Mayan warrior. He was fighting with the Mayans in Chactemal against the Spanish, and would resist all appeals to return to 'civilization'.

Guerrero had apparently told the Maya that the newcomers – the Spaniards – were men 'who suffer death like other men', and perhaps this is why the Mayans seem to have understood from the start that the Spanish were not divine, but simply 'a powerful cruel enemy': a new group of invaders who had come to conquer and rob. The dark presence of Guerrero was disturbing; the idea that a good Spanish Christian could become the Other was a threatening one, which must have cast a shadow as Cortes and his men sailed on, along the low surf-beaten shore that was fringed with palm trees and dotted with gleaming white pyramids.

Cortes journeyed on round the tip of the Yucatan. It is about 400 miles by sea, along the coast of the Yucatan, travelling first south-west, then turning northwards up to the Bay of Mexico. Stopping in the steaming jungle at the mouth of the Tabasco river, Cortes disembarked at Potonchan, a large native settlement (now the town of Frontera). The natives were nervous. They gave him small offerings of food and a gold mask, but asked the Spanish to go: 'We wish neither war nor trade,' they

◄◄ The Tabasco river, into which Cortes sailed in March 1519.

◄ Taken from the sixteenth-century Duran Codex, this illustration shows that the Aztec ruler Montezuma was aware of Spanish explorations along the coast, and his spies watched every move Cortes made.

told Cortes. Word had obviously spread in the Yucatan about the newcomers. 'We have no more gold – you will be killed if you do not leave…'

Several days were spent jostling for position, while the natives evacuated their women and children from the town. This edgy time ended in a battle in which twenty Spanish were wounded but, using their guns and crossbows, they gained an easy victory. Four hundred Indian warriors were driven off with heavy losses. It was another important lesson for the inexperienced Cortes: the value of artillery against Bronze Age warriors, and its shocking impact on people who had never seen guns. The Spanish weaponry meant that, even outnumbered ten to one, they could still expect victory at little cost to themselves.

'As Beautiful as a Goddess': Malinche

▲ Malinche interpreting between the Spanish and the Aztecs. This illustration from the mid-sixteenth-century Florentine Codex, compiled from Aztec eye-witnesses in the Nahuatl language and illustrated by native artists, shows speech signs coming from the protagonists' mouths.

CORTES SPENT THREE WEEKS BY THE TABASCO RIVER. The Indians submitted and gave the Spanish gifts, including twenty women to cook tortillas and serve them. Cortes gave these women to his commanders – one of them, named Malinali, to a home-town friend, Portocarrero. Malinali, or Malinche as she is generally known, spoke Mayan, but Cortes later overheard her talking to women further up the coast in Nahuatl, the Aztec language. This was a crucial moment: Cortes had stumbled upon the key to his ambitions – through Geronimo de Aguilar, he would be able to talk to Malinche in Mayan, and then through her speak with the Mexicans in Nahuatl.

Cortes now took her back from Portocarrero and made her his mistress. From this point, all the way to the fall of Mexico, the two appear inseparable, seeming at times to speak as one person – especially in the Aztec version, which records with shock 'that a woman of our race was leading the Spaniards to Mexico'.

Malinche's father had been a local lord of the village of Painala, inland from the Tabasco river. But, after her father's death, her mother remarried, and Malinche was disinherited and eventually sold to merchants. Some said she was as 'beautiful as a goddess' – and there is a faint suggestion of this in the most vivid of our pictorial sources, the Lienzo of Tlaxcala, which represents her with an oval face and long hair, standing by Cortes's side, controlling events in her characteristic check-patterned costume.

She has been a problematic figure ever since. Portrayed as mother, whore, betrayer, goddess of the dead, few people in history have had to live an afterlife so freighted with anachronism. She is now known in Mexico as La Malinche – and any *Malinchista* is a sucker-up to American global culture, a betrayer of the nation who delivers Mexico to foreigners. The truth, of course, is more complex – especially when viewed in the light of the shifting politics of sixteenth-century Mexico.

What we do know is that Cortes worked closely with her from that moment onwards, and that she rapidly learned Spanish. Becoming the duet we see in our sources, they combined eloquence, subtlety and piety with threats, sophistication and brutality. All important communications went through Malinche, and in a sense she manipulated events. She seems to have had more freedom and power than any other woman of her time, from either of the two cultures. She remains one of the most enigmatic and intriguing characters in history – tantalizing because her story can never be told, her agenda never known. Her loyalty to Cortes, though, seems to have been complete. Language is a crucial means of conquest, a companion of empire, and in her Cortes found his companion.

First Contact with the Aztecs

THE FLEET PRESSED ON and reached the Isle of Sacrifices (where Grijalva had landed the year before) on Maundy Thursday, 20 April 1519. It is a small island, sheltered by a reef, and marked by a line of roaring surf. There is a sandy beach on the landward side, and a pale tide of white coral and driftwood along a shore fringed with palm trees. The island is a military post today, and throughout the night its lighthouse sends out a slow eerie flash, lighting up the sea. To the west, the red shore of the mainland stretches away, flat, low, surf-beaten and crowned by tall palms. On a clear day, from the crow's nest of a ship, one can see far inland to the majestic 20,000-foot snow-capped volcanoes of the Orizaba range. What lay beyond? Cortes was soon to discover.

Canoes paddled out from the shore, bearing messengers from the local governor. The people were Totonacs, who remembered their previous Spanish visitors with affection. Grijalva had been careful to be kind to the natives, who had even thought that the Spanish might be possible allies in their war of liberation against the Mexicans. The locals gave Cortes gifts: meat, fish, tortillas, turkeys, cloaks and ornaments. They also asked after some of the men they had met with Grijalva: 'How is Benito, the tambourine player?' (He had danced with them the previous year, and did so again, to much laughter.) Cortes gave them some presents for their chiefs: cloth shirts and doublets.

The jolly atmosphere changed two days later when a messenger arrived from the great king of Mexico himself, accompanied by a huge train of bearers, who brought food supplies for Cortes.

The next day, Easter Sunday, the steward of the Aztecs came in person. They met on the shore by a little white-walled Totonac town where Veracruz now stands. The steward's name was Teudile and, like all functionaries of great kings, he was very aware of his own high status, gorgeously turned out in a parrot-feather cloak.

The emperor of Mexico (if we may so call the *tlatoani* – the 'Great Speaker' of the Aztecs) was Montezuma II. He had, Teudile said, heard of the new arrivals; he knew of the Grijalva expedition, and had heard of the battle on the Tabasco river. He had instructed his steward to supply and feed his guests, and to offer them gifts of precious stones and featherware. Teudile put a damp finger to the earth and raised it to his lips (to 'eat dirt' was a gesture of respect in Aztec diplomacy), then he lit incense and, to the Spaniards' surprise, bled himself and offered them his blood on straws.

It was the formal beginning of Spanish acquaintance with the elaborate customs of the Aztec universe – and an insight into the symbolic value that the Aztec culture placed on blood. Teudile also offered them food, sprinkled with blood, at which one or two Spaniards nearly threw up. On a more practical note, he thoughtfully put 2000 servants at Cortes's disposal to build wood and palm leaf huts, 'as the rainy season was approaching'.

The Aztecs then watched perplexed as the Spanish performed one of their own characteristic rituals: kneeling and saying their Easter prayers to a simple wooden cross placed in the sand. After this, they ate together, with Aguilar and Malinche haltingly translating.

Cortes presented himself as the ambassador of a king who ruled 'the greater part of the world'. The king had heard of Mexico and had sent Cortes as his representative. Cortes asked after Montezuma: 'Where is he? We would like to meet him.' Teudile replied that Montezuma was also a great king, who was served by lesser rulers. Concerning Cortes's arrival, he would, of course, send a message to Montezuma to find out his wishes. In the meantime, he offered them, in Montezuma's name, a chest containing gold objects and cotton cloths. Cortes rustled up some gifts in response: beads and pearls, a studded chair, and a crimson cap, which Teudile accepted, giving the impression (one of the Spaniards observed) that he thought them 'excrement'.

Cortes then took the opportunity to give the Aztecs a demonstration of his guns and horses. His cavalry charged along the beach at full tilt with swords flashing and bells tinkling. If that were not intimidating enough, the big cannon were fired, at which Teudile and his men literally fell to the ground in fear. By now Cortes understood, of course, that the Mexicans lacked guns, and wished to impress them with the killing power of his weapons.

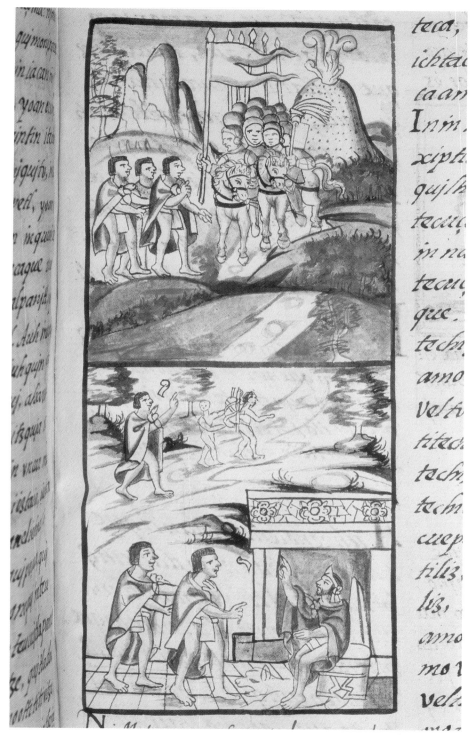

◀ Two more scenes from the Florentine Codex, our most valuable record of the Aztec side of the story. Emissaries of Montezuma meet Cortes on the road (above). They return to the distraught Montezuma (below): 'My heart burns as if it has been washed in chillies.'

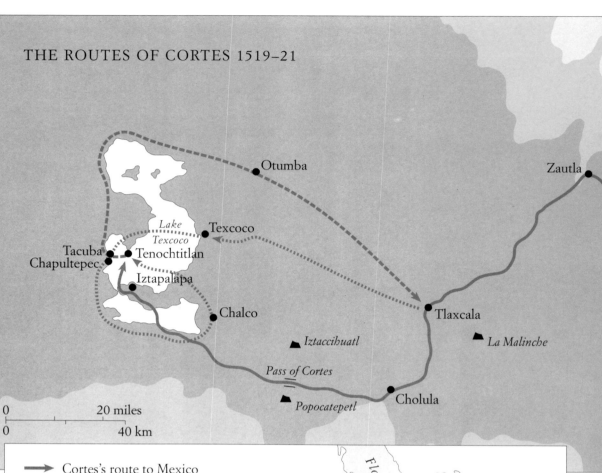

THE ROUTES OF CORTES 1519–21

Otumba

Zautla

Lake Texcoco

Texcoco

Tacuba
Chapultepec
Tenochtitlan

Iztapalapa

Chalco

Tlaxcala

▲ *Iztaccihuatl*

La Malinche ▲

Pass of Cortes

▲ *Popocatepetl*

Cholula

| 0 | 20 miles |
| 0 | 40 km |

→ Cortes's route to Mexico

Florida

Gulf of Mexico

Havana

CUBA

C. Cartoche

Chichen Itza

Cozumel

San Juan de Ulua

Campeche
Yucatan

Tulum

Santiago

Tabasco
Potonchan

MEXICO

Caribbean Sea

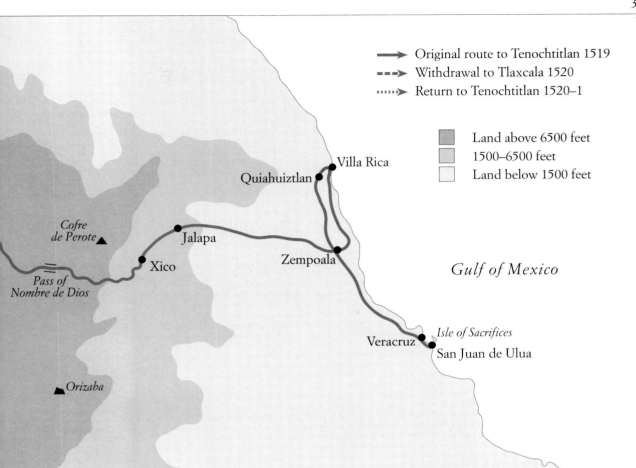

The men who carried the story back to Montezuma reported the thunderous sound, the smoke, the spurt of fire, the foul smell; they described how the shot cannon ball had 'dissolved' a hill and 'pulverized' a tree. But did the Aztecs really understand that this was a weapon to be used against human beings?

Although the Spanish publicized the 'fierce and unnatural cruelty' of the Aztecs to the outside world, they also knew that the Aztecs were men without guns, steel, gunpowder or horses. More important still, perhaps, the Aztecs lacked the Spaniards' confidence in being able to shape and manipulate the world. Cortes knew that the Aztec civilization was, in many ways, beautiful and extraordinary; he was sensitive to their arts and crafts, which he thought 'superior to any in the world'. But their civilization was at the level of the Bronze Age and, although his numbers were few, the superiority of his technology was overwhelming. So, too, he thought, were his mental toughness and flexibility.

Before Teudile left, there was a last emblematic exchange. Cortes could not, of course, let such a momentous meeting end without asking if they had more gold. 'It is good for a bad heart,' said the supreme ironist. 'You see, my men suffer from a disease of the heart which can only be assuaged by gold.' Teudile replied that they did have more – lots of it. It was, to say the least, a dangerous admission.

In the Court of Montezuma

O Master, O our lord, O lord of the near and nigh, O night, O wind, now in truth I come to appear before thee... Let me not encounter your anger, O compassionate one...lessen your rage...your city is as a baby, a child. I throw myself before thee...

The *tlatoani,* the Great Speaker of the Aztecs, sits on a richly carved stool, while black-clad priests move across the floor, their dreadlocked hair matted with blood, their fingernails dirty and uncut, the flesh of their ear lobes lacerated by the daily blood-lettings. A smouldering brazier flares with incense, the aromatic wood bark masking the cloying smell of death in the House of Snakes.

Five messengers come forward, travel-stained from the road. They have hurried from the coast with news of the arrivals from across the sea. But before they speak they must be purified with the blood of sacrifice: 'For they had gone into great danger...they had looked into the very faces of gods...' So, first, naked prisoners are brought from their cages, already drowsy from the hallucinogenic mushrooms which will dull the pain of the 'sweet obsidian death'. They are covered from head to toe with chalk. Then, one by one, they are stretched on their backs on the altar, their hearts cut out with obsidian blades. The messengers are sprinkled with their blood; only now may they speak of the wonders they have seen.

Montezuma (Motecuhozuma as we should strictly call him, but we will stick to the best known form of his name) is about fifty years old, although he looks ten years younger. He is 'of good height, well proportioned spare and slim', his hair cut just over his ears. He has a short, thin, black beard, and his face, although rather long, is cheerful. He has fine deep eyes, and (so said one who knew him) 'in his demeanour could express geniality or, if needed, a serious composure'. He may laugh heartily, giggling with delight when off duty, and when entertained by his jesters and dwarfs, his jugglers who balance logs on their feet, but in his public duties he is always contained: 'astute, learned, discerning and capable' was a Spanish judgement on him.

If *we* were able to look into his face (and, remember, no one may cast eyes on him in such meetings), we would no doubt think him extremely reserved –

◄ Montezuma, by an unknown Spanish artist of the seventeenth century. Although probably imaginary, some of its details are convincing (compare the picture on page 94), especially the feather cloak and buckler. The face allows us at least to picture a man 'astute and learned', as the Spanish describe, 'with fine deep eyes'.

repressed even – for when suitors speak to him, he looks at the floor and replies in a voice so low that 'he hardly seems to be moving his lips'. But this was the courteous etiquette of the day. ('As polite as a Mexican Indian' was a well-known phrase in seventeenth-century Spain. And it is still true today that traditional Mexican people have an innate politeness and deference, which many would trace to their ancestors.) This natural diffidence was accentuated in the poetic rhythmic speech of the court, inculcated in the colleges of the nobility. Such public speaking was most admired, and 'when Montezuma spoke he drew the sympathy of others by his subtle phrases, won them over by his profound reasoning'.

Montezuma was, then, a noble king, and kept his court with great majesty. An experienced ruler, he had been 'on the mat', as the Aztecs would say, since 1503. He had won many victories against subject peoples, taking numerous noble captives for sacrifice, and he had rebuilt the beautiful city on the lake with its magnificent ceremonial precinct. But his was not a time of blind confidence, but of growing anxiety. Recently, military failures, economic trouble and social unrest had appeared on the horizon. The old Aztec military virtues and the rigid class structure had loosened, and their ethic was under threat. No innovator, Montezuma had attempted to centralize power and maintain the over-extended empire as bequeathed to him. A rigid character by repute, he had tried to crack the whip, hectoring generals and refusing public ceremonies for armies which failed. But at the heart of his problems was the very idea of the empire. Rapidly expanded over the Valley of Mexico, and into Central America during the fifteenth century, the empire still existed for prisoners, tribute and food levies. There was no idea of consolidation – and nothing in it for the client peoples. And still its rulers and priests demanded human sacrifice to feed the insatiable appetite of its gods, who, it was believed, needed the gift of human hearts, the most precious lifeblood, to ensure their cooperation in maintaining the precarious and terror-laden order of their cosmos. It was, literally, a fatal obsession.

So now was a dangerous moment. In their external relations were still unresolved antagonisms. Their subject states, especially the Tlaxcalans, still resisted their rule. But looking inward, there was also a loss of confidence in themselves, in the imperial cosmology that had stood them well during their rise to power. In such times of uncertainty, all states have recourse to the certainties of the past, but for the Aztecs the certainties of the past were ambiguous indeed. For among the prophecies that were central to their ideology was the one that called into question their continued primacy in their adopted home in the lake: the one that told how the exiled god Quetzalcoatl would one day return to reclaim his mat.

So Montezuma now urgently consulted with his leaders and kinsmen. Perhaps they met inside the sacred enclosure in the House of Eagles. Its precinct, the main

theatre of the Aztecs' ritual drama of cosmic terror, is a vast stuccoed court, 500 yards square. In their victorious heyday, thousands of prisoners queued to be sacrificed here, their broken bodies thrown down the steps. The House of Eagles – a splendidly decorated single-storey building on a massive plinth, 170 feet long by 100 wide – lies in the shadow of the great pyramid. From the portico of the house we can look out on to a cluster of small shrines, altars and skull racks, and behind them rises an immense white stucco wall, which gleams in the glare of the Mexican sun: the great pyramid of Tlaloc, the god of weather and rain, which looms 120 feet above us; that of the war god Huitzilopochtli lies behind. From the House of Eagles we cannot see the crusted river of dried blood on the pyramid steps but, despite clouds of copal incense wafting from the altars, we can smell it.

In a splendid cloak shimmering with macaw feathers, Montezuma mounts the steps between eagle heads painted in bright orange, brown and yellow. At the top he walks through a colonnaded patio into the inner hall past life-size statues of the élite Eagle warriors. This room is among the most private of the Aztec state. Here, out of the sun's glare, it is cool. Round the wall is a low bench with a sculpted procession of warriors painted in bright greens, blues and deep reds. In the shadows are eerie, larger than life figures of the gods of the dead, with skeletal bodies, claw-like hands and huge grinning heads; from their viscera the livers hang down like tumescent banana plants. Such images are not designed to be comforting (but then we all take our religious images for granted, and to some non-Christians, a tortured figure on a cross is no less disturbing).

Although as yet untouched by the newcomers, Montezuma's priests and magicians, the 'keepers of books', the Eagle warriors, are in no doubt they have reached a crisis. They now need to categorize these aliens. All clues are scrutinized, no detail too small. The aliens' food will be subject to analysis, like rocks from another planet. (It proves to be 'white and sweet tasting'). Teudile, the Aztec ambassador from the coast, has brought artists with him who had sketched the foreigners on cloth, with their guns and horses, as we would take photographs. These paintings are now shown to Montezuma with descriptions of what they signify. He already knows of the earlier Spanish landings on the Yucatan, and has doubtless heard stories about the one true God, the great king overseas, and the strangers' hostility to human sacrifice. Everything he hears causes alarm. The strangers:

…completely covered their bodies with clothes except for their faces. Their faces were white, their eyes like chalk. Their hair often fair is sometimes, though, black and curly. Most of them had a long beard. Their battle array was of iron. They clothed themselves for war in iron, covered their heads with iron, and used iron for swords, shields and lances.

▲ 'In their wicked sacrifices they worshipped the devil as their god, believing they could offer no finer tribute than human hearts'; from the sixteenth-century Duran Codex. The Spanish saw the conquest as a punishment for human sacrifice.

▸▸ The god Quetzalcoatl emerges from the jaws of the earth, enigmatic, pale-faced and bearded. Like the Spanish, he opposed human sacrifice – a disturbing coincidence for the Aztecs.

The devil, as always, is in the detail: one of the helmets given by Cortes, an old morion parade helmet with faded gilt, was shown to Montezuma, who confirmed that it 'resembled what the god Huitzilopochtli wears in the great temple at Tenochtitlan'.

Other phenomena were no less unnerving: the noise of the guns, with their foul smell and power to splinter trees, the foaming horses and slavering dogs. And for Montezuma himself, equally sinister and threatening, was the arrogant demeanour of the strangers in asking after him: 'What sort of man was

Montezuma? Old? Young? Strong-minded or feeble?' What sort of beings asked such impertinent questions, beyond the pale of any civilized diplomatic etiquette?

Montezuma, a former priest, a man of the cloth, is adept at reading signs. He grows pale: 'My heart burns as if it is washed in chillies.' When the analysis comes from his wise men, it is bleak: 'We are not as strong as they. We are nothing compared to them...'

On this reading the course of events will hinge.

Montezuma's Dilemma: Gods or Men?

IN THE MINDS OF MONTEZUMA and his wise men, of course, it was not simply a case of either/or – that the Spanish were either men or gods, as the Europeans have so often represented it. They could, after all, be invaders, as had been reported in the Yucatan, 'subject to the pains of death as other men were'. They could be ambassadors of a great king far away, although they did not behave as such.

But there were other possibilities. For example, could they be gods or supernatural beings unknown in the Mexican pantheon? The perplexing behaviour of the Spanish, to any common-sense view inhuman, might even suggest they were a similar kind of being, but of a different creation. Or they might be creatures connected with the divine – remember the army of hunchbacks who accompanied Quetzalcoatl across the mountains when he left Mexico? Gods, after all, like earthly kings, had their followers. And Aztec gods were not like the Christian deity, omnipotent and righteous; they were more like Greek gods – playful, capricious, wilful, quarrelsome, full of human vices, vengeful, cruel, sadistic even...

But another possibility was the most disturbing. Perhaps the Spaniards were long-lost rulers or deities of the Aztec pantheon, in particular, Quetzalcoatl, 'the feathered serpent', who had once ruled at the ritual centre of Tollan, in the Valley of Mexico, a place charged with a peculiar and potent destiny in the foundation myth of the Aztec state. Quetzalcoatl was a figure who exposed radical tensions in the Aztec thought-world, for he had been expelled and had vanished across the sea eastwards, near Veracruz (where Cortes had landed), promising that one day he would return to claim his kingdom.

Quetzalcoatl stood for the solar light, the morning star. He was the warrior of dawn, 'the white hero of the break of day', who would at some point come back from the place where the sun rises. Some said he was white-skinned, bearded; he was the fount of all arts and knowledge, and he was opposed to human sacrifice. Unnerving as these coincidences were, there was one factor that was positively spine-chilling: for the year in which Quetzalcoatl was born and died, and the year in which the astrologers were expecting him to come was 1-Reed, which in the

Aztec calendar came round only once every 52 years. By an extraordinary coincidence, 1519 was that year.

The Aztec version of the story, although written down some thirty years later, seems to confirm that this was uppermost in the Mexicans' minds. 'He has appeared! He has come back!' says Montezuma. 'He will come here to the place of his throne and canopy, for that is what he said he would do when he departed.' This motif in the tale is often claimed as a *post hoc* invention – an Aztec attempt to explain the conquest in terms of their own beliefs – so that even though the Spanish triumphed, they triumphed *within* the rules of Mexican history. But, while the events were actually unfolding, we cannot be sure what the Aztecs were thinking – and perhaps they were not sure themselves. Whatever the case, none of the possibilities was comforting, and they seem to have left Montezuma's brain swimming.

There were perhaps those in the Aztec court, for example young Cuitlahuac, Montezuma's eventual successor, and his kinsman Cuauhtemoc, who argued that the Spaniards were simply 'cruel enemies', international terrorists as we would call them. But Montezuma was a clever man. The possibilities to him were real, the observable phenomena deeply disturbing and well capable of supernatural interpretation. And one thing was sure, in the Mexican view of the cosmos: none of this had happened by chance.

Cortes 'Burns His Boats'

CORTES NOW KNEW WHAT LAY AHEAD. He had not yet seen the magical city, but he knew it was there, 200 miles away, over mountains whose gleaming distant peaks he had glimpsed from out at sea. He now does a very clever thing. He cannot return to Cuba where he faces imprisonment or even death for defying the governor, so his only alternative is to conquer and settle part of the land. In order to do this, he has to constitute and set up a legal Spanish authority.

Cortes is a man trained in the law, and he has all the legalistic tricks up his sleeve. He gets his supporters to install a municipal government (the first Spanish authority in mainland America), and resigns from the post conferred on him by Velasquez so that the legally constituted 'town council of Villa Rica' can offer him the post of captain-general. After long protestations that he cannot possibly accept, Cortes allows himself to be persuaded to take the post and severs his connection with Velasquez. His direct authority is now the Spanish crown which is several thousand miles away. In practice, he has freedom of action for the foreseeable future.

Camped amid the millions of mosquitoes of Ulua, Cortes made contact with the local kingdom of Zempoala, up the coast, whose leader saw his chance to

throw off Aztec rule. During these contacts, Cortes received a reconnaissance report that there was a much better anchorage, forty miles up the coast, the other side of Zempoala, at a place called Quiahuiztlan. Moving his army there, he refounded his municipality of Villa Rica nearby.

It is still there, a pleasant little fishing village, amid emerald forests of palm trees, along a beach of dark volcanic sand, with sugar-loaf hills rising up behind. Close by the beach is a steep little hill, with a flat top a couple of hundred yards across. Here among the fruit trees are the ruins of a small fort, with the footings of a simple church, a stable block, a prison and stores. This was the first permanent Spanish base on the mainland of the New World. In its tiny plaza the treasures that Dürer saw in Brussels were packaged up.

In his talks with the Zempoalans, Cortes lectured them about the Christian faith, and they agreed to install an image of the Virgin Mary on the top of their main pyramid. In an amazing twist, three Zempoalan priests washed and cut their matted hair, and were instructed by Cortes in some basic rituals for the Christian Mother of God. Unbaptized 'devil worshippers' they may have been only hours before, but now they were men of the Church! Cortes was nothing if not pragmatic.

During this time, the Zempoalans also gave Cortes crucial intelligence about the Aztec empire, and about its many subject nations which were hostile to Montezuma's rule. Most important, he learned, were

▼ Aztec artisans making a buckler like that shown on page 14. (below). The Spanish were quick to recognize the Aztecs' mastery of arts and crafts, such as their featherwork, but what they really wanted was gold, which Aztec craftsmen cast into various gold objects (below right).

the Tlaxcalans, who were traditional enemies of Mexico. Cortes now saw a possible strategy: a military alliance using the manpower of the Native American kingdoms against the Aztecs.

Then, while Cortes was still on the coast, quite by chance Montezuma's tax inspectors arrived at Quiahuiztlan, the neighbouring Totonac town. Cortes now encouraged the Totonacs to arrest the Aztec emissaries, who were roughed up and imprisoned. That night, Cortes secretly set them free and sent them back to Mexico, making them believe he was not to blame but was really Montezuma's friend. It was the first of many tactical ploys to wrong-foot the Aztecs – and, of course, it also pushed the Totonacs on to his side.

All this must have seemed increasingly risky – even mad – to some of his men, especially to the associates of the governor of Cuba who made up part of his force. And now came the first serious threat to the enterprise – a rebellion by the Velasquez faction, who had grown impatient with Cortes's attempts to hitch them on to his dreams, and not least to exceed the terms of his licence to explore. Their plan was to seize a ship and escape to Cuba. Cortes moved swiftly, hanged the ringleader, and cut off

➤ An anonymous Spanish painting from the sixteenth century shows Cortes scuppering his boats in the bay at Villa Rica. A master of bluff, gamble and subterfuge, Cortes calculated all his risks carefully – and they nearly all came off.

the feet of another rebel. The last thing he wanted was for news of what he was doing to get out. To make sure this did not happen again, he decided, on the pretext that they were not seaworthy, to scuttle his ships.

The ships were stripped of everything useful – metalwork, rigging, sails, gear, oars. These were stored in the fort on the hill above the beach. The ships were then sunk (not burned, as legend has it). As his ships settled on the bottom, just inside the windswept headland, Cortes had made another gambler's throw. He had left his men with 'nothing to rely on save their own hands – and the certainty that they must either win the land or die in the attempt'.

March into the Interior

WHAT EXACTLY DID HE HOPE TO DO? To march into the interior seems an almost irrational course of action – unless, of course, his plan from the start was conquest. In his letter to the king of Spain, he says that he had always planned to deliver Montezuma to him, but as this was written after the fall of Mexico, he would say that.

Perhaps he hoped to negotiate the Aztecs' submission to Spain? To persuade them, by demonstrating Spanish technological superiority, to accept Spanish rule and the Christian religion? He knew that the Aztecs were a Bronze Age people who did not have guns and horses (and were terrified of them) and that, in the view of European civilization, they were an archaic, 'primitive' polity. He knew the Spaniards were 'superior' in technology, more flexible in their 'mode of thought' and in their thinking. That was probably enough. So he marched off into the interior, searching with a gambler's instinct for ways to strengthen his hand – whether this was by persuasion, intimidation or force.

We followed, crossing the green plain, across the Actopan river, past the lovely town of Antigua, with the ruined house of Cortes entwined by ancient creepers. His route leads through the picturesque towns of Xalapa and Xico from where the ridges of Perote and the snow-capped range of Orizaba begin to block the view.

The path Cortes took under Perote is disused today. It goes up to a chilly 11,000 feet (the Spanish in their cotton armour suffered from the cold, and some of the Caribbean slaves died). This was the more northerly of the two routes to Mexico and was obviously chosen to avoid the main route through Cholula which might be defended.

At an open-air market in Zautla, we met an old farmer who told us there was a crumbling *hacienda* at the upper end of valley where, according to his father, 'Cortes had passed the night on the way to Tlaxcala'. This seemed entirely probable. It was here in Zautla that a local chief gave Cortes a first detailed description of the great city of Tenochtitlan on its lake and told him that the place was impregnable. With a mixture of fear and anticipation, the Spanish pressed on.

The route led up the lovely valley of Zautla, where a wall built across the valley mouth marked the edge of the territory of the Tlaxcalans. The Tlaxcalans, an old Mexican federation of four towns, were resolute enemies of the Mexicans, but none the less, after a long debate, they decided to fight Cortes.

You can see the battle site when you come out into the plain, which opens out from the end of the valley of Zautla, just past the remnants of the old wall which Cortes passed that summer. From here, there is a wonderful view of the 14,000-foot volcano, La Malinche (named after Cortes's mistress), with rolling fields stretching towards Tlaxcala: the route the Indian army took. Here ploughmen still pick up fragments of obsidian and other battle debris.

Cortes estimated the Tlaxcalan numbers at 150,000. But even if there had been a tenth of that number, it would have been a terrifying sight:

They were very well armed in their fashion. They used cotton jackets, cudgels and swords, and a great many bows and arrows. Many of them carried standards and gilded shields, and other insignia, which they wore strapped to their backs, giving them an appearance of great ferocity, since they also had their faces stained, and grimaced horribly, giving great leaps and shouts and cries. They put so much fear into us that many of the Spaniards asked for confession.

It was a desperate battle, with terrible losses suffered by the Tlaxcalans to the Spanish guns, but by nightfall the Spanish were reeling on the brink of defeat, and took refuge on a 'round hill where there was a settlement and an Indian shrine on the top'. Here, Cortes's forces held out for two weeks, making forays to get food and drinkable water. The hill is still known by its native name of Tzompantepec; there is still a shrine on top, and on its lower slopes is the bright yellow church of San Salvador, which tradition claims was founded by Cortes after the battle to thank God for his victory, because, as the locals say, 'it was a miracle that the Spanish had survived'.

But the Tlaxcalans could not dislodge the Spanish. With their losses mounting daily, they eventually brought gifts and sued for peace. The council of the four towns met with the newcomers and, after lengthy negotiations, they gave Cortes what he most wanted. They agreed to go with him to Mexico.

The alliance with the Tlaxcalans was the turning point of the war. More even than the superiority of European technology, it would be the support given by Native American peoples which would eventually lead to Cortes's victory. Still today, the Tlaxcalans are bitterly criticized for siding with 'the enemy', or 'betraying' Mexico. But, of course, that is to apply the assumptions of our own time to the politics of the sixteenth century. As the Tlaxcalans saw it, these powerful

▲ The church of the Virgin of Remedies founded, apparently,
by Cortes, stands on the ruined pyramid at Cholula.
The pyramid, the largest in the world in terms of the area
it covered, was the focus of pilgrimages from
c. AD 1000 to 1500.

▸▸ Travelling in Cortes's footsteps, we retraced his journey over the
'Pass of Cortes' (above) under the smoking cone of Popocatepetl
(below) which now, as then, was erupting.

people from across the sea were a means by which they might overthrow the hated Aztec state. Since the sixteenth century, the 'most loyal city' of Tlaxcala has defended this view in works of history, paintings, and even in a cycle of murals with which their Town Hall was adorned in our own time. In Mexico City, on the other hand, a proverb still declares: 'The Tlaxcalans are to blame.'

'Death Came to Cholula' SO CORTES MARCHED ON WITH THE TLAXCALAN WARRIORS at his side, whooping their war cries. The next stage of his journey was to the important city of Cholula, some thirty miles from Tlaxcala. Cholula was the greatest pilgrimage city of the Americas, the city of Quetzalcoatl, who was still worshipped there in a grand temple. According to one of Cortes's men, there were: 'fifty or sixty thousand houses', all of them well built with solid roofs and freshwater wells. 'We were amazed at the number and grandeur of its temples.'

'Viewed from beyond, it is one of the most beautiful cities imaginable,' says Cortes's secretary, Gomara, 'many towered with as many temples as there are days in the year…the land is rich and covered with farms which are irrigated and so thickly populated that not a palm's breadth is unoccupied.'

No one is certain about what happened at Cholula, but the Aztecs blamed the Tlaxcalans, who 'hated, detested' the Cholulans, even though their cities were so close. 'They inflamed the Spaniards, saying, "The Cholulans are evil, they are enemies of ours, as powerful as Mexico…and friendly to Mexico."'

Malinche heard rumours via the Tlaxcalans that the Cholulans were planning to trap Cortes inside the city and then massacre his army. True or not, Cortes was not a man to give anyone the benefit of the doubt. The Cholulan leadership and many of their warriors had gathered, unarmed, in a great enclosure by the pyramid temple of Quetzalcoatl. This is now San Gabriel, a huge church made from blocks of the ancient temple.

There, they were massacred by the Spanish and the Tlaxcalans. 'With no warning, they were deceitfully slain,' say the Mexicans. Many said that it was a deliberate act of terror. According to Las Casas (who knew Cortes), the aim was a 'punishment…to inspire fear and terror among all the people of the territory'. Cortes claimed that he killed 3000; others said nearly twice as many. The role of Malinche is particularly problematical for, according to the Spanish, it was she who first heard of the alleged plot to kill the Spaniards. The Aztec version, however, is simple: 'The Tlaxcalans induced the Spaniards to do this.'

So the possibility of resistance in Cholula, the wealthiest trading town on the major trade routes into Mexico, was shattered. And a message was sent ahead: 'The effect on the people of Mexico was immediate; they came out in crowds, alarmed as if by an earthquake, as if there were constant shaking of the surface of the earth. They were terrified…'

Cortes pressed on. From Cholula, the old royal road, now a dirt track, winds through farm fields, the volcano Popocatepetl gradually filling the view ahead. Then you turn off through pine forests carpeted with ash, up to the 'Pass of Cortes', on a great shoulder of the mountain at 13,000 feet. To the south, now as then, the crater of 'Popo' smokes ominously, occasionally spewing out fire and cinders.

Here Montezuma's ambassadors met Cortes with gifts of gold necklaces and precious feathers – and they watched, fascinated by the Spaniards' reaction:

The Spaniards appeared to be much delighted…they seized upon the gold like monkeys, their faces flushed. For clearly their thirst for gold was insatiable; they starved for it; they lusted for it; they wanted to stuff themselves with it as if they were pigs. They went about fingering the streamers of gold, passing them back and forth, grabbing them one to the other, babbling, talking gibberish among themselves.

Journeying down into the valley, with his Indian allies in a column behind him, Cortes sent ambassadors to the lesser rulers on the lake, and they submitted. The alliance of kingdoms and cities that made up Montezuma's empire was crumbling. Decades of cruelty and high-handedness by the rulers of Tenochtitlan were reaping their reward. As the Spaniards came down from the mountains, they began to glimpse the huge bowl of the Valley of Mexico, and caught their first distant sightings of the great lake, pale blue, shimmering in the haze. They were still too far off, however, to see the city and its causeways: 'And still Montezuma did nothing. He commanded no attack against them,' says the Aztec version. 'No one was to resist them with force. He only commanded they should be cared for, that all be done for them. And in all this, Mexico lay as if stunned. None went out of doors. Mothers kept their children in.'

Finally, the Spanish column reached the shore of the lake, and even the most experienced conquistadors could hardly believe what they were seeing:

And when we saw all those cities and villages built in the water, and other great towns on dry land, and that straight and level causeway leading to Mexico, we were astounded. These great towns and temples had buildings rising from the water, all made of stone, [and it] seemed like an enchanted vision... Indeed, some of our soldiers asked whether this was not all a dream. It is not surprising therefore that I should write in this vein. It was all so wonderful that I do not know how to describe this first glimpse of things never heard of, seen or dreamed of before.

Tenochtitlan was indeed a City of Dreams: 'the most beautiful thing in the world', Cortes would call it. He had coaxed and bullied his men this far; dream-led, dream-fed them into his gamble; lured them to acknowledge their own most extreme fantasies of wealth, glory and fame; persuaded them, by his leadership, that their fantasies were realizable and that his City of Dreams could be captured and delivered intact to the king of Spain with Cortes himself as governor. Early the next day, 8 November 1519, the Spaniards marched on to the causeway:

...which is eight yards wide and goes straight to the city with no curves... It was so crowded with people that there was hardly room for them all, so we could hardly get through the crowds that were there. The towers and the temples were full, and they came in canoes from all parts of the lake. And no wonder, since they had never seen horses, or men like us, before... With such wonderful sights to gaze on we did not know what to say, or if this was real that we saw before our eyes. On the lakeside there were great cities, and on the lake many more. The lake was crowded with canoes. At intervals along the causeway there were many bridges, and then before us was the great city of Mexico. As for us we were scarcely four hundred strong and we well remembered the many warnings we had received to beware of entering the city of Mexico, since they would kill us as soon as they had us inside. What men in all the world have ever shown such daring?

This wonderful description by an eye-witness, the conquistador Bernal Diaz del Castillo, is augmented by fantastic images in the Aztec account, which suggests how the Mexicans saw the newcomers at the moment they marched along the causeway for the first time: 'The Spaniards now put on their war gear...their battle dress [and] marched in order...' The Aztecs saw the cavalry of the advance guard – rather like a president's bodyguards continuously scanning crowds – 'peering hither and thither, watching on every side, scanning all areas...between

▶ Two seventeenth-century paintings by the Spanish artist Miguel Gonzales, showing Cortes being welcomed at the court of Montezuma. In the first, Cortes accepts food before entering the palace.

▶▶ The formal reception in the palace portrayed in a Renaissance setting: the coat of arms of Mexico and images of earlier Aztec kings are shown on the walls. The two thrones are mentioned in both Spanish and Aztec accounts.

the houses, up on the roof terraces'. The crowds watched fascinated as the horses reeled, the bells on their harnesses 'jingling in a shattering jangle'. Certain details particularly struck them: the behaviour of the dogs 'continually sniffing each object, continually panting'; the sweating horses, 'flecks of foam flying from their mouths like soap suds'; the standard-bearer with his parade-ground tricks, swirling the standard round 'so it stiffened in the wind, rose like a warrior, twisting and rising up, filling itself out'; the swordsmen, flashing their swords…the crossbowmen 'testing wielding their weapons as they marched'; and, in the rear behind Cortes and his bodyguards, the triumphant Indian allies 'prancing, whooping, shrieking as they struck their palms against their mouths…'

Everything about this display communicated menace – and was intended to. Ever mindful of detail, Cortes was a master of signs and psychological warfare.

The causeway stretched for nearly five miles through the lake, linking smaller islands from Iztapalapan. Finally, the Spaniards reached a great fortification with two towers. There, they waited one hour for various ceremonies to be performed by a Mexican welcoming party; then they were allowed over the bridge on to the main island where the city stood.

The moment had come when two worlds would meet. Cortes, with his European conception of time and history, knew who the Aztecs were. How soon would Montezuma and the Aztecs understand Cortes's true nature?

The Meeting of Two Worlds

AS FAR AS WE KNOW, this was the first time in history that two civilizations, which had no previous idea of each other, had met. According to Aztec tradition, the place of that first encounter was Xoloco – now a crossroads in a run-down part of Mexico City, close by the derelict Monastery of San Antonio Abad. At this point in 1519, a canal intersected the main causeway road. This is now filled in, but the cross-street, which marks its line, still bears the ancient name of the canal, Chimalpopoca. According to the Aztecs (and they take great care to remember the details of the tragedy), this is the spot where the two worlds first met. 'The rooftops of the houses were brimming over with people,' said one of Cortes's men. Two great processions of people came down the wide road from the city centre:

In the centre was the great king Montezuma in a litter draped with fine cotton mantles. He could be seen by no one and none of the Indians accompanying him dared glance at the litter which was borne on the shoulders of the lords. Then Montezuma emerged from the litter and placed necklaces of gold and precious stones round Cortes's neck.

Flowers were also given. These were formal greetings for foreign ambassadors (for that is who the Aztecs took Cortes to be). Then: 'With all courtesy, Montezuma bade him welcome, saying this was the Captain's home.'

It may have been at this point that the ever-suspicious Cortes said, through Malinche: 'Are you Montezuma?' Montezuma replied that he was. The Aztecs say that they then led the Spaniards back up the street into the heart of the city, to a place called Uitzillan: 'a very large and beautiful building', according to Cortes. (The Hospital of Jesus stands here today, with its charming colonnaded courtyards full of flowers.) There they entered a great room facing out on to a wide courtyard, a place: 'large enough to accommodate more than two thousand people'.

There the Spanish were to be quartered, and as they arrived, the Aztec account mentions another intimidating detail:

When they entered the palace assigned them, the Spaniards fired repeated
volleys from their arquebuses. And each one exploded, crackled, thundered as it
discharged...smoke spread suffused, massed over and darkened the ground.
It spread all over, its fetid smell stupefying us, robbing us of our senses.

Trying hard to control his emotions, Montezuma took the Spanish leaders into the hall and sat Cortes down beside him. More wonderful gifts were now brought forward: gold, silver, splendid featherwork: 'several thousand fine garments and many other beautifully woven textiles'.

Far from being a sign of submission, this largesse was a statement of power. These were superb gestures of wealth and liberality, made more glorious by the humble and self-abnegating words which accompanied them. This was the arrogant humility of a great king who bestows more than his inferiors can possibly give in return. However, these dazzling things spread before them can only have further excited the cupidity of Cortes and his men, who must now have been almost beside themselves with excitement.

Then Montezuma sat on his throne and spoke. How his words are interpreted lies at the very core of how we understand this meeting of the two worlds. Our earliest version of the speech is reported by Cortes himself, written less than a year later, in a letter to the king of Spain. This is what Cortes *says* Montezuma said (as understood and interpreted to him, we should remember, by the enigmatic Malinche):

For a long time we have known from the writing of our
ancestors that neither I, nor any of those who dwell in
this land, are natives of it, but foreigners who came from

▸ The great market of Tenochtitlan, showing all the classes of Aztec society, depicted by Diego Rivera in a mural at the National Palace, Mexico City. This is part of the re-imagining of Aztec Mexico that has taken place since the Mexican Revolution in order to reclaim Aztec roots. Although imaginary, it projects the sense of wonder felt by the conquistadors when they first saw the city.

very distant parts; and likewise we know that a chieftain of whom they were all vassals brought our people to this region. And he returned to his native land and after many years came again, by which time all those who had remained were married to native women and had built villages and raised children. And when he wished to lead them away again they would not go, not even admit him as their chief; and so he departed. And we have always held that those who descended from him would come and conquer this land and take us as their vassals. So because of the place from which you claim to come, namely from where the sun rises, and the things you tell us of the great lord or king who sent you here, we believe and are certain that he is our natural lord, especially as you say that he has known of us for some time. So be assured that we will obey you and hold you as our lord in place of that great sovereign of whom you speak; and in this there shall be no offence or betrayal whatsoever. And in all the land that lies in my domain, you may command as you will, for you shall be obeyed; and all that we own is for you to dispose of as you choose. Thus now as you are in your own country and your own house, rest now after the hardships of your journey.

Interestingly, Cortes does not give us his own reply, saying simply: 'I replied to all he said as I thought most fitting, especially in making him believe that your Majesty was he whom they were expecting; and with this he took his leave.'

What can we make of this? Of course, it seems totally inconceivable to us that Montezuma should be willing to give away his kingdom. (Nor, we might think, was it possible for the *tlatoani* to do this, ignorant as we may be of Aztec constitutional procedures.) The Spanish assumption that Montezuma was a tyrant represents, of course, a European view of the situation: evidently many among the Aztecs were hostile to his willingness to welcome these 'ambassadors' from another world.

We must remember, too, that Cortes's letter was sent to the king in October 1520, nine months after the dramatic change in his fortunes when he was expelled from Mexico City, and still in rebellion against royal authority. Desperate to re-establish his credentials, he portrays himself in the letter as the creator of his own legend: exemplary soldier, magnificently daring in strategy, endlessly resourceful, and yet a simple-hearted loyalist, unreservedly obedient to the king – and to the letter of the law.

But, of course, this will not wash. The letter is a clever fiction. The key to Cortes's legalistic strategy was that Montezuma had voluntarily ceded his empire to Spain. Cortes was adept at depicting himself as the simple discharger of the royal will, but actually he was the very opposite. We know him by now as an arch manipulator – even more so when we remember that, at the moment of writing the letter, he was nursing wounds suffered during a catastrophic reverse in which he

had to represent Montezuma as having gone back on his original fealty as a vassal. So the letter cannot be taken as a reliable source for what happened and, without corroboration, certainly cannot be believed.

So what did the Aztecs say about the meeting? Their version is equally fascinating and, for different reasons, just as problematic. Their version of Montezuma's speech was written down in Nahuatl from Aztec eye-witnesses, but long after the event, in around 1550.

The English translation which follows tries to capture the formal poetic quality of the Nahuatl – the alliterative, repetitive figures of speech of the public discourse of a high-ranking Aztec figure. This was in part standard politeness in Aztec high society, but is there also a hint here of a nervous staccato quality? Perhaps though this may be an illusion stemming from the rhetorical qualities of Nahuatl, rather than a deliberate attempt to reproduce Montezuma's tone of speech. On the other hand, we have to remember that, at this moment, Montezuma was a man under peculiar and intense stress. Whatever the truth, it is one of the most poignant documents in history:

Our lord, thou hast suffered fatigue, thou hast endured weariness. Thou hast come to arrive on earth. Thou hast come to govern thy city of Mexico; thou hast come to descend upon thy mat, upon thy seat, which for a moment I have guarded for thee. For thy governors are departed – the rulers Itzcoatl, Montezuma the Elder, Axayacatl, Tizoc, Ahuitzotl, who yet a very short time ago had come to govern the city of Mexico... O that one of them might witness, might marvel at what to me now hath befallen, at what I see now that they have quite gone. I by no means merely dream, I do not merely dream that I see thee, that I look into thy face. I have been afflicted for some time. I have gazed at the unknown place whence thou hast come – from among the clouds, from among the mists. And so this. The rulers departed, maintaining that thou wouldst come to visit thy city, that thou wouldst come to descend upon thy mat, upon thy seat. And now it has been fulfilled; thou hast come. Thou hast endured fatigue, thou hast endured weariness. Peace be with thee. Rest thyself. Visit thy palace. Rest thy body. My peace be with our lords...

It is electrifying in its immediacy, as breathtaking as a historical source possibly can be. The text seems to catch the dignified, poetic diction of the Aztec aristocracy: a meditative, ruminative tenor also evidenced in Aztec poetry with its profound strain of melancholy about fate and the transience of life. It suggests a discourse that is very different from European modes of speech, or Cortes's manipulative, tricksy ambiguities. Interestingly enough, the Aztecs record more of Cortes's reply than he thought fit to at the time:

And when Montezuma's address which he directed to the Marquis was ended, Malinche then interpreted it, she translated it to him. And when the Marquis had heard Montezuma's words, he spoke to them in a barbarous tongue [quijnoalpopolotz]; he said in his barbarous tongue, 'Let Montezuma put his heart at ease; let him not be frightened. We love him much. Now our hearts are indeed satisfied, for we know him, we hear him. For a long time we have wished to see him, to look upon his face. And this we have seen. Already we have come to his home in Mexico. At his leisure he will hear our words…'

It is a wonderful text. Nothing could match it today unless we were to meet people from another planet. But how far can we go in accepting the text as a primary historical source? For all its apparent immediacy, it was recorded much later than Cortes's letter, although taken down from 'men of good judgement', and possibly with access to earlier written accounts that were in existence by the late 1520s.

Its oral formulaic quality may also owe something to having been structured for tale-telling, so we should be wary of assuming that the tone is authentically that of Montezuma. But it comes from a memorizing society, from witnesses trained to remember, educated in the colleges in the finer points of the rhetoric of kingship. They would be expected to recall the gist of what Montezuma said at this defining moment for Mexico. And, clearly, some of the same ideas are referred to in both speeches – in particular, the idea of the divinity returning, but even the memorable form of welcome ('Thou hast endured weariness. Rest thyself.') come out the same in Spanish and in Nahuatl.

All in all, then, it is hard not to believe, for all Cortes's twisting of words and meanings, that *something* like this was said. But what Montezuma *meant* by it is another matter altogether. Cortes's own slanted interpretation would be a key factor in justifying what he did: namely that Montezuma had ceded his kingdom to him and willingly become a 'vassal' of the king of Spain. This 'ceding of the kingdom', however, is easy to dismiss – and it usually is by scholars – as a mythical construction, a contamination of the way the Spanish represented events – a distorted version that attempts to make sense of Montezuma's fatal errors and his apparent cowardice.

But is it really that simple? The story of the returning god is there in Cortes's letter – and in other Spanish eye-witnesses, such as the conquistador Tapia. Whatever we make of that, it must have been one of the issues raised between Cortes and Montezuma.

More than that, though, we cannot say. Cortes declared that he came as an ambassador and, although this was a lie, he seems to have been received by Montezuma as such. We then see a man who, having claimed to be an ambassador,

persistently swears friendship to Montezuma's representatives. Accomplished in the duplicitous language of diplomacy, so modern that we hardly give it a second thought, he merely blames Montezuma for not recognizing it as such, for being stuck in the framework of his own assumptions about diplomacy.

But Montezuma was a great king with a magnificent court. Perhaps it was impossible for a ruler of his stature simply to attack in secret and kill the Spaniards, even if he had recognized them for what they were. So he dealt in gifts and protocols, the liberality of a great king to lesser people. And the Spanish had neither the wit nor the means to reciprocate (cartwheels of gold and silver were matched by a cup of Italian glass and 'three Holland shirts'!).

From this moment, there seem to have been signs of disaffection among some of Montezuma's lords. We do not know how they responded to the sinister insistence by the Spanish on the need to see Montezuma's face. We can only guess that as no one in Aztec society was allowed to look on the king's face, this would have seemed uncannily threatening. So, too, is the moment when the speeches were over, which is recorded by Father Sahagun, when the Spaniards held Montezuma by the hand:

Already they went leading him by the hand. They caressed him with their hands to make their love known to him. And they looked at him; they each looked on him thoroughly. They were continually active on their feet; they continually dismounted in order to look at him.

This is so vivid, dark and intimidating that it sounds like a genuine memory, and surely must have been a violation of the strict taboos of divinity which hedged Aztec majesty. Touching the *tlatoani*, especially by strangers, was forbidden. This is perhaps confirmed by a note at the end of this section of the Aztec account. This circumstantially names the Aztec nobles and their rank, who accompanied Montezuma at this meeting. It goes on to tell us that when Montezuma was 'made captive, they not only hid themselves and took refuge, but abandoned him in anger'.

This may be retrospective bias, but one may suspect that Montezuma's position was already being undermined in the eyes of his nobles, especially those who had counselled him not to let the strangers into the city. Among his followers, it may have been already understood that the Great Speaker of the Aztecs had made a fatal error in allowing Cortes to enter Tenochtitlan and that in so doing he had compromised both his ritual status and his real power.

That night of 8 November, the mood in the city was as if some powerful beings from space had landed – aliens with powers which could not yet be categorized. Not only had Cortes arrived in 1-Reed, Quetzalcoatl's year, but that

day, 1-Wind, was Quetzalcoatl's day in his attribute of the whirlwind. It was the day when robbers and wizards do their worst, robbing and violating, stealing treasure while their victims sleep in a trance-like state. People went to bed that night 'as if everyone had eaten stupefying mushrooms…as if they had seen something astonishing. Terror dominated everyone, as if all the world were being disembowelled… People fell into a fearful slumber…'

Of course, the Aztecs knew by now what the Spanish had done in Cholula; that they had the ability to be (as the Aztecs saw it) irrationally and unpredictably cruel – in a way, perhaps, that only gods behaved. It was as if they had given shelter inside their city to a monster.

The Phoney War Begins

FOR THE SPANISH, THE DAYS THAT FOLLOWED were days of wonder and anxiety. Inside the strange and magical city, quartered in fairytale chambers, the rough soldiers of Estremadura and Castile, many of them illiterate, had never seen the like. All around were 'wondrous artefacts, beautifully made furniture, beds with mattresses and pillows of animal skin and tree fibre, fine quilts'. There was strange food, too: 'fowl and cock and turkey; quail, pigeons and other birds; every kind of river and sea fish, all kinds of fruit from the sea coast…very many different kinds of bread…kneaded and very tasty so that the bread of Castile was not even missed'. When they went into the streets, they gawped at such incredible sights. Yet they knew they were isolated in an alien land; and there was a darker side to the city – especially the bloody sacrifices, which took place across the rooftops to the beating of the 'dismal drum of Huitzilopochtli'. All around them was the smell of death.

They were, though, fascinated by the daily routine of Montezuma: his rituals, food, women, and his manner. Aguilar was one Spaniard who later came to know him well when he was in Spanish custody:

Montezuma was of medium height and slender build with a large head and somewhat flat nostrils. He was very astute, discerning and prudent, learned and capable, but also harsh and irascible, and very firm in his speech… He was very considerate with those of us who were respectful and took off our caps and bowed to him; he gave us presents and jewellery, and dishes of the food that he ate. All this I saw with my own eyes, for I had charge of guarding him many days.

Wandering the streets of today's Mexico City, trying to recover a sense of these events on the ground requires an effort of imagination. Montezuma's city is long gone. The vast filigree of waterways, teeming with thousands of private canoes, the fish jetties, innumerable shrines, and palaces, grand houses, vast outer suburbs

with low-rise adobe houses, the huge market where thousands came every day, and the great white painted pyramids, are no longer to be seen. As Tapia said:

This great city is built within the salt part of the lake, its circumference about two and a half or three leagues. Most of the persons who have seen it, judge it to have about 60,000 inhabitants or more [Aguilar says there were 100,000 houses, and the population was estimated at 240,000 or 300,000 people]. The city has many beautiful and wide streets… The great market, about three times the size of the square of Salamanca, has porticoes all around it, and every day about 20–25,000 people are there buying and selling. On market day, which is held every five days, there are 40–50,000…

In places, though, the outline of the old city is still there, for example, in the pattern of streets north of Tenochtitlan, towards Tlatelolco, in a neighbourhood of run-down barrios, to the west of the great modern throughway up to the shrine of Guadalupe. There, in the earliest detailed city maps of the eighteenth century, we can see part of the ancient network of canals and streets: 'all of which,' as the Spanish said, 'save the three great main avenues are water on one side and earth on the other'.

SO CORTES DISCOVERED THE CITY, and Montezuma took him up one of the pyramids for a wonderful view over- *Gods and Devils of Mexico*
looking the vast market place where the produce of Central America was for barter. And in a scene paralleled only in science fiction, they entered the shrine on top to be confronted by the gleaming eyes of the war god Huitzilopochtli. In front of them, freshly extracted hearts burned in a brazier. Cortes was horrified, but remained cool: 'I marvel that a man as intelligent as you could think that these are good things: these are very bad things known as devils.'

He then asked permission to put a Christian altar there.

Montezuma said: 'We hold these things to be good: they bring us fertility, and rain, say no more to me about it.'

Cortes had time to reflect on these matters. But what should he do next? He had got himself inside the City of Dreams; nothing terrible had befallen him yet; he and his men were still treated as guests, and the Aztecs – despite all the chats about Christianity, comparative religion and human sacrifice – still seemed to be pretending that all was normal. Days passed. In the end, on 16 November, Cortes decided he had to use the cards he had. He arrested Montezuma and told him he had to stay inside Cortes's lodgings, and to continue issuing orders as if all was well.

▲ The war god Huitzilopochtli, to whom Spanish captives were
sacrificed. During the siege, his image was removed by the Aztecs
to a cave at Tula, and was never found; perhaps it still exists.

The scene was set for another fantastic drama. Montezuma was horrified and, at times, during the hours in which neither side would budge, he was in tears. But in the end he bowed to Cortes's threats. Once Montezuma was Cortes's prisoner, psychologically their relationship became more like that of hostage-taker and victim. Cortes tried to govern through Montezuma and, control freak that he was, became angry when he couldn't get what he wanted. He made the mistake of thinking that Montezuma had absolute power, but that was not the case – even though his men looked to him to provide the lead in interpreting and negotiating with the newcomers. The fact was that Montezuma's power was dwindling in the eyes of his people. Despite Spanish claims, the Aztecs were rational beings and Montezuma could no longer command them without question.

Having tried out his power and seen that it worked, Cortes continued to use it. Some of his men had been attacked and killed on the way to the coast. Cortes wanted the local leaders there punished. Montezuma was told to summon them, and Qualpopoca and his sons, and fifteen other chiefs, were brought into Mexico. Like a torturer, alternating sweet talk with threats and coercion, Cortes told Montezuma that he thought he himself must have given the orders to kill his men, but, nevertheless, he 'wouldn't hurt him for all the world'.

No sooner was Montezuma reassured than Cortes told him he must order Qualpopoca and the others to be burned in the great square. To make the fire, they used a great stock of weapons from the armoury and Montezuma was forced to watch in chains. Around them, the Mexicans looked on in complete silence. Such a terrible punishment was seldom used in the Aztec world, except for notable acts of betrayal, and these events must have been absolutely shocking and horrible for the onlookers. It must also have been plain to all now that Montezuma's government had irretrievably broken down.

For the next few weeks, there was a weird interregnum while Montezuma continued the rituals – even performing human sacrifices – taking ritual baths, seeing suitors, enjoying his jesters and jugglers. He also played Mexican gambling games with Cortes, learned a bit of Spanish, and was friendly with some of the Castilian guards, giving them jewels and girls as gifts.

Meanwhile, the Spaniards got used to Mexican tortillas, water fowl, and stranger forms of food, such as the larvae of the salamander, and the green scum off the lake. They drank pulque, a beer made from the fermented juice of the maguey plant, which is still widely drunk today by country people in Mexico. And, just as the Aztec lords did, Cortes would have smoked tobacco after dinner in painted pipes of baked clay. Other diversions included 300 native women who were provided as 'servants'. As well as enjoying the affections of Malinche, Cortes had sexual relations with other women, including a daughter and a niece of Montezuma.

What was Cortes up to? What did he hope to gain from the situation now? Despite all the pleasures on offer in the capital, he could not stop thinking about his predicament. Militarily speaking – and experienced captains would have hammered home this point – he was marooned on the island, as the bridges on the causeway could be taken up at any time.

In late November, he gave orders to construct ships, sending some of his men to the coast to collect the materials which had been salvaged from his fleet –

▲ A prisoner of Cortes, Montezuma pleads with the Aztecs not to attack the Spanish. It was at this moment that his people finally turned against him and attacked him, injuring him, perhaps fatally, with stones and missiles.

anchors, sails, rigging. They built four brigantines, each one thirty or forty feet long and big enough to take cannon. Montezuma was told that these were for pleasure, and was taken on a boating expedition across the lake to hunt on the southern shore. At first sight, they did appear to be pleasure boats – and Montezuma enjoyed the outing.

For Cortes, the trip afforded him valuable information about the lake's character, its landing places and its depth. From then on, frequent trips were made to explore all parts of the lake, on which they saw the local traffic of thousands of canoes, merchants coming in with their goods along causeways, and long-distance traders and tribute-payers from as far away as Guatemala and Oaxaca. The Aztec world was still turning, said the Spanish; 'all on surface was order and harmony'.

As might be expected, this could not last. There were now frequent quarrels over religion and demands for the Aztecs to accept the rule of Spain. There were also relentless requests for gold. Cortes wanted to send expeditions to the gold-producing areas of the empire, and Montezuma agreed. Most contentious, Cortes still wanted to place an image of the Virgin on top of the great temple. Montezuma, however, still resisted this: 'How can you expect us to lose our whole city…? Our gods are very annoyed with us, and I do not know if they would even stop at taking our lives were we to do as you ask.'

In the New Year, resistance broke out among the people of the powerful lake-side ruler, Cacama of Texcoco. Captured with several other lords in circumstances that are still unclear, Cacama was tortured by fire. It was at this point – perhaps with a growing sense of unease about his situation – that Cortes decided that he needed to formalize Montezuma's vassalhood and enact a ceremony of formal submission (as a lawyer, Cortes always liked to see things done by the book).

Cortes insisted that Montezuma should summon the leading lords of the empire. At a meeting in the palace, Montezuma narrated the story of the myth of strangers from the east and, according to the Spanish, he and his lords agreed to submit to the king of Spain. The conquistador Tapia, who had learned some Nahuatl, agreed that this was said, but another eye-witness said he did not understand what was going on, 'but it seemed according to the interpreters that they accepted what Montezuma had requested'.

Later, stories emerged from the Aztec side that Montezuma had not understood the ceremony because of the inadequacy of the translation. Montezuma is said to have cried profusely afterwards when he and other Mexican lords were forced to give brothers, daughters and children as hostages to guarantee their oaths. Cortes was tightening the screw.

His next move was against the Aztec religion. He installed Christian images on the great pyramid, and made the first attempts to destroy the Mexican idols. Still

trying to be reasonable, Montezuma suggested an astonishing compromise: the placing of his gods on one side, the Christians' gods on the other. He even admitted that it was possible they had made one or two mistakes in their beliefs. Forewarned, the Aztecs removed their idols from the top of the pyramid, brought them down on mats and rollers, and secreted them away. They have never been seen since.

In the midst of all these secret moves, the Mexicans tried to gather an army of resistance. The details, however, are very unclear. The Spanish seem to have thought they were still free of worry in Mexico ('things were still in a peaceful state and we were free of strife and alarm', says Aguilar) when, suddenly, there was a dramatic new turn of events. At the beginning of April 1520, news came that a large Spanish force, under a man Cortes knew, Panfilo de Narvaez, had landed on the coast. A punitive expedition had been sent by the governor of Cuba, Velasquez, to arrest Cortes. His past was catching up on him. The gambler's plans were undone.

It was a key moment for Cortes. With the situation still unresolved in Mexico-Tenochtitlan, he had to act. He left Alvarado in the palace in charge of a part of his army (about 120 men, including many sick), and an arsenal of weapons, and with Montezuma and many other nobles in chains. Cortes then marched his main force to the coast to stop Narvaez. Only by another gamble could he retain the possibility of victory – the fantasy he had sold his men – but, to do so, he would have to fight his own countrymen. It was 'winner take all, loser lose everything'.

On a night of pouring rain, Cortes mounted a surprise attack on the Spanish camp in the pyramid enclosure at Zempoala, leaving Narvaez wounded in one eye. (Narvaez lived to fight again, and play a role in the extraordinary tale narrated in Chapter 6) For Cortes, the outcome was better than he could have hoped. Thanks to Narvaez, he was now reinforced by a large group of front-line troops. He would need them.

Massacre in the Temple

WHILE CORTES WAS AWAY ON THE COAST, things came to a head in Mexico. We will never know whether, as the Spanish claimed, the Mexicans were planning an armed assault on the Spanish but, as we have seen, there are hints that they were trying to organize an alternative government and had raised an army of resistance. The Spanish mention no troubles, but one of the earliest and most interesting Aztec accounts – a brief set of annals, written in Tlatelolco, in the north of Mexico City, in 1528 – gives some crucial clues.

During the time Cortes was absent fighting Narvaez, Alvarado imprisoned two important leaders, including the military chief of Tlatelolco. He hanged another chief, and murdered the king of Nautla by shooting him with arrows and burning

▲ 'The Spanish attacked the Mexicans first.' The massacre in the temple precinct, from the Duran Codex.

him alive. So the situation had already taken a turn for the worse when the time came for the great Aztec spring festival: 'That was why our warriors were on guard at the Eagle Gate…sentries from Tenochtitlan at one side; Tlatelolco on the other.'

In other words, the Aztecs were expecting trouble. But at Montezuma's specific request, according to the annals, the festival still went ahead. The Aztec annals, although laconic in the extreme, differ from the more detailed accounts in Spanish, and from the eye-witness reports gathered later by Father Sahagun. According to the Aztecs, the first day passed as normal: the idol of Huitzilopochtli was made and dressed and the celebrants sang their songs without interference. It was on the second day that the Spanish struck:

They began to sing again but without warning they were all put to death.
The dancers and the singers were completely unarmed. They brought only their
embroidered cloaks, their turquoises, their lip plugs, their necklaces, their clusters
of heron feathers, their trinkets made of deer hooves. Those who played the drums,
the old men, had brought their gourds of snuff and their timbrels.

The Spanish attacked the musicians first, slashing at their hands and faces until
they had killed all of them. The singers – and even the spectators – were also killed.
This slaughter in the Sacred Patio went on for three hours. Then the Spaniards burst

◀ A detail from Charles
Ricketts's 'Death of
Montezuma', *c.* 1924; the
tlatoani was perhaps killed by
his own side, but rumours
persisted that he was
garrotted by Cortes.

into the rooms of the temple to kill the others: those who were carrying water, or bringing fodder for the horses, or grinding meal, or sweeping the floor…

Those are the bare facts, undisputed by either side. In the Florentine Codex account, which gives a report from an Aztec eye-witness who was present that day, there is an horrendous, agonizingly painful, and detailed description of the slaughter that triggered the Mexican uprising against Cortes. Through his words, we watch in slow motion as the camera turns from one horror scene to the next in the wide stuccoed courtyard: the sun beating down, the turquoise-blue and emerald-green feathers of quetzals and macaws, the gorgeous finery of the warriors, the flash of gold arm-rings, the liquid sheen of jade lip plugs. The Spanish suddenly move forward in their armour, bearing their long swords of Toledo steel. The first Mexican victim, we are told, was a drummer. First his hands were severed, then his neck: 'Of some they slashed open their backs, then their entrails gushed out. Of some they cut their heads to pieces… Some they struck on the shoulder; they split openings…they split bodies open…'

Although the Mexicans had heard reports of what happened at Cholula, they had never seen Spanish swords at work first-hand. What was the meaning in this cutting of unarmed warriors? The Mexicans, for all their 'fierce and unnatural cruelty', as the Spanish describe it – and as we still tend to see them today – had very precise rules about the conduct of warfare, and very precise rules about violence to the human body. As their sacrificial ceremonies show, their cruelties were strictly controlled, ritualized. The idea of this kind of pre-emptive strike – a punitive massacre, like that at Cholula – was incredible to them, and the tone of the Aztec account is full of incredulity. For them, it was the Spanish who exhibited 'unnatural cruelty'.

The massacre in the temple is a key inciting moment in the tale: why did it happen? Did Alvarado panic? Obviously Cortes knew that Alvarado was impetuous – and, doubtless, in the way that calculating people are drawn to their opposites, this was why Cortes was drawn to Alvarado. Cortes must have left Alvarado with contingency plans, and these must have included the use of force if Alvarado believed they were threatened. But with that act of violence, the spell exerted by the bearded foreigners was broken. The upshot now was war: 'It was the twentieth day after Cortes left for the coast… We allowed the Captain to return to the city in peace. But on the following day we attacked him with all our might, and that was the beginning of the war…'

Cortes had returned on 25 June 1520. By 30 June, his situation was desperate. The causeways had been cut, the bridges taken away and the net had closed. The Spanish were now denied food supplies and there was an acute shortage of

drinking water. With growing terror, they found themselves imprisoned in the heart of the City of Dreams.

What happened next on the Aztec side is shrouded in mystery, but we have to assume that, in secret rituals, they stripped Montezuma of the power of *tlatoani*, and appointed a successor – something which had never happened before in Aztec history. Did Cortes know this before he took his next step? We do not know, but he now forced Montezuma to speak to the crowds from the rooftop to try to pacify them. But, having already lost his power, Montezuma was forced to duck back under a hail of missiles.

The Spanish later claimed that Montezuma was wounded and later died of his injuries. But, hurt or not, when he was taken back to the palace, it seems clear that the Great Speaker was now understood by Cortes to have lost all his power and was, therefore, of no further use to the Spanish. The other captive nobles were also considered to be an encumbrance who should not be allowed to go free. That night, as the crowd roared outside, Cortes conferred with his captains and decided that Montezuma should be killed. Then, according to Father Sahagun's Aztec informants, he 'garrotted all the nobles he had in power'. The bodies were thrown off the roof into the courtyard below. The gambler had staked all.

The Night of Tears

AS THE NEWS OF THE KILLING OF MONTEZUMA and the other great lords spread, there was uproar in the city. The terrible scene that unfolded is told with nightmarish power by Aguilar:

After night fell, about ten o'clock, a terrifying mob of women appeared carrying torches and flaming braziers. They came for their husbands and relatives who lay dead in the porticoes. And they came for Montezuma, too. And as the women recognized their men (which we could see by the great amount of light from the rooftop where we kept watch) they threw themselves upon them with great sorrow and grief, and raised such a wailing and crying that it filled one with fear. I was on guard duty then and I said to my companion: 'Have you not seen the hell and flood of tears over there? For if you have not seen it, you may witness it from here.'
In truth, in all the war and in all the terrors I went through, I was never so afraid as I was when I heard that awful lamentation…

Cortes had to get out of the city, and as fast as possible. The date set was the night of 1 July, three days before the new moon. In frantic haste, he tried to parcel up the gold and spread it out between the troops, but also found time in the hours leading up to the departure to take another mistress, a sister of Cacama. (He also prayed to his favourite Virgin, Los Remedios of Seville.)

Copolco
3oī mīcca ȳ
capītan.

▲ The Spanish defeat on the 'Night of Tears' copied from the finest Mexican representation of the Conquest – the lost Lienzo of Tlaxcala.

Eye-witnesses remember that the night was bright and a light rain was falling as they prepared to move off. The route chosen was the one out to the west, which was the shortest causeway to the mainland. The Mexicans had removed the bridges, so the Spanish improvised a portable bridge made from roof-beams of their palace, which was carried by sixty Indian assistants.

Accompanying the Spaniards were a huge number of people, including their Indian allies, women, baggage, several cannon and large quantities of gold, melted down into bars and mounted in boxes on horses, or carried by the men. The remainder was tied in bundles carried by Tlaxcalan auxiliaries. At midnight, they filed out of the palace, their horses' hooves muffled, all orders passed along in whispers – no trumpets allowed for military signals.

◄ Attacked by the Aztecs, the Spaniards found themselves trapped inside the city. Their attempt to escape has all the qualities of a nightmare. Many men were weighed down by gold and their superiority in weapons was largely nullified. Perhaps two-thirds of the Spanish army were killed: the biggest disaster suffered by Europeans arms in the Americas.

Moving down the causeway, they crossed four of the canals towards the lake shore. Then, at the 'Tolteca canal' (today marked by a post office on the Tacuba road), they were caught. A woman up late saw them: 'Mexica come quickly, our enemies are leaving. Now that it is night they are running away as fugitives!'

The word spread like wildfire. A few minutes later, there was a shout from the temple top, a drum beat, and the male population rose up: 'To your canoes of war…' Within minutes, the Spanish were hurled into panic and chaos. It was hellish in the darkness as canoes closed in on all sides. 'Speeding like arrows' was how the Aztecs remembered their warriors that night. The Spanish column still tried to press forward, and in the confusion hundreds of people fell into the canal. At one point, the Spanish seem to have killed their own Indian auxiliaries by pushing them into the water and crossing on their bodies: 'All fell in there, the Tlaxcalans, the Spanish, their horses, some women were dropped in there. The canal was full of them…and those who came last only crossed over on dead bodies…'

The Spanish conquistadora, Maria de Estrada, gave as good an account of herself as any man, swinging a Spanish sword. At one point, Cortes himself fell into the water and, as Aztec canoes closed in on him, he was pulled out just in time by two of his men. 'But soon it was a matter of each man saving his own skin…'

Over 600 Spanish conquistadors were killed (some estimates ran to over 1000), many no doubt weighed down by the gold they were carrying; several thousand Tlaxcalans were probably lost too. Among the dead were many Aztec collaborators, including no fewer than three of Cortes's Aztec mistresses: 'Dona Ana' and 'Dona Ines', daughters of Montezuma, and 'Dona Ana', daughter of Cacama. A measure of how fast they planned their escape was that their departure time, or their full plan, was not communicated to 270 men billeted in another part of the city who never moved off. Trapped and starved out, they fell into the hands of the enraged Aztecs and were sacrificed to the war god.

The elemental horror of that night was never forgotten. It is still called 'La Noche Triste' ('The Night of Tears'). Diaz del Castillo's harrowing description of the distant sight of his comrades, dragged up the temple steps for sacrifice, forced to dance naked, embodied the worse nightmares of the Spanish. The prisoners were not given the status of warrior captives – as the Aztecs saw it, they had been captured ignobly running away like cowards, and an honourable warrior's death was not for them. They were stripped of their battle equipment, armour, clothing, and only then, when they were naked, and reduced to 'slaves', were they dragged up the temple steps and held down on the *chacmool* for the priests to cut out their hearts. And no doubt, they were refused the hallucinogenic mushrooms which made it easier to face the 'obsidian death'.

At most, a quarter of Cortes's force fought their way through to the shore at Tacuba, where legend has it that Cortes sat down at dawn beneath a kapok tree, whose gigantic stump still stands at the roadside. The great gambler had lost his throw, and the story is always told that he shed tears at this moment (a scene portrayed on calendars and posters still sold round the city today). But Cortes had not lost his key helpers, the two interpreters, Malinche and Aguilar, or his friends, Alvarado, Sandoval and Tapia.

According to an eye-witness, when he reached the Tacuba side, Cortes asked after one person, and one person only – the master shipbuilder and carpenter, Martin Lopez, 'a very clever and skilful man', who had built the boats in the lake. Had he survived? He had, but badly wounded: 'Okay let's go, for we lack nothing,' said Cortes – an incredible display of bravado and self-belief at such a dire moment. Cortes had not given up – far from it: 'For from those words', said one who was present, 'we understood that through this Martin Lopez, the city which had been lost, might be regained.'

The Enigma of Montezuma

CORTES RETREATED IN A WIDE CIRCLE through the north of the valley and over the mountains back to Tlaxcala. The next few days were a struggle for survival, and at Otumba he fought a desperate battle in which he was very lucky to drive off his pursuers. Indeed, it is still a mystery as to why the Aztecs were unable to crush the weakened Spanish survivors when they were almost at their mercy. It was a lost opportunity that they would bitterly regret. But Cortes was able to retrace his steps to Tlaxcala, there to lick his wounds, and to consider his next move.

As for poor Montezuma, the mystery of his actions is still impossible to sift. Perhaps his fascination with the Other was as big a factor as any in what happened – in his failure to classify and counteract the strangers. Did he see the future? Was he trying to save his empire, city, people, position – or merely his own skin? We cannot tell. Short of finding a draft of his famous welcome speech in a manuscript, written by the priest of the House of Darkness, we will never know Montezuma's intentions. What he said, or meant to say, what significance the belief in a returning god had on all these events, we cannot say. Perhaps he thought he had done what was best for his city and his people.

2
THE WAR OF
THE WORLDS

SO, THE FIRST MAJOR EUROPEAN MILITARY INCURSION into the New World had ended in disaster. Despite superior European technology, Cortes had narrowly escaped total defeat and, with the loss of a huge proportion of his expedition, had been humiliatingly expelled from the Valley of Mexico.

It is easy to forget, because we know the eventual outcome, that defeat was not inevitable in July 1520. After the initial confusion about how to classify and respond to these strangers, the Aztecs had begun to come to terms with the tremendous culture shock of their discovery of the Other – the knowledge that, over the ocean to the east, there was a world peopled by beings whose moral order was very different to their own – but humans none the less, who died, and could be beaten.

To focus on that summer of 1520 in Mexico City, with a year or more to go before the final tragedy, to sit with Cuitlahuac and his nobles, and go over the nightmare of the last six months, is to crowd the mind with 'what ifs'. What if the Aztecs had been able to reorganize, capture or trade Spanish weaponry, and force their prisoners to show them how the crossbows and guns worked?

What if they had been able to exploit the differences between the colonial powers – as, for example, the Maya of the Yucatan were able to do in the nineteenth century, when they fought for independence from Mexico, and negotiated with Queen Victoria's British empire which ran them guns through Belize?

And what if the Tlaxcalans had decided not to support Cortes further? What if disease had not devastated the Mexican population? What if Cortes's defeat had been total at the bridges, ending, say, in the death of all the Spaniards?

When the news spread through all the distant provinces that Mexico was destroyed, their chiefs and lords could not believe it. However, they sent their chieftains to congratulate Cortes on his victories and to yield themselves as vassals to His Majesty, and to see if the city of Mexico, which they had so dreaded, really was razed to the ground. They all carried presents of gold to Cortes, and even brought their small children to show them Mexico, pointing it out to them in much the same way that we would say:
'Here stood Troy'.

•

BERNAL DIAZ DEL CASTILLO
The Conquest of New Spain, c. 1565

◀◀ The emblem of the war god: a gold and turquoise breastplate in the form of a shield with four ceremonial arrows.

All of this was certainly within the realms of chance (Cortes himself only narrowly survived on several occasions). What a different story it might have been. Perhaps, though, history was against the Aztecs: at this very moment Magellan was in the Pacific, and the world was changing around them even before they had time to understand it.

For just a short time, though, the situation looked hopeful for the Aztecs. According to them, 'When the Spanish left, the Mexicans thought they had gone for good and would never return'. Convinced the Spanish would not come back, they cleaned the temple courtyards and celebrated their fiestas again in the traditional way. The old sacrifices were made once more on the great pyramid of Huitzilopochtli.

They had a new ruler now, too. Wisdom and good counsel were key qualities in being the Aztec *tlatoani*, as well as bravery and ritual expertise – and the man they had chosen possessed these in good measure. Decided upon, perhaps, even before Montezuma's death, the successor was Cuitlahuac – one of several who had warned against allowing the Spanish to enter Tenochtitlan in the first place. He did not, however, have long to enjoy the royal mat.

Pestilence Strikes

OMENS, BOTH NATURAL AND SUPERNATURAL, crowded the last months of the Aztec world. And the natural ones – those now capable of scientific explanation – seemed at the time no less astounding, dreadful and portentous than those which we can only interpret in the realms of the psyche. The most ominous, though, was all too visible and tangible.

At the end of September 1520, at Cuatlan in the Valley of Mexico, people started to die of a mysterious and alien illness which had horrifying symptoms of 'racking coughs and painful burning sores'. The pestilence began to spread and soon crossed the causeways into Tenochtitlan. It lasted seventy days, until late November, and killed a vast number of people. The disease was smallpox.

Previously unknown to the people of the New World, it had come across the Atlantic with the Spanish emigrants and conquistadors. We can trace its track as closely as an army on the move. It devastated the island of Hispaniola from December 1518, where one third of the people died; then Puerto Rico, Jamaica, Cuba during 1519, crossing to the mainland Yucatan in spring 1520, and then moved into the interior.

An invisible killer, travelling with Cortes's army – apparently (so it was believed) with one of Narvaez's troops who had come back from the coast with Cortes. Smallpox is communicated through droplets of breath, and is one of the easiest diseases to pass on in the crowded conditions of a great city, and one of the most virulent once it has taken hold. Tragically, the immune systems of New

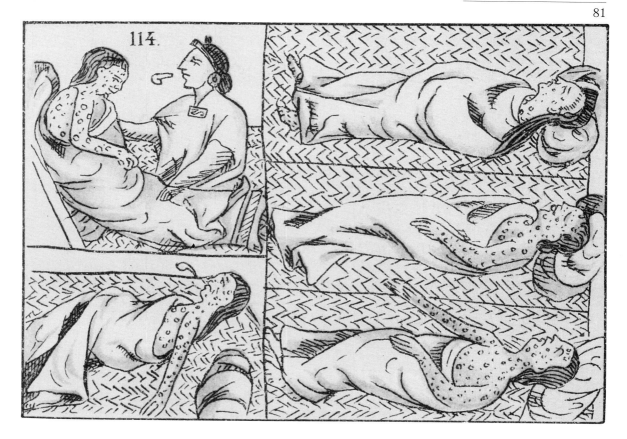

World natives had no ability to resist such infection, and the population was devastated. The description in the Aztec account of *huey zahuatl* ('the great rash') is as exquisitely painful to read as anything in that memorable text:

▲ The 'great rash': victims of the smallpox pandemic of autumn 1520. Note the speech symbol, bottom left: 'they cried out in agony'; from the Florentine Codex, *c.* 1570.

Sores erupted on our faces, our breasts, our bellies, we were covered with agonizing sores from head to foot… The sick were so utterly helpless that they could only lie on their beds like corpses, unable to move their limbs or even their heads. They could not lie face down or roll from one side to the other. If they did move their bodies, they screamed with pain.

According to Cortes's secretary, Gomara, the Indians called the sickness 'the great leprosy' and later counted the years from it, as if it had inaugurated some new cycle of time, which, in a way, it had. Among the dead was the new king, and his young son.

As so often happens when pestilence devastates a population, the side-effects can be shattering, too. Belief in social norms breaks down; the fields are not cultivated; the harvest is left to rot if there are not enough able-bodied survivors; people are paralysed, and lapse into stunned inaction. As we can see in other great plagues in history, the disaster is psychological and social, as well as physical – a blow of fate so implacable and inexplicable that, in the short term, people lose the will to rebuild. 'Many died from hunger for they had no one left to look after them,' said the Aztecs. 'No one cared about anyone else.' Timing is everything in history.

Cortes Prepares the Fleet

MEANWHILE, CORTES NURSED HIS WOUNDS and consolidated himself in Tlaxcala. His long lines of communication with Cuba and Spain, although on one level isolating, on another enabled him to mask his actions, cover up his defeats and bide his time while he put together another gambler's hand.

First, he convinced the Tlaxcalans to stay with him and, with them, subdued wavering Indian allies who were questioning the wisdom of an alliance with the strangers. Then he rebuilt his military force, with reinforcements which had come in during the autumn. By the winter, he could muster over 500 infantry with eighty crossbowmen and arquebusiers, with forty horses and eight or nine small cannon. His first attempt to bring the Aztec empire under Spanish rule had been by a mixture of cajolery, blackmail and discreet violence. Now, with the promise of 10,000 Tlaxcalan warriors marching with him, he decided to attempt the overthrow of the Aztec empire by war.

It was at this time that he wrote his long second letter to the king of Spain, outlining his actions since his arrival into Mexico-Tenochtitlan, structuring the whole tale to fit his story. In it, he presents himself as a simple, loyal, devoted servant – an invented persona, we have to say, when compared with the ironic manipulator who comes out in face-to-face meetings described by people such as Las Casas. He now declares his intention to return to take the city, and bring it under the rule of the king.

Having staked all on that outcome, he had no alternative, of course. He had to win, and still believed he could. It is a measure of Cortes's nervousness, though, that the letter dated 30 October 1520 was not actually dispatched until March the following year. Perhaps too many imponderables remained for such self-serving optimism to convince even its own writer. Better to send it, perhaps, when the wheel of fortune had more clearly turned in his direction.

The events of the Night of Tears had shown Cortes that the key to victory would lie in the hands of whoever maintained control of the lake. So he decided

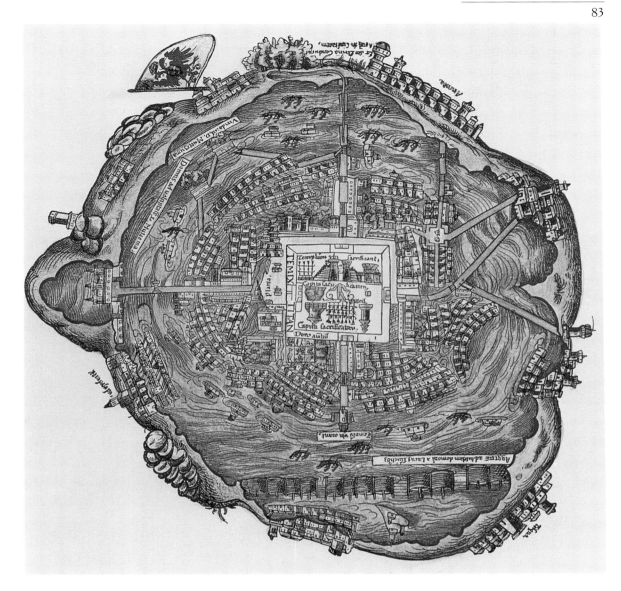

to build a fleet of boats in Tlaxcala and transport them in prefabricated sections across the mountains and reassemble them on the lake itself. It was a plan of breathtaking ambition. The construction of the fleet, and the forging of alliances with the Tlaxcalans and their followers, would allow him to lay siege to the city of Tenochtitlan. This is the most amazing example of Cortes's character – his ability to devise a grand strategy while at the same time paying close attention to the practical details.

▲ Map of the Aztec city of Tenochtitlan, published with Cortes's second letter to Charles V; a woodcut of 1524, it may have been based on an Aztec painting.

Impressive above all is his maintenance of the precarious web of political alliances with his native allies – all sustained by intimidation, charm, blackmail, promised rewards and theatrical use of punishment and cruelty. What comes out again and again is Cortes's extraordinary capacity to sustain a complex vision by constantly scanning shifting and unstable factors. Nothing in his earlier life that we can discern would have prepared us for it. Dislike him as we may, the man certainly had a talent for control of himself, and of others.

First, a blueprint for the boats. One brigantine had been spared during the sinking of the fleet and he had this dismantled and transported – with the remaining bolts, nails and tackle from the ships destroyed on the beach – back to his old base on the coast at Villa Rica. The parts were then laid out under the supervision of the expedition's master shipbuilder, Martin Lopez. The Tlaxcalans, meanwhile, sent out parties to cut the wood in the forests on the slopes of the volcano, Malinche.

Back in Tlaxcala, under Lopez's instructions, they cut the wood and shaped it. The shipyard was on the banks of the Zahuapan river, which they dammed to form a small lake on which to try out the stability and soundness of the boats. Thirteen brigantines – big enough to mount cannon in the bows – were constructed; each was, perhaps, forty feet long.

At the end of December 1520, the army moved on Tenochtitlan; the boats followed later, transported in pieces overland by 8000 native carriers. As an example of implacable resolve and masterful pragmatism, one can only be reminded of Alexander the Great's siege projects on the mountain tops of Central Asia and the Hindu Kush. Nothing was going to stand in Cortes's way.

The Siege of Mexico

THE NEW KING, CUAUHTEMOC, was in his mid-twenties, the son of Montezuma's uncle, Ahuitzotl. The Spanish describe the king as a graceful person, lighter skinned than most Mexicans with 'grave eyes which never seemed to waver'. He was personally brave and was an experienced warleader. Like any Aztec ruler, he was also ruthless. To forestall any whiff of appeasement, he ordered two sons of Montezuma to be killed.

To Cuauhtemoc fell the task of organizing the resistance of the shrinking Aztec empire and, for as long as he lived, he did so bravely. Unlike Montezuma, his image can still be seen on posters, calendars and statues all over Mexico today.

Cortes camped by the lake, and made reconnaissances to assess the rebuilt causeways, and the likeliest lines of attack. At the lakeside town of Texcoco, his master shipbuilder reassembled the boats, and Cortes supervised the digging of a canal to the lake, dredging part of the lake bottom to ensure a successful launch. The incredulous reaction of the Aztecs soon turned to dismay as they realized that the fleet had the potential to cut off their access to the outside world.

The early stage of the siege saw the surrender of towns all round the lake to the point where the Aztecs were shorn of almost all their former allies, vassal states and tribute-payers. The cruel and overbearing nature of Aztec rule was coming home to roost. By the end of the siege, ten native kings were in Cortes's entourage.

With the wind blowing this way, Cortes had hoped to take the city without serious fighting, expecting to intimidate the Mexicans by the steady reduction of the city states around the lake, and by histrionic acts of violence – by what his critic Las Casas calls the 'deliberate use of terror'. By punishing any resistance with exemplary cruelty, he thought he would bring Cuauhtemoc to negotiation and surrender. But events did not turn out that way.

At the beginning, there were divided opinions among the Aztec leadership, and the Aztec annals of Tlatelolco note that the Mexicans were already fighting among themselves. Several high-ranking nobles were put to death, 'killed because they tried to persuade the people to bring corn, hens and eggs to the Spaniards. They were killed by the priests, captains and elder brothers... But the great chiefs were angry at these executions. They said to the killers: "Have we all become murderers? Only sixty days ago our people were slaughtered at the fiesta of Toxcatl!"'

But these dissensions, if we are to believe the accounts which survive from the Aztec side, carried on. At one point the Tenochtitlan warriors killed four of their own chiefs for their failure to lead from the front. And recriminations continued between different groups, right till the bitter end. The people from Tlatelolco, the once independent northern part of the island, insisted to the last that, 'We were the ones who fought all the main battles: the warriors of Tenochtitlan were nowhere to be seen...they hung back, but as for us, our humblest warriors died fighting bravely as captains.'

Divided purposes, even more perhaps than technology, were decisive in the fall of Mexico.

So, the net closed and the native kingdoms of the Valley of Mexico all went over to the grand alliance of the Spanish and the Tlaxcalans. Soon it must have been plain that Tenochtitlan was doomed. But the Aztec leadership would not surrender, even when only the city on the island was left. And so a siege proper began, with the Spaniards now resorting, as Diaz del Castillo put it, to a 'new kind of warfare'.

Siege was a quintessential European strategy. Cortes himself was not experienced in such warfare, but among his forces were Greek, Genoese and Spanish soldiers who had fought in the Mediterranean. They understood the principle of siege warfare: that maximum pressure has to be exerted on the entire population – the old, the women and children – to cut them off and reduce them to starvation and despair.

For the Aztecs, so far as we can tell, this was a new kind of war – indeed not war at all. They had destroyed cities on occasion and enslaved their populations, they knew about putting their army round a city to persuade its warriors to come out and fight, but the systematic starving of a population and the deliberate targeting of non-combatants was not part of their experience. Indeed, within their chivalrous rules of war, it was possible that they would provide food for enemies in order that victory might be seen to have been won without unfair advantage.

That said, they adapted: changing their tactics, using captured Spanish swords, for example, tied to long spears to get at the horses' bellies; learning to avoid the crossbow bolts by taking cover when they were cranked up, 'listening out for the hum of the bolt'. But the Aztecs never lost their contempt for enemies who hid behind cannon and guns, who fled without shame and killed brave warriors at a distance, unfairly, with guns and crossbows.

The images of battle from both sides vividly convey this sense of two different orders of thought – two kinds of moral combat. The Spanish were perplexed by the ferocity and determination of the resistance, even when all was lost, and angered by the Aztec failure to understand, acknowledge and submit to their rules. The Aztecs, on the other hand, were embittered and frustrated by the Spaniards' constant flouting of their chivalric code of fighting. Almost to the very end, the two sides persisted in their failure to communicate with each other.

Our greatest account of the siege is from the Aztec eye-witnesses, which is full of memorable scenes, sprinkled with memories, gestures, names and places, as vivid in its human detail, and as grand in its sense of destiny, as Homer's *Iliad*.

Here, for example, told with the same refinement that Homer gives to the arming of Achilles, is the Aztec hero Tzilacatzin, a man who:

…scorned his enemies, Spaniards as well as Indians, so that they all shook with terror at the mere sight of him. When the Spaniards found out how dangerous he was, they tried desperately to kill him. Therefore, he wore various disguises to prevent them recognizing him; sometimes his lip plug, gold earrings and full regalia…then head uncovered to show his hair clipped Otomi style…sometimes he wore cotton armour with a thin kerchief wrapped round his head…but sometimes the full finery, a plumed headdress with the eagle symbol on its crest, and gleaming bracelets of gold on arms and ankles. He was one of only three captains who never retreated. They were contemptuous of their enemies and gave no thought whatsoever to their own safety…

This was the kind of detail to delight an aristocratic warrior class and, in the retelling in later years, to provide some solace for the eventual outcome, affirming

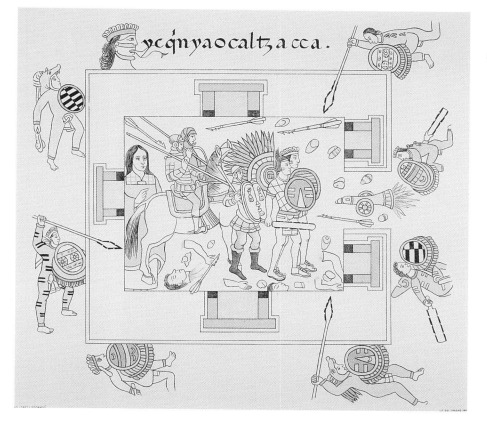

ycq́nyaocaltz̧acca.

◂ The battle for Tenochtitlan,
copied from the lost Lienzo
of Tlaxcala. Malinche (behind
the horseman) still appears
as a *dea ex machina*.

that the true values of the old culture of Mexico did not fail, even if history, or fate, had been against them.

Cut off by besiegers whose numbers they estimated at nearly 250,000, the Aztecs defended their island as best they could. They sent a party to protect the aqueduct – the city's crucial source of fresh water which came down from the hills at Chapultepec. They made underwater barriers of sharpened stakes to deter Cortes's brigantines. But, in the end, all the individual battles came down to the firepower of guns, and crossbows, and the terrible cutting edge of Toledo steel swords. The weaponry of the Aztecs was primitive and, for all their courage, the Eagle and Jaguar warriors could not keep the Spaniards and their allies at bay.

Cortes and his allies landed their forces in the south of the island, and fought their way through the city, street by street, and house by house. Even though the weight of weapons was on their side, the Spanish still suffered reverses. In a ferocious battle at the 'House of the Arsenal', fifteen Spaniards were captured and sacrificed. A tremendous struggle inside the north of the city ('at the place where San Martin is today', says a later Aztec witness) ended with 2000 of Cortes's Indian allies killed, and no fewer than fifty-three Spanish captured along with their standard. All of these men, and four horses, were sacrificed, with lingering ceremonial, on the temple platform at Tlatelolco, in full view of their comrades.

In the Aztec account, we can taste the sharp relish of the beleaguered defenders as the Spanish captives staggered about 'drunkenly', weak with terror, before they were taken, one by one, up the temple steps to suffer 'the sweet death of the obsidian knife'. Their heads (and those of their horses) were displayed on skull racks to cheer the defenders and strike fear into their assailants.

The Aztec resistance was desperately brave, men and women together rushing out under cover of dark to clear canals which had been filled in by the Spanish advance. But the odds were stacked against them; and when the Spaniards cut off their fresh water supply, the vast population trapped inside the city was left in desperate straits:

There was no fresh water to drink, only stagnant water, and the briny water of the lake, and many died of dysentery. The only food was lizards, swallows, corn-cobs and the salt grasses of the lake. The people also ate water lilies and chewed on hides and pieces of leather – they ate the bitterest seeds; they even ate dirt.

Gradually, the whole southern part of the island, the original city of Tenochtitlan, fell to the Spaniards. The defenders, who were estimated at 300,000 people by one contemporary account, became concentrated in the northern part of the island, formerly the separate city state of Tlatelolco. This became the centre of the battle, and the main idol from the temple of Huitzilopochtli was brought here to be set up in the 'House of Young Men', that is, the college close to the temple and the great market. Most of Father Sahagun's informants, including eye-witnesses, came from this part of the city and, for this reason, the narrative now takes on the tragic dimension of first-hand war reportage.

The Last Stand: An Aztec Iliad

Nothing can compare with the horrors of that siege and the agonies of the starving. We were so weakened by hunger that little by little the enemy forced us to retreat. Little by little they forced us to the wall.

They fought for eighty days. The Spaniards had total control of the lake by now. The causeways were cut off, and the survivors were concentrated into the north-eastern corner of the island. Although the Spanish now knew that they would win, they were angry that the Aztecs refused to accept the inevitable. But the rules of war had gone beyond the point where they understood each other or

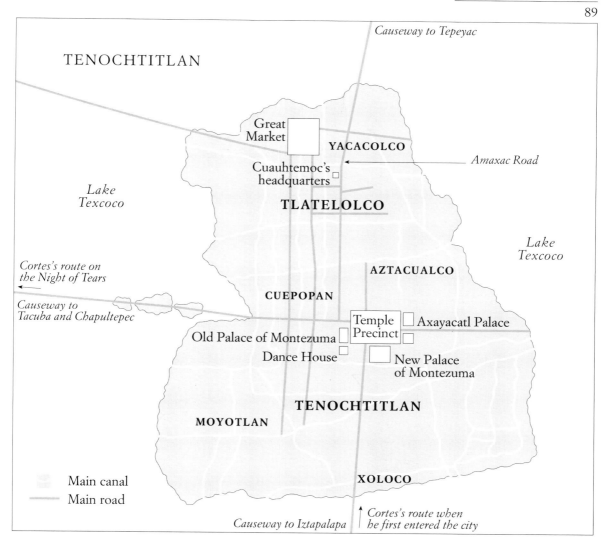

had any common ground. The Spanish conduct of war was so despicable to the Aztecs that they chose to ignore 'their rules'.

This drove Cortes to distraction because he was now compelled to reduce the city district by district. Ironically, to possess the city of his dreams, he was forced to demolish it.

The Aztec annals of Tlatelolco, written within a few years of the events, record how, at one point in a lull, the Spaniards and Tlaxcalans approached some defenders on the front line and asked for a parley. A group of Tlatelolcans agreed and were taken under safe conduct to Cortes ('in the House of the Mist in Nonhualco: along with Malinche, Alvarado and Sandoval, with a number of native chiefs').

▲ An eagle warrior – one of the Aztec élite; a lifesize statue from the House of Eagles in the ceremonial precinct. Such men led the fight against the Spanish.

The text next reproduces what Cortes said to them, as interpreted by Malinche. It has a high-handed brusqueness, a casual brutality that, to the reader at least, suggests the real-life Cortes, when the mask has slipped:

Malinche said to the guards: 'Come forward! The Captain wants to know: what can the chiefs of Tenochtitlan be thinking of? Is Cuauhtemoc a stupid, wilful little boy? Has he no mercy on the women and children of his city? Must even the old men perish? See the kings who are with me' pointing to ten kings around him: one of whom spoke: 'Do the people of Tenochtitlan think they are playing a game? Already their hearts are grieving for the city in which they were born. If they will not surrender we shall abandon them to their fate, and let them perish – bring a senseless destruction on themselves.'

The tensions and contradictions in the position of the native rulers, allied to Cortes, are pitifully exposed in this scene. But the Aztecs were no longer prepared to acknowledge the Spaniards' superiority, and the battle now moved on into that sinister zone where men fight to the death. The women, too, joined in the fighting, hitching up their skirts and shooting arrows at the enemy.

By now, the action had been compressed into the north-east part of the island, around the plaza of the great market, the temple precinct of the great northern pyramid (of Tlatelolco), the grand noble mansions and colleges, and the warren of lesser houses along the filigree of canals. The Aztec account tells how, stage by stage, their resistance was broken down: the moment, for example, when the Spanish cavalry burst into the market place for the first time and set fire to the temple, causing a huge conflagration. And, again, they tell it with vivid immediacy:

This battle lasted for many hours and extended to every corner of the market place. There was no action along the wall where the vendors sold lime, but the fighting raged among the flower stalls, and the stalls offering snails, and all the passageways in between them.

CONQVISTA DE MEXICO POR CORTES. *G7*

These last dark days are also recalled in Aztec poems, written in Nahuatl in the aftermath of defeat. They portray images of the city in flames, the air black with smoke, the stench of the uncremated dead in the streets, the guns flashing in the darkness. Most severe was the

▲ The battle for Tenochtitlan. Cortes and his army cross the causeway, depicted by a sixteenth-century artist in the manner of a heroic European battle painting. In reality Cortes's forces were largely made up of his native allies.

battle for the canal line in Yacacolco, in the north-east of the island. As Father Sahagun's eye-witnesses remembered: 'The Tlatelolcans…took up positions on the opposite side of the canal, hurling stones and shooting arrows across it. The enemy could not advance or capture any of the bridges.' This battle, which saw the great market fall into Spanish hands, lasted five days, and, during it, the 'great warriors of the Tlatelolcans', the Eagle and Jaguar warriors, were defeated, and 2000 Tlatelolcans were killed. The end was now only a matter of time:

Our warriors rallied to the defence of the city. Their spirits and courage were high; not one of them showed any fear… The warriors of Tlatelolco were very alert; very cautious and vigilant, and watched intently to see where the crossbow shots were coming from. But step by step the Spaniards gained more ground and captured more houses. And they forced us backward along the Amaxac road.

Amaxac was the scene of the final tragedy. The witnesses were very careful at this stage of their act of remembrance to name each precise location of the story, and handed down to us an intimate sense of this part of the Aztec city, to the south and east of the great market.

These place-names were later explained to Father Sahagun by his Aztec informants. Yacacolco, for example, the great house where the fifty-three Spaniards were sacrificed, some by Cuauhtemoc himself, stood 'where the plaza of Santa Ana is today'. This place is still there, a whitewashed church set in a little garden square, full of palms and flowers. If we look at the eighteenth-century street maps of Mexico City, we can place today's plaza into the old Aztec plan with its canals and lanes.

At that time, the colonial capital of New Spain was still within the boundaries of the ancient lake; many of the old canals had survived, and the lake itself was not yet drained. In the pattern of eighteenth-century streets around Santa Ana, we can see something of the layout of the city which Montezuma knew. And, today in this little corner of Mexico City, which has not yet fallen prey to the developers, it is still there. The canals have been filled in and trams rumble over them now, but you can stand in the plaza of Santa Ana and, with a little imagination, picture, amid today's hustle and bustle, where the heaviest fighting took place in the last desperate phase.

The area then, as now, was mainly low-rise houses. The nineteenth-century residences, with their faded stucco walls and little gardens, are the same sort of height as the sixteenth-century buildings. The grand noble houses were of double-storey height, with heavy-beamed roofs from which warriors could fire slings and throw spears and stones.

So, imagine: thousands of women and children camped in the streets around us, off the main thoroughfare. The Amaxac road goes north through this area where, later, Santa Ana will stand. Between us and the temple pyramid there is a big north-south canal which is the Aztec defence-line against attacks from the west; right by Yacacolco (the Santa Ana plaza), there is an east-west canal cutting across the Amaxac road, the main Aztec defence-line against attack from the south. All the crossing places have been broken; there are barricades of beams, rubble and adobe from the demolished houses across all the roads.

Over the rooftops to our left, the great pyramid is now fire-blackened, the shrines on its summit smashed and torched. Below it, columns of smoke rise from the huge square of the market, which has now ceased to function. To the north of us are the grand buildings of the colleges of the Aztec nobility; in one of these, the image of the war god is still being worshipped. From the rooftops around us, through the pall of smoke, we can still catch glimpses of the blue lake where the brigantines of the allies have now broken through the inside of the great weir with their cannon, and are firing at will over the Aztec defences, leaving smudges of black smoke hanging over the water.

This north-eastern corner of the great island city is the last enclave of the resistance. And nearly 500 years on, walking round its decaying nineteenth-century shops and houses, it is moving to find that some faint imprint of that past history of the city should have survived here and nowhere else.

The Final Omen

FROM THE NATIVE ACCOUNTS, we can see that Cortes's final push was over the canal which ran east-west crossing the Amaxac road, the Aztecs' last line of defence before the north-eastern corner of the island. Once this fell, they were pushed around the area now marked by the little sixteenth-century church of La Concepcion (La Conchita) in Tepito, a popular church in a bustling neighbourhood of a city that is famous for its low life, its sports clubs, and especially its boxers.

There is an open-air market in the streets outside the church, whose walls (made in part of reused Aztec stone) butt on to a warren of tenements bristling with TV aerials. It is a place where you will sometimes hear Nahuatl spoken by the old folks who migrated here from the countryside before the Second World War. In the immediate vicinity of where the whitewashed courtyard of La Conchita is now situated, the battle came to its climax.

The Spanish, the winners, wrote the history and ever since the sixteenth century we Europeans have been taught that this was a triumph against the odds – a victory not merely of technology but of cultural, mental and moral qualities. A few hundred heroic Europeans, we have been told, against vast armies of Aztecs, whose society was irrational, whose cruelty was 'fierce and unnatural'. A triumph of character and moral fibre, then, as well as of weapons. And, in this myth, Cortes himself becomes the model of the European Renaissance man: superbly rational in his manipulative intelligence, his strategic flexibility, his ability to improvise. Like we post-moderns, he is a specialist in human communication.

This myth informed the most famous account of the conquest, by William Prescott in the 1840s, and we are still taught it today. It is these qualities which are deemed to be supremely European, which enabled the Europeans, and their American offshoots, to overcome the traditional civilizations in the world; they are still held up as the attributes of global civilization.

But, as we have seen, it would be wrong to say that the conquest of Mexico was easy, or that the Aztecs remained till the end paralysed by this encounter with the Other – unable to respond to the Europeans' singular ability to think rationally and to improvise. The Aztecs learned to read the signs, whether physical ones,

▸ This depiction of a late-fifteenth-century Mexican lord, with his fine clothes and elaborate courtly adornments, helps us imagine the Aztec warriors educated in the 'college of nobles', who rallied round Cuauhtemoc in the final siege.

▸▸ The implacable face of the Aztec gods. Mexican defeat was understood as being within the framework of Aztec belief and time: 'the will of the "Giver of Life".'

whose laws were alien to them (how crossbow bolts and bullets flew, for example), or cultural ones, the kind of rules the Spanish worked by and what their words and behaviour actually meant. Most of all, too late, the Aztecs came to understand who the Spanish – aliens from another world – actually were.

But people are only human and in crises it is only natural for them to seek refuge and comfort in older ways of thought, in ancient rituals. Even in our post-religious age, people still do, so we should not be surprised that the Aztecs appealed to the supernatural, especially as, at this moment, they had no reason to suppose that defeat would mean the end of them as a people, the end of their ancient beliefs.

Once defeat was finally understood to be inevitable (and for them, with their fatalistic view of history, the fact that it was defeat meant that it had always been inevitable), Cuauhtemoc consulted with his captains who sought a guiding omen – rather as Alexander the Great had in India at the Beas river – to have the gods validate what they already knew must be:

...they dressed a brave captain up in the finery of the quetzal owl...the combat regalia of the great Ahuitzotl, who had ruled before the despised Montezuma. The king placed in his hands the magic object which was the most important part of the regalia. This was an arrow with a long tip and an obsidian shaft...

This was the obsidian-tipped arrow of the war god Huitzilopochtli. Should the arrows twice hit their mark, they would still win. Magnificent in his long green plumes of quetzal tail-feathers, the hero raced towards the enemy and vanished into the smoke and confusion. For a time they thought they could follow his movements as he reclaimed stolen gold and quetzal plumes, and took captives. Then he dropped from a terrace and out of sight. No Spanish account mentions this great warrior, but then the Spanish were oblivious to the signs which distinguished the Eagle warrior from the Jaguar, or the supernatural charge carried by the quetzal owl. But the omen had failed. An eerie calm followed:

Suddenly the battle ended. Neither side moved against the other, the night was calm and silent, with no incidents of any kind. On the following day, absolutely nothing took place, and neither the Spaniards nor the Indians spoke a word. The Indians waited in their defence works, and the Spaniards waited in their positions. Each side watched the other closely but made no plans to launch an attack. Both sides passed the whole day in this fashion, merely watching and waiting.

Then that night, or so it was told later, the omen was seen. No Spanish source mentions a sign, a comet, a meteor or any other kind of strange celestial visitation. So perhaps what is described only happened retrospectively in the hands of tale-tellers, who were striving to put the final collective acceptance of defeat into a meaningful literary form. But, years later, the old eye-witnesses recalled the final omen as plain fact:

At nightfall it began to rain, but it was more like heavy dew than a rain. Suddenly the omen appeared, blazing like a great bonfire in the sky. It wheeled in enormous spirals like a whirlwind and gave off a shower of sparks and red hot coals, some great and some little. It also made loud noises, rumbling and hissing like a metal tube placed over a fire. It hovered for a while above Coyonacazco. From there it moved out into the middle of the lake where it suddenly disappeared. No one cried out when this omen came into view: the people watched in silence, for they knew what it meant.

The Aztec Surrender

THE AZTEC LEADERS NOW GATHERED to discuss what to do, how best to surrender to the strangers, and 'what tribute to pay' (a phrase which shows that they had not yet understood the total nature of the war: that the very existence of their culture and religion would be ultimately forfeited by defeat). Then they put Cuauhtemoc – plus a captain, a servant, and 'boatman named Cenyautl' – into a war canoe. (How typical of the Aztec account that they preserve the name of the man who punted the last Aztec king. Cenyautl, the boatman, is one of the little people who, for a brief moment, played his part in history.)

Cuauhtemoc was led to Cortes, who was standing under a multi-coloured canopy on the roof of one of the noble's houses – 'Lord Aztautzim's house near Amaxac'. Cortes 'stared at him for a moment and then patted him on the head'.

The meaning of this apparently demeaning gesture seems to be revealed in the account of Alva Ixtlilxochitl, the son of one of the allied kings who fought for Cortes:

Cortes received him with all the respect due to a king. Cuauhtemoc then asked Cortes to kill him: 'for you have already destroyed my city and killed my people'.

He spoke other grief-stricken words which touched the heart of everyone who heard them. Cortes consoled him and asked him to command his warriors to surrender.

Alva Ixtlilxochitl says his father was so touched by the tragedy 'that he was eager to clasp Cuauhtemoc's hand'. Even the Aztecs' hereditary enemies were overwhelmed by the scale of the disaster which had engulfed the city, and by the bearing of the brave young king with his pleasant open face and his steadfast grey eyes.

Father Sahagun's eye-witnesses mention, too, that the king's feathered dress was now 'soiled', a tiny detail which stands out after all the earlier formulaic descriptions of gorgeous royal finery. The king no longer had a pristine dress: ritual propriety had gone by the board. As for Cortes's gesture of consolation, it may have been genuinely felt at that moment. But in the end it would not stop him torturing Cuauhtemoc to find out the whereabouts of the gold lost during the Night of Tears or from subsequently killing him when he had outlived his usefulness.

Visions of the Vanquished

THE SAME DAY AS THE SURRENDER, the Spanish looted the city while their native allies ran amok, taking revenge against their ancient tormentors. The rule of plunder was gold for the Spaniards, precious stones, jade and feathers for their confederates. 'Many more people died now,' say our native informants, and the streets were full of the 'sickening stench of the rotting bodies' which could not be cremated. 'And this is when the flight from the city began.'

Many people fled to the mainland by canoe in daytime, most by night, 'crashing into each other in their haste'. There were humiliating scenes on the crowded causeways, where roadblocks had been set up under Spanish supervision to search the fleeing population:

They were looking only for gold…they paid no attention to jade or turquoise or quetzal feathers… Many noblewomen covered themselves with mud, dressed in rags, and hid what wealth they had on their person, but the Spanish searched all the women without exception.

The Aztec annals colour this with an image of the violation of the Mexican women, of a kind we read in so many accounts right across the New World: 'The Christians searched all the refugees. They even opened the women's skirts and blouses and felt everywhere: their ears, their breasts, their hair…'

And, amid all this, Father Sahagun's Aztec eye-witnesses give us another tiny human detail which lets us enter into the feelings of the defeated Aztecs. As the

▲ The end of the battle: the surrender of Cuauhtemoc, who was punted in his canoe by the boatman Cenyautl; detail of a sixteenth-century Spanish painting.

long lines of famished refugees poured out along the causeways, '…the grown-ups carried the young children on their shoulders. Many of the children were weeping with terror, but one or two laughed and smiled, thinking it was great sport to be carried like that by their parents along the road.'

Alva Ixtlilxochitl helps us conjure up the mixed feelings which the fall of the city aroused, even among the Aztecs' enemies:

On the day that Tenochtitlan was taken, the Spaniards committed some of the most brutal acts ever inflicted upon the unfortunate people of this land. The cries of the helpless women and children were heart-rending. The Tlaxcalans and other enemies of the Aztecs revenged themselves pitilessly for old offences and robbed them of everything they could find. Only Prince Ixtlilxochitl of Texcoco, an ally of Cortes, felt compassion for the Aztecs, because they were of his own homeland. He kept his followers from maltreating the women and children as cruelly as Cortes and the Spaniards did... The anguish and bewilderment of our enemies was pitiful to behold. The warriors gathered on the rooftops and stared at the ruins of their city in a dazed silence, and the women and children and old men were all weeping...

AND SO IT WAS ALL OVER. Some thought 100,000 Mexicans had died in the siege: 'We had to walk over the heaped bodies to get into the middle of the city,' said the Spanish. 'The day we laid down our shields and admitted defeat was the Day 1-Serpent in the Year 3-House,' said Father Sahagun's informants, carefully adhering to the old calendar even as their time closed. The date in the Christian almanac was 13 August 1521. The siege had lasted eighty days – not the legendary ten years of the siege of Troy, but this was real, and no less powerful in the literary form in which it has come down to us. The Aztec accounts are worthy of being set alongside the *Iliad* and the *Aeneid*. Several other post-conquest native sources record laments and poems about the fall of Mexico-Tenochtitlan. The earliest is a remarkable annal, written perhaps as early as 1528 in Nahuatl, but already using the Spanish alphabet. Probably the oldest prose account of the conquest in a native source, it preserves this wonderful poem:

'Our Inheritance Is Lost'

> *And all these misfortunes befell us.*
> *We saw them and wondered at them:*
> *we suffered this bitter fate.*
> *Broken spears lie in the roads;*
> *we have torn our hair in grief.*
> *The houses are roofless now, and their walls*
> *are reddened with blood...*
>
> *We have beat our hands with despair*
> *against the adobe walls*
> *for our inheritance is lost and dead.*
> *The shields of our warriors were its defence,*
> *but they could not save it...*

It is a final acceptance of the wheel of history: no self-pity, none of the lengthy self-justification of the victors for their terrible acts. For the Aztecs, defeat had been revealed as inevitable in the pattern of eternally recurring time, and they simply accept that the 'bundle of years', with its inscrutable permutations, had been stacked against them. For all the 'fierce and unnatural cruelties' of which the Spanish accused them, the Aztec polity was, unquestionably, a moral order with a deep, if tormented, spirituality; and it was with spiritual insight that an Aztec poet, writing soon afterwards, summed up these terrible events: 'These are the acts of the Giver of Life'.

The Visions of the Victors

CORTES COULD NOW WRITE HIS THIRD LETTER to the king of Spain in the full assurance of victory. The gambler had won. Fame and fortune, estates, treasures and the viceroyship followed. He was now 'Marquis of the Valley'. A flood of Spaniards followed him into Mexico – settlers, profiteers, administrators and, of course, the representatives of the main orders of the Catholic Church, anxious to begin the task of converting the peoples to Christianity. Many of the Aztec aristocracy were allowed to convert and keep their estates and status; and so many intermarried with the newcomers that a mixed (*mestizo*) society very rapidly developed, particularly in Mexico City itself. In this mingling lay the beginnings of a New Mexico.

Of the other characters in this drama, some like Alvarado died fighting on other New World battlefields; others like Bernal Diaz reached a ripe old age and regaled their grandchildren with tales of 'things never heard of, seen or dreamed of before'. Malinche disappears soon after from history: she was too problematic a character to be allowed any public role, although her shadow has haunted Mexican culture ever since.

As for Cortes, the greatest gambler in history, the remainder of his life betrays a curious emptiness, a sense of disappointment, as if, perhaps, it would never be possible for him to live so intensely, so fully, as he had during those two astonishing years. To be sure, there was glory in full measure to be had in Spain. Embraced by the king against whose agent he had acted, he was heaped with honours, land, estates and slaves. But he had also made many enemies and, animated by bitterness and envy, some of his old comrades soon turned against him, accusing him of war crimes and the misappropriation of Montezuma's gold. There were also dark whisperings as to what had really happened on the Night of Tears, and why so many good Spaniards had perished. A sinister story, from the year after the conquest, reveals the latent violence and anger in his make-up.

In 1522, his wife, Catalina, finally came over from Cuba to join him in Mexico. That November, they had a very public row at a banquet when Cortes flew into a fury at her unthinking reference to the Mexicans as 'my Indians'. '*Your* Indians? Let me hear no more about *your* Indians,' he snarled. Catalina left the table sobbing; later that night, she was found dead in bed – her face blue, bruising round her neck.

There were many who were sure that Cortes had killed her after another rage. It was said that he had often thrown her out of bed, and that Catalina had confided to a friend: 'One day you will find me dead, the way we live together.' Those arguing for Cortes said that Catalina had a congenital heart problem, and was prone to minor attacks, that she had had a heart attack after a row that was really about his 'infinite number of mistresses, Spanish and native'.

Cortes had tried to revive her, his defenders claimed, and the bruises had come from his shaking her in panic. But no one else saw her before she was buried, and his descendants were still paying compensation to her family a hundred years after. In later years, it was said that tears came to Cortes's eyes whenever he talked about his dead wife. But were those shed for grief, or for the memory of losing self-control?

Catalina's death was one of several clouds which darkened Cortes's later years. After being feted in Spain, he returned to live in Mexico. He led great expeditions to the Pacific, at first still hoping to find a strait that would offer a short cut to the Moluccas, the Spice Islands and Cathay. He discovered – and named – California, but only after great privations, and the loss of half his men.

By now, he had lived through enough adventures to fill several lives. But, by the 1540s, he had become something of a background figure, disliked by many. He retired to live in Seville, where he recounted his adventures to the local nobility and was received at court from time to time. Among those who met him then was Las Casas, the great fighter for Indian rights, who tells another revealing story in his *History of the Indies*.

'But by what law did you take Montezuma prisoner?' Las Casas asked Cortes, surrounded by a crowd of adulatory courtiers. Cortes replied with one of those Latin tags which came so easily to him, and which seem to have convinced Las Casas that he was a 'good Latinist': '*Qui non intrat per ostium fur est et latro*' ('Anyone who does not enter by the front gate is a thief and a robber').

When Las Casas looked at him for further illumination, Cortes added: 'Let your ears hear what your lips say.'

'Read my lips.' Those present in the room burst into laughter. But not Las Casas, whose eyes filled with tears at this further evidence of what he took to be Cortes's strangely callous amorality.

Cortes died in Spain at Castilleja de la Cuesta, near Seville (the house is still there), in December 1547, at the age of sixty-two, leaving behind vast property,

▲ 'And all these misfortunes befell us, and we beheld them with
wonder.' Aztec prisoners depicted in the Florentine Codex,
compiled around 1570 from earlier materials.

▸▸ Portrait of Cortes as a Spanish gentleman, with parade armour,
coat of arms and regalia of a marquis; from the painting in the
Hospital of Jesus, Mexico City (see page 104).

colossal wealth and many children. His greatest interests and talents, which had been noticed in Cuba well before his fame, that is, being a gambler and a seducer, had served him well.

Would it all have happened without him? It is hard to say. Even with him, if his defeat on the Night of Tears had not been followed by a pandemic, things might have been different. And, as we saw earlier, if the Tlaxcalans had turned against him then he would surely have been lost, for there can be no doubt whatsoever that their help – as warriors, porters, suppliers, and in providing him with a sanctuary after his defeat – was essential to him.

It is a pleasing fantasy to imagine the Aztec state continuing into the nineteenth century, moderating its views on human sacrifice as the values of the European Enlightenment percolated into their culture through European visitors and residents; surviving as a beautiful archaic polity like the late Ching empire or the Meiji era in Japan. To the orientalist vogues in early modern European art, we might have had to add the impact of Nahuatl-speaking poets and artists resident in the Enlightenment courts of Spain and the rest of Europe. (And no doubt, given the wonderful quality of Aztec art, sculpture and poetry, we are the poorer for that loss.)

But in the end, we have to admit that it was Cortes himself who shaped the course of this history. His speed, daring and audacity, his ability to act swiftly and

ruthlessly when needed, his ability to assess risks and act on them, were gamblers' skills. And, still more than that, perhaps, was his ability to come up with heroic grand plans. Finally, he also had the charisma and ability to seduce: his own men, the fat caique at Zempoala, the leaders at Tlaxcala, the great Montezuma, all fell for him.

Is that perhaps what made him tick? Could it really be that simple? History, alas, is never so straightforward. Cortes, we have to admit, remains an enigma, a character whose past does not help explain the astonishing moment when he found himself in the eye of the storm of history. It is, after all, given to few people in history to demolish an ancient civilization.

In his early days in Cuba, Cortes boasted that he would die on a gallows or with his sword in hand, and he certainly had plenty of chances to die in one of those ways, as did so many of the other great figures of the conquest. Francisco Pizarro was murdered in Peru, his brother Gonzalo was executed; Hernando de Soto died of disease on the banks of the Mississippi; Orellana was lost in the Amazon; Alvarado was killed in the saddle in Guatemala. Cortes, though, died in bed in Spain, not as covered with glory as he might have wished.

Today, there are no statues and images of Cortes in the streets of Mexico City, where – after the revolution – he became reviled. His monument on the 'Pass of Cortes' by Popocatepetl has been vandalized. He only survives now, in public, in cartoons and satires, and on the popular calendars that you can buy on the streets: a handsome dark-eyed seducer with the film-star beauty of Malinche by his side, the mother-betrayer of the nation.

The ninety-year-old woman with an Indian face, who sells these souvenirs near the Ministry of Defence, told me: 'He was a good-looking guy, and the girls wanted to have him. I don't blame them. Look, it was fated. There was no other way it could have ended. We are their children whether we like it or not.'

There is, though, one statue of Cortes in Mexico City that is still cared for. It is kept not in a public place but hidden away in a beautiful courtyard full of roses and acanthus. This is the Hospital of Jesus, which Cortes founded for the good of his soul after the fall of Mexico. The statue stands on the spot where he met Montezuma. In the hospital boardroom, they keep some relics of the founder: an old chair, and a sixteenth-century oil painting, which is our best and most authentic likeness. It is the image of an older man: the hair is long, the beard somewhat unkempt, the stocky frame bent by age; tired eyes and a gaze empty with piety. Done by a painter of provincial skills, it tells us that, for all his dark past, Cortes has made his peace with God.

There are no clues in such conventional devotions. Can this *really* be the man who, at Zempoala, washed the Totonac priests, cut their blood-caked hair, and

taught them how to light candles for the Virgin? Is this the masterful Renaissance man who calmly watched his boats sink into Villa Rica bay, or stood by unmoved as his men strangled the captive lords of Tenochtitlan? In the end, the tremendous will that we encounter in those two astonishing years eludes us.

▲ There is no public statue of Cortes today in Mexico City. But in films and plays, in cartoons, on calendars and even on car bonnets, his presence still haunts modern Mexico. 'Are we children of Cuauhtemoc? Or of Malinche and Cortes?'

One of the most inscrutable characters in history, Cortes leaves us with a dark and perplexing puzzle: the gambler who gambled all and won, but who found in his victory a strange hollowness. Like the person of God in Karl Kraus's epic of the modern holocausts, *The Last Days of Mankind*, who stares down at a world ruined by war, and says: 'I did not mean it to happen this way.'

3
THE CONQUEST OF THE INCAS

IN SEPTEMBER 1513, Vasco Nunez de Balboa and his party of conquistadors hacked their way through the forests of Panama to be confronted by a great ocean. They were the first Europeans to see the 'Southern Sea', the Pacific. Among Balboa's senior officers was a veteran called Francisco Pizarro. He, along with Hernan Cortes, is one of those characters who, by his own deeds and force of personality, changed the course of history.

Then in his late thirties, Pizarro was the illegitimate son of a captain from Trujillo in Estremadura, the same region from which Cortes came, and to whom he was distantly related. Having served as a soldier in Italy, he arrived in the New World in 1502 with deep experience of war. He became a citizen of the new colony of Panama when it was founded in 1518, with farms and Indian slaves, and was part-owner of a gold-mining company. A bachelor of sparse tastes, he was a very different character from Cortes, but they shared a similar drive. Like Cortes, Pizarro was wealthy; he could have retired in Panama on his profits or gone back to his home town of Trujillo and built himself a fine house with his bust on the frieze and a coat of arms on the door. But he wanted more.

As the war in Mexico was reaching its climax, the Spanish in Panama began to explore the north-west coast of South America. In 1522, an expedition from Panama under Pascal de Andagoya, seeking a tribe or province around a river called Biru (or Viru), sailed as far as the San Juan river in what is now Colombia. Andagoya became too sick to continue and, under the auspices of the governor of Panama, Pizarro and his financial partner, Diego de Almagro, acquired Andagoya's ships and prepared for an 'exploration'.

When I set out to write for the people of today and of the future, about the conquest and discovery that our Spaniards made in Peru, I could not but reflect that I was dealing with the greatest matters one could possibly write about in all of creation as far as worldly things go. And what I mean is this: Where have men ever seen the things they have seen here? Where was it known that so much wealth could come from one land?... And a land so extensive, so rich, so abundant that it cannot be bettered. And to think that God should have permitted something so great to remain hidden from the world for so long in history, unknown to men, and then let it be found, discovered and won all in our own time!

•

PEDRO DE CIEZA DE LEON *Chronicle of Peru,* 1545

◂◂ A portrait of Francisco Pizarro: steely, uncompromising and without illusions.

Earlier expeditions, such as those of Cortes in Mexico, had employed men on salaries. But now that investors had woken up to the fantastic profits to be gained from the New World, it became the practice to form military companies, groups of men each in charge of his own equipment and weapons, who received no salary but a previously stipulated share of the spoils.

With the huge financial returns made in Mexico, such companies inevitably became caught up in the web of international capitalism. Merchants and financiers from Genoa, Nuremberg, Florence and Hapsburg, as well as cities in Spain, who were previously dedicated to mining, trade and plantations, now directly involved themselves in financing conquest expeditions – the first globalizers. Although illiterate, Pizarro had a mind for business. He understood the workings of the sixteenth-century venture capitalists and, from the start, his goal was to carve himself a kingdom – and also to 'discover the unknown'.

First Contact

IN NOVEMBER 1524, PIZARRO and his partner Almagro made their first voyage with eighty men and four horses. It was not a success: they only got a short way below the isthmus of Panama, as far south as the aptly named 'Port of Hunger'. Almagro lost an eye in a skirmish; no riches were found and the landscape, with its intractable mangrove swamps along a coast plagued by insects, deterred any idea of colonization. On their return they had some difficulty in persuading backers to finance a further attempt.

Still, on 10 March 1526 in Panama, Pizarro and Almagro drew up a formal business contract. Their second voyage, from November 1526 to late 1527, was a much bigger affair, with 160 men and several horses carried in two ships. After some initial probing, they split up: Almagro went back to Panama for reinforcements and supplies; Pizarro camped by the San Juan river in Colombia; the pilot, Ruiz, sailed on, crossing the Equator for the first time. Then, suddenly, came the first contact with people from another civilization.

A brisk northerly was gusting down the coast when Ruiz encountered a large balsa trading raft with a huge triangular cotton sail. On board were twenty crew and passengers (see illustration page 111). Such ocean-going rafts, with a cabin, and deck space for cargo, were still used in these waters up to the early nineteenth century. The raft was on a trading mission to barter Inca artefacts for corals and crimson spondylus shells. The Spanish boarded and, to their delight, saw:

…many pieces of silver and gold…belts, bracelets, body armour, clusters of beads and precious stones, rattles and strings…mirrors decorated with silver, cups and other vessels; there were many wool and cotton mantles and tunics, and other pieces of dyed clothing…different kinds of figured embroidery depicting birds, animals,

fish and trees. There were small stones in bead bags, emeralds, chalcedonies and other jewels and pieces of crystal and resin.

Some of the crew jumped from the trading raft, some were later allowed to go, but Ruiz kept three people to be taught Spanish and to be trained as interpreters, ready for the time when they would make first contact with the mysterious Other in the land of 'Biru'. Through sign language, the captives told him that their gold came from a land far to the south, a land of wonders.

Ruiz returned to Pizarro with his prisoners and their trade goods, and then ferried him and his troops onwards to explore the coast of Ecuador. But, by the middle of 1527, the expedition had again separated, and the initial expectations raised by the treasures on the raft were long forgotten. By now, Pizarro's men had grown sick of the promises of their craggy leader, and he found himself, with his army, camped on an uninhabited island, just off the steamy mangrove coast of Colombia. Mutiny was in the air. And this was the turning point in the story and, indeed, a turning point in history. The place was called Isla del Gallo, 'Isle of the Cock'.

TODAY, YOU GET TO THE ISLAND from the little port of **'A Line in the Sand'** Tumaco on the Pacific coast of Colombia – a down-at-heel sort of a place, subject to the floods and storms of El Nino, with many dirt streets, and ramshackle wooden houses built out on stilts over the sea. It rains most of the year here, on a population now mainly black – descendants of slaves brought over when the native Indian peoples died of disease. The island is close to the shore on the northern side of the bay, washed by the warm brown swell of the Pacific, and frequently shrouded in mist. Situated almost dead on the Equator, it is uninhabited except for seasonal fishermen who will take you out there in fishing boats and land you under a creeper-hung cliff.

On this leashore, away from the Pacific breakers, a ragged band of desperados camped – just eighty left. Their leader, Francisco Pizarro, was now approaching fifty and had seen better days, his face bearded, sunburnt and gaunt like the rest of his men. In some he inspired great loyalty: 'the bravest man I ever met,' said one. He always took the lead, fished and hunted to feed his men, and went through all the hardships they endured, and more. Behind his twinkling eyes, though, was a cool calculating man who had already evaluated the societies of the Americas, and learned the technical and ideological skills needed to survive as a conquistador.

Pizarro was practised in deception and had the capacity to be unflinchingly cruel. He had personally tortured and burnt alive chiefs in Panama to make them

▴ Detail from a world map of 1526 showing South America as known on the eve of Pizarro's exploration. It is a wonderful example of the speed with which mental landscapes were transformed in the Age of the Conquistadors. Magellan had already sailed around the globe; Pizarro was reaching into what was still unmapped, but no longer unknowable.

give up their possessions. 'Perpetrating cruelties on the Indians,' said one historian of the time, 'was a habit Pizarro knew off by heart – he'd used it for years.' There is no mystery about Francisco Pizarro. He knew the world, and knew himself, before he ever set foot in Peru.

But, at that moment, he had reached the end of the line. His starving men were eating snakes and shellfish. Two or three were dying of disease every week; others were on the edge of mutiny. He had promised them a world beyond – a world where they could make their fortunes. But most of these men, recruited in Panama, no longer believed in his dreams. Some had already smuggled a message out with Ruiz's boat which had left them there: a message pleading to be rescued. Pizarro, they claimed, was a lunatic, a 'butcher' who insisted on them hanging on in this hellish place.

The message reached Panama and, at the end of August 1527, the governor ordered the rescue of any men who wished to get out. When the boat arrived, a memorable scene ensued. Pizarro took his sword and drew a line in the sand: 'Comrades and friends, on that side lies the part which represents death, hardship, hunger, nakedness and abandonment; this side here represents comfort. Here you return to Panama – to be poor! There you may go on to Peru – to be rich. You choose which best becomes you as brave Spaniards.'

▲ An early nineteenth-century illustration by the explorer and naturalist Alexander von Humboldt of a balsa trading raft off Ecuador. Such craft were encountered by Pizarro early in 1527.

Only thirteen – the famous 'glorious thirteen', all of whose names are known – crossed the line. But the historian Cieza de Leon has a different take on this epic scene on the beach: he was a young soldier at the time and talked to some of those present. This is what they told him:

Pizarro was downcast when he saw they all wanted to go. He quietly composed himself and said that of course they could return to Panama and the choice was theirs. He had not wanted them to leave because they would have their reward if and when they discovered a good land. As for himself, he felt that returning poor to Panama was a harder thing than staying to face death and hardship here. And he told them one thing more. He took satisfaction in one thing: if they had all gone through hardships and starvation, he had shared it with them: indeed he had always gone first. Therefore he begged them to re-examine and re-examine their options, and to follow him, taking a sea route to discover what lay beyond. After all, the Indians that the pilot Ruiz had seized said such marvellous things about the land ahead.

Most of the troops, says Cieza de Leon, did not want to hear his words and abandoned their friends, 'weeping with joy as if this had ended the captivity in Egypt'. According to him, the thirteen who stayed 'did so out of compassion for Pizarro', or because they did not wish to go back to Panama. As he prepared to leave, the ship's captain refused a request to leave them a small boat. However, he agreed to drop Pizarro and the thirteen on another island which they knew from earlier in the voyage. They named it Gorgona (the Isle of the Gorgon), after the snake-headed monster of Greek myth.

On the Gorgon's Island

THE CAPTAIN SAILED IN CLOSE ENOUGH to drop Pizarro and the thirteen into the surf, pausing only to unload the maize rations he had agreed to leave them, dumping the provisions loose on the sand, where some were spoiled and rotted. Pizarro made a last request: he wanted the Indians, whom Ruiz had captured, to stay with him so that they could be trained as his interpreters. After an argument, the captain reluctantly agreed, and cast them ashore before pulling away and sailing off over the horizon. Effectively they were marooned. What on earth had Pizarro hoped to do?

'Those who have actually seen Gorgona, as I have,' says Cieza de Leon, 'will not be surprised at how much stress I lay on what the Spaniards went through. It is a vision of hell. The rain, thunder and lightning are continuous. The sun is rarely seen. There are enough mosquitoes to wage war on all the armies of the Grand Turk.'

But, apart from the many dangerous snakes, it was safe. When the clouds lift, which is not often, it can be a magical place, covered with lush tropical forests, although it is hot and very humid, and has almost continuous rainfall. And it was large enough to sustain them. Six miles long, it has an abundance of fresh water, and, although there are no big mammals, there are many small animals: monkeys, lizards, bats and birds. An hour's walk through the forest from the shore, there is a little lake containing freshwater turtles, and in the breeding season sea-turtles come ashore to bury their eggs on the beaches. Unlike the Isla del Gallo, the Spaniards could survive here.

Up on the lonely northern edge on the landward side is a cove still called 'Pizarro's Beach'. Here they made huts of leaves and wood to keep off the incessant rain and just about managed to survive. Feeling entirely responsible for having hitched the thirteen to his dreams, Pizarro took it upon himself to go out every day to make sure that his men had food to eat. He made a canoe from a fallen kapok tree and went hunting for capybaras, the island's largest rodents, with his crossbow.

For seven months, Pizarro and his thirteen companions lived like castaways, while he dreamed of lands of gold far to the south – lands unknown to the rest of the world, which were described to him by the Indian men and women who had stayed with him on the island.

And, in the middle of the night, as Pizarro heard the breakers roll out in the Pacific, the Inca ruler of those vast lands to the south slept with his beautiful *coyas*, his queens, unaware of the strangers on the edge of his world, lying on their beds of palm fronds and seaweed under the stars by the roar of the Southern Sea.

'We Thought This Was the Whole World…'

AT THAT MOMENT, in fact, the emperor was not so far away as the crow flies – in Quito. The Inca, Wayna Capac, was sixty-three, not much older than Pizarro himself. Born in 1464, he had been on the throne since 1498 and was one of the most experienced kings in the world, although he himself had no knowledge of any world save his own. A formidable man, tough, composed, he was good at weighing up people and situations. When guests saw him on his golden throne or his red jewel-studded war litter, his trademark tunic 'divided into squares like a chessboard', they saw a man 'short, but stocky, well made with a fine face and a grave expression'.

According to tradition, he was 'handsome and charming…widely esteemed by the people and friendly in his manner'. Like all successful kings, he was a skilful diplomat, a charismatic army leader; 'a man of few words and many deeds' was how those who knew Wayna Capac described him to Cieza de Leon. But Wayna Capac also had the common touch: he could talk as a man to the lowly, and was a 'great friend of the poor' (not to mention a man who could out-drink three people, but was never seen drunk).

As the Peruvians calculated their dynasty, Wayna Capac was the eleventh Inca (or, to be absolutely correct, Sapa Inca, as his followers would have addressed him. The word Inca strictly applies to the ruler, not the people. It means the 'model' or 'archetype' – and the Sapa Inca was the 'Unique Inca'). For nearly thirty years, he had overseen the Tawantinsuyu, the 'Land of the Four Quarters', which, for the Incas, constituted the whole of the known world – an empire which, if laid across Europe, would stretch from Spain to Moscow. By now, he and his council believed they had united the world, that virtually all the peoples were under their rule. For, as his grandson Titu Cusi would say later, 'Until the Spanish came, we thought this was the whole world, for we knew of no other.'

It was an empire whose deep antecedents grew up with no outside contact. During the fifteenth century, it had expanded rapidly to embrace Ecuador to the north, Bolivia and northern Chile to the south, and the subtropical forests beyond the Andes to the east – what is now Peruvian Amazonia. They had even latterly sent expeditions into Amazonia, but the suffering of the troops had been severe, matching those of the great Spanish expeditions of the sixteenth century. In the end, the Inca had deemed it unnecessary to extend his rule over such uncivilized peoples who, in Inca eyes, rather as in the European myths of the time, were barbarians, subhumans who 'mated with monkeys'. So the frontier of the Tawantinsuyo was drawn at the Andes. What lay beyond was beyond the pale of civilization. Racial prejudice is by no means a monopoly of the Europeans.

This, then, was Tawantinsuyu – the Land of the Four Quarters. We call it an empire, as the Spanish did, but, if it was, it was very different from our conception of empire. Quite separate from all other civilizations, the Inca world in 1527 had developed in isolation and – as we understand it now – was at about the same level of development as the Bronze Age civilizations of the Old World. In fact, the Inca world offers many fascinating parallels with early dynastic Egypt or, even better, Shang dynasty China, to which it was distantly related, particularly in its shamanistic religion, its mountain worship, and in the importance of astronomy and divination.

▸▸ The Virgin of the Mountain at Potosi in Bolivia, the greatest source of silver in the Americas. At the foot of the mountain, between the Pope and King Charles V, is the small figure of the last great Inca, Wayna Capac.

Like all known Bronze Age civilizations, the Incas practised human sacrifice – not on the horrific scale of the Aztecs, but still extensively, especially on prisoners of war after battle; at great festivals 'when innocent unblemished boys and girls' were buried alive; at royal

funerals when hundreds of human beings, and thousands of animals, might die to accompany the spirit of the dead Inca to the Lord Sun.

Like all early states, the working of the empire combined the highly practical with the most idiosyncratic. The central ritual of the state, for example, was the cult of the dead Incas, whose mummies were 'brought out at the great festival and put on show in the open air, dressed in their best clothes with feathers in their heads, sat in litters and carried through streets and squares'. Treated as if they were living potentates, which, in a sense, they were, this cult of the royal dead was as characteristic of the Inca monarchy as belief in human sacrifice was to the Aztecs.

But the empire also functioned in very practical ways. It was linked by a system of roads which stretched from Quito down to southern Chile and across the Andes into Argentina. It is easy to underestimate the power of the so-called primitive Bronze Age states, but long after the conquest, and in the farthest reaches of the empire, traditions survived of the Inca armies and caravans which linked Ecuador with the far south of Chile.

Over this whole vast area, the royal commands were carried by a system of runners, known as *chasqui,* who wore sunhats made of white feathers and carried shell trumpets, cudgels and slings. Organized in two-mile relays, they were 'so fast that a snail picked off a leaf in Tumi [Cuenca in Ecuador] could be delivered to Cuzco still alive'. In this way, even without horses or wheeled transport, it was possible to control the movement of supplies, minerals, food and troops. But the Inca state was still primitive in the sense that it relied on force, on the importance of garrisons, on tribute-paying, gift-giving, hostages, and on the participation of vassals in its rituals. It was only in the recent past that the Incas had united peoples of different race and language under their rule – and not all welcomed it.

Like Ancient Egypt, theirs was a redistributive economy, and they had commerce – including long-distance trade – up the coast and over the Andes into the jungles. Warehouses were kept by the Inca in all four provinces. Frozen and dried potato, cooked potato, dried meat and wool were usually stored all over the central province. Maize, sweet potato, cassava and chilli were kept at points spread all over the rest of the land – 'each warehouse corresponding to a particular farming area'. As the sixteenth-century Peruvian historian Waman Poma says, 'Some belonged to the local community, some to the Inca, some to the temples: all came under the control of the central farming administration.'

To be a good Inca, then, was to care for the people, to provide and ensure a surplus so that everybody could be fed, and to establish a network of storehouses and roads so that famine or dearth in one part of the land could be alleviated by surplus from another.

In the winter of 1527/8, Wayna Capac was, indeed, a great king. Waman Poma, who was half Inca and had had a Spanish education, writing after the conquest with the knowledge of a wider world, stated with pardonable exaggeration:

Having read accounts of the various kings and emperors of the world, I am sure none of them had the majesty or power of Wayna Capac Inca. The monarchs of Turkey and China, the Roman emperors, Christian and Jewish rulers, the kings of Africa: none of them enjoyed such esteem or wore so lofty a crown.

During the previous ten years, Wayna Capac's generals had been fighting northern campaigns which had pushed the empire's final extent deep into Ecuador. There had been times when it seemed they might have been driven out, but it was at the triumphant conclusion of this northern war, when Wayna Capac was in the Quito region, that disturbing news came of an unknown disease which was ravaging the population of Cuzco. This was smallpox, sweeping from north to south in advance of the Europeans. As we have already seen, it began in Hispaniola in December 1518, where it spread to Mexico during September 1520, and devastated the Aztecs. Between 1525 and 1527, the epidemic ran along the Caribbean coastlands and travelled down the Andes through the valleys of Colombia and Venezuela.

By the end of 1527, the pestilence suddenly had appeared in Peru, apparently brought by traders or travellers straight to Cuzco, the navel of the earth. Early in 1528, the news came by royal runners, travelling the 1000-mile journey to Quito along the Inca roads. The Inca learned with deep concern that some of his kinsmen and family, his favourite generals and the governor of Cuzco had died, along with many common people. Ominously, the practitioners of traditional healing reported that their medicine was of no use.

Part of the Inca's job was to protect his people from famine and disease, to mediate on their behalf with the gods through the elaborate and ceaseless round of royal rituals. This sudden eruption of an unknown plague in the Land of the Four Quarters required urgent and deep discussion with his wise men, the council of the land, the high priest, the leaders of the great lineages. What did the plague portend?

The synchronicities of history are sometimes extraordinary: 'Wayna Capac was doing his last great deeds in Quito at the very same time that Francisco Pizarro was languishing in the mangrove swamps,' says Cieza de Leon, 'his men waiting for release as if for the salvation of their souls', still hoping that his partner in Panama would send a ship: 'When we saw clouds on the horizon we took them for a sail…'

Three of the thirteen were seriously ill by now, one dying. When they finally reconciled themselves to the idea that the ship was not coming back, they sank into exhausted depression. Their only hope was to build a raft to try to escape. The gamble had not paid off: they were starving to death on a Pacific isle that was aptly named after the Gorgon, the malevolent goddess who turned all who gazed on her to stone.

AT THE END OF MARCH 1528, Pizarro's horizon remained bound by the equatorial Pacific's interminable warm

First Contact with the Incas

rainy days where sky and sea merge in a brown haze. By now, he and his men had despaired of rescue. Then, one day, far out at sea, they saw a ship: 'At first they thought it a log, or something else…but as it drew nearer they saw the white of the sails, they realized it was the thing they had longed for, and became hysterical… speechless with excitement.'

It was a ship from Panama, sent by Pizarro's partner Almagro, and piloted by Ruiz. They all hugged each other with joy.

After their seven-month ordeal one would have thought that Pizarro would have been anxious to get back to the home comforts of Panama, but that was not his way. Determined not to waste this opportunity – and anxious to see for himself the unknown world which had been described to him by his Indian captives – he left the sick behind with Indian helpers, and sailed south to Peru.

Accompanied by Ruiz and the Indian interpreters, Pizarro travelled down the mangrove coast of Colombia and Ecuador, and entered the region where the coastal landscape changes and the brown Peruvian desert comes right down to the shore. They encountered more balsa rafts now, whole clusters of them apparently ferrying supplies in a civil war that was raging inside Peru. They sailed on and, after twenty days, the Indians recognized the coast of their home town of Tumbes. The Spanish pulled in close to land, presumably near the little port now known as Puerto Pizarro, and anchored in the brown somnolent sea. It was now late April 1528.

On the shore, the Inca town of Tumbes stood a couple of miles to the northeast of the modern town at San Pedro de Los Incas, on today's Pan-American Highway. Here the two worlds met for the first time: 'When the indigenous people saw the ship coming on the sea they were amazed, as this was something they had never seen before,' says Cieza de Leon, who had talked to Inca eyewitnesses. 'They were astonished.' But they prepared food for the Spaniards, as 'it was proper to give a warm reception…and sailed out to the ship on balsa rafts without any guile or menace but rather with joy and pleasure to meet such new people'.

◂◂ Inca road with water channel in Peru. 'We were amazed by the extent of their road system,' said a member of Pizarro's army.

There then followed a series of wonderfully open exchanges, all the more poignant to us now because of what we know will happen later. At this point, Cieza de Leon says, the Spanish were as 'astounded' by it all as the Indians. Pizarro's interpreters explained their story: how the whites were 'searching for lands' and had been 'staying on an island for a long time'.

The local governor told the Spanish that they were 'welcome to come ashore and provision themselves with water and whatever they needed without fear of harm'. Pizarro replied that he had no misgivings about trusting people 'who are so *rational*'. The Inca governor, too, took his visitors for 'very *rational* people since they were not causing any harm', and freely gave what he had with him. None the less, the governor thought it right to send an official report about the strangers post-haste to his king, the great Wayna Capac.

It is fascinating to read these eye-witness accounts and to learn that, from the start, each side took the other for 'rational beings'. The Inca governor now proceeded to question the newcomers so thoroughly and acutely that the Spanish 'were taken aback by such a wise and knowledgeable man'. This first recorded conversation between representatives of the Inca and the European worlds, which is reported to us through Pizarro's interpreters, is enough to dispel some of the weird modern theories about the Incas' initial perception of the Europeans. And it is, by the by, an interesting testimony to the quality of mind of the civil servants in the Inca empire:

He asked the captain where were they from, what land they had come from, and what were they looking for, or what was their purpose in going by sea and land without stopping? Francisco Pizarro replied that they had come from Spain, where they were native, and that in that land there was a great and powerful king called Charles, whose vassal and servants they were, and many others because he ruled wide territories. They had left their land to explore these parts, as they could see, and to place what they found under their king's authority, but primarily, and above all, to let them know that the idols they worshipped were false, and that to save their souls they had to become Christians and believe in the God the Spanish worshipped, who was in heaven, because those who did not worship him would go to hell, a dark place and full of fire. Those who know the truth and take him as God, the only lord of Creation, will live in heaven forever.

The Inca governor 'was astounded on hearing this', as well he might be. But Pizarro's brief account of Christianity seems to have been received with interest, or even amused disbelief, rather than disquiet. The Spanish were now invited ashore, and two of their party disembarked – Alonso de Molina and an unnamed

African servant, who caused a commotion among the locals who 'made him wash to see if his blackness was his own, or an applied colour: and so many came to see him that did not have time to eat'.

The Spaniards walked around Tumbes and saw fine buildings, planted fields and irrigation canals. This, no question about it, was a well-ordered and advanced civilization. Meanwhile, as news of the strangers spread, crowds of people came into the streets and followed them, coming up full of interest and fearlessly asking questions. (A salutary warning for us against believing stories that the native people were so 'primitive' that they believed the Europeans to be gods.)

As Molina walked freely around the streets, 'many Indian women who were beautiful and well dressed came up to talk with him using sign language' – an interesting pointer to the independence of *runa* – women – which is still true in traditional Andean society today. One 'very beautiful woman' in the group suggested that he might stay and take one of her friends in marriage. The warmth of the welcome, the lively interest in them, the independence of mind of the people, and their humorous curiosity, all made a great impact on the two men who were lucky enough to experience that first moment.

When Molina and the African servant returned to the ship to tell their story, Pizarro found it difficult to believe them and ordered someone else ashore. This was Pedro de Candia, a Greek artillery man, who was experienced in siege warfare – a 'calculating man', a 'crafty so and so'. Pizarro instructed him to 'reconnoitre the land and see where it would be best to enter *when they returned*'.

Once ashore, Candia, a giant nearly seven feet tall, caused an even bigger stir than the black servant. People invited him to sit and eat, and even the *mamaconas* – the sacred virgins in the local temple – begged the governor to let them see him: 'They loved seeing Candia…they were women skilled in working with wool, of which they made fine cloth. Most of them were beautiful and all were very affectionate.'

Needless to say, the combination of beautiful women and gold on temple walls was made much of by Candia, and his shipmates became 'ecstatic'. (These twin themes of women and gold run throughout the tales of the conquistadors.) Others, though, were profoundly moved by the openness and beauty of the people. One, Pedro Halcon, fell in love with a woman chief, a *capullana*, of which there were many on this coast, and had to be restrained in irons when he said he wished to stay. A sailor called Bocanegra jumped ship, 'because he wanted to remain among *such good people*. As for Molina: 'When he got back to the ship he was so overwhelmed by what he had seen, that at first he could not speak.'

Further contacts only confirmed those first impressions, the Spanish reiterating their surprise at the 'rationality' of the natives; that 'there was so much reason…that they were so "civilized"'. On their part, if we are to believe Cieza de Leon's Peruvian informants, the Incas' first impression of these outsiders was that they were 'white and bearded and did not harm, rob or kill, but rather gave of what they were carrying and were very pious and humane'. ('A reputation more exaggerated than real,' says Cieza de Leon, 'but human beings, even if barbarous, delight in seeing new things, no matter how strange and unbelievable.') As a prelude to one of history's greatest and most tragic events, these judgements could hardly be more poignant.

Before he left, Pizarro took the opportunity to perform the rituals of submission, with which all Spanish captains sailed to the New World, announcing to the chiefs that he was 'taking their land on behalf of the king of Spain' and that they should refrain from the worship of idols. 'But they took it as a joke and laughed heartily,' says Cieza de Leon.

Before Pizarro moved on, Molina and another sailor named Gines asked to stay. On reflection, Pizarro decided it would be useful to leave men behind to learn the Inca language, so he left them at Tumbes. What became of them has never been discovered.

These precious accounts of the fringe of the Inca world before its fall are full of vivid human detail and, as mentioned before, the scene of the first contact at Tumbes is all the more touching because we know the outcome, and so we cannot fail to be moved. Cieza de Leon was only too aware of the painful irony, and adds at the end of his account that:

Had Pizarro tried to wage war against them for money before the divisions which followed Wayna Capac, he would never have succeeded. But had he wished to convert them with kind words, this people were so gentle and peaceful that all he needed was those few people with him and he could have done it. But the matters of the Indies are the judgements of God, and come from His profound wisdom, and He knows why He permitted what happened.

The Death of the Inca

THE INCA GOVERNOR AT TUMBES had sent his runners with all speed to Quito, to the Inca Wayna Capac, a journey of perhaps only three days. And now the significance of the timing of these events becomes clear. Both Spanish and Inca sources suggest that, at this moment, Wayna Capac was still near Quito, resting after battle and reorganizing the northern part of the empire prior to his return to Cuzco.

No doubt, too, he was weighing up the sinister news of the outbreak of pestilence in the heart of his empire. But he had moved only a short way south – he was near the city of Cuenca (known then as Tumi or Tumibamba), 150 miles south of

Quito – when the disease struck the Inca camp. The incubation period of small-pox is only a few days, and in no time it swept through the army. Many of his trusted generals died; and then the Inca himself caught it. The date was now perhaps late April or May 1528.

As his health rapidly worsened, the Inca was asked to name a successor to be ratified by his council of wise men. There is some suggestion that he was so gravely ill that he had become confused and named, as his first choice, an infant, for whom not surprisingly the auguries proved inauspicious. Sources disagree over his second choice: some said it was his twenty-five-year-old son, Atahuallpa; some said it was twenty-one-year-old Huascar – Atahuallpa's younger brother by a different queen. (Their relative ages were unimportant: primogeniture was not a factor in the Inca royal succession.)

Fate could not have played the Incas a worse card. From this unforeseen disaster, cataclysmic events would follow, upturning the Andean universe which had developed untouched by the outside world for millennia. As we have remarked already in this book, timing is everything in history.

Not surprisingly, later historians, writing after the conquest, told of sinister omens: Pedro Pizarro, Francisco's half-brother, heard a tale from Peruvians that three dwarfs had come as auguries of the Inca's death; Waman Poma says the Inca hid himself away to die in a lonely cave; Pachacuti Yamqui (in his *Antiquities of Peru*, 1613) recounts a most fantastic and eerie story of a dark-clothed super-natural messenger, bearing a box of paper-thin, butterfly-like things whose escape was the harbinger of doom:

The Inca went to Quito to rest after battle, and to issue new laws and taxes. Then from Cuzco came the news that there was a pestilence of smallpox. And when he turned towards the sea with his army there was seen at midnight visibly surrounding them a million men, and none knew who they were. And they say that he [the Inca] said they were living souls which God had shown to them, signifying that so many were about to die of pestilence... And when he sat down to eat there came a messenger with a black cloak, and he gave the Inca a kiss with great reverence, and he gave him a 'pputi', a small box with a key. And the Inca told the same Indian to open it, but he asked to be excused saying that the Creator had commanded that only the Inca should open it. Understanding the reason why, the Inca opened the box, and there came fluttering out things like butterflies or scraps of paper, and they scattered until they vanished. And this was the smallpox plague. Within two days the general Mihicnaca Mayta died, with many other distinguished captains, all their faces all covered with burning scabs. And when the Inca saw this, he ordered a stone house to be prepared for him in which to isolate himself. And there he died.

It sounds almost like a parable of germ warfare. One wonders whether the tale might have originated from the message from the coast concerning bearded strangers – along with a box sent by the Spanish? Most likely, though, it needs to be understood as one of those folk tales which encapsulate the agonizing process of history, and the terrifying, almost supernatural malevolence of the new disease – an Inca version of Pandora's Box. Some said, too, that before the emperor died, he warned his people to prepare for an invasion by people from another world.

The Inca's funeral cortège wound its way slowly along the royal road, 1200 miles from Cuenca in Ecuador to Cuzco. Wayna Capac's mummified body, dressed in his finest clothes, was carried on the shoulders of his sons, cousins and brothers, and the 'most important people in the empire'.

According to the Spanish chronicler Murua, his entry into the capital was preceded by the triumphant return of the army, bearing a gold statue of the king; the great nobles dressed in their finery, carrying trophies – heads and loot – and parading their captives; each of the three army corps making a spectacular day-long entrance while the nobles sang their songs of victory. It was the last great public triumph of the old Inca world.

When the military ceremonies were over, the dead king made his entry into Cuzco 'in a lifelike posture', accompanied by great displays of grief. His funeral ceremony saw the sacrifice of hundreds of retainers, servants and women, with a thousand llamas – black, brown, white and red. Then his mummy was carried through the painted gateway of the *casana*, his own towering palace enclosure, on the great square of Cuzco. This huge palace-cum-mortuary temple – the largest and most beautiful of all the city's palaces – had a sacred pool and a royal festival hall which sheltered no fewer than 3000 people.

As the great gate of his house of eternity closed behind him, the late Inca's councillors knew the era was over. Already wounded by pestilence, the empire now faced further troubles – the enmity between the brothers, Atahuallpa and Huascar, and civil war.

The chronology of these events has never been worked out. But it is probable that Wayna Capac lay dying in Cuenca, in May 1528 on the Western calendar: 'They say when the news of the Spanish arrival came, the Inca was already dead,' says Cieza de Leon. But others said that the Inca had actually received the first news, and had asked for one of the Christians who had elected to stay behind to be brought to him, but that he had died before he was able to meet face to face with the stranger from another world. At all events, our sources indicate, as Cieza de Leon says, that 'Wayna Capac died the same year and *at the same time* that Pizarro arrived on the coast of his land.'

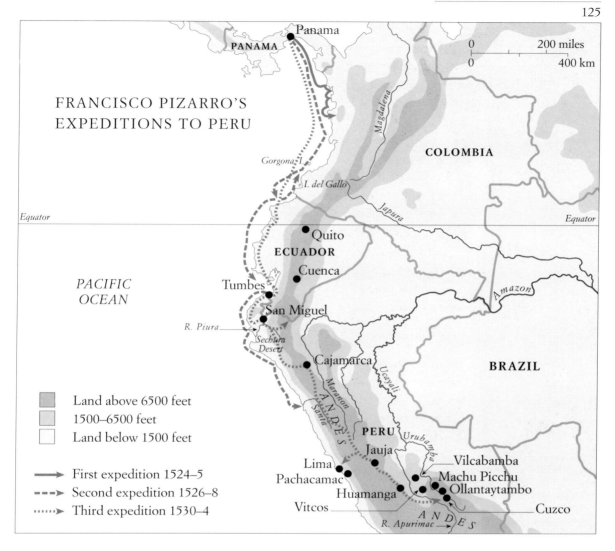

FRANCISCO PIZARRO'S
EXPEDITIONS TO PERU

*PACIFIC
OCEAN*

Land above 6500 feet
1500–6500 feet
Land below 1500 feet

First expedition 1524–5
Second expedition 1526–8
Third expedition 1530–4

PIZARRO HAD PUSHED ON DOWN THE PERUVIAN COAST
as far as the Santa river, making further landings which
only confirmed the magnitude of his discovery. There was no doubt now that a
high civilization on the scale of Mexico – or even grander – lay south of the
Equator, quite unknown to the outside world: 'A land which was the best and richest in the world.' He had glimpsed the edge of a great civilization, which had
grown up in complete isolation from the rest of mankind.

Pizarro returned elated to Panama, and there the partners formulated their
plan of conquest. He then took a ship to Spain, seeking backers and royal
approval. In mid-1529, he was well received at court by King Charles V and

'To Discover and Conquer Peru'

showed the king Peruvian pottery, metal vessels, fine clothing, embroideries and small worked pieces of gold, winning 'the applause of all the city of Toledo'.

There, too, by coincidence, he met his distant kinsman Hernan Cortes, who, aglow with his own achievements, was showering the court with presents of Aztec treasure. The two men spoke privately – we can imagine on what subject. Much encouraged, Pizarro returned to his home town of Trujillo to recruit young, tough, ambitious men who would be the next generation of conquistadors – men who would not baulk at seven months' starvation on a desert island.

On the evidence presented, the king and his advisers were convinced of the need to sign a deal with such experienced conquistadors as Pizarro and Almagro. At Toledo, on 26 July 1529, the queen granted Pizarro a licence 'to discover and conquer Peru', which is described as 'a rich and fertile land, inhabited by people *more reasonable* than any other which has so far been discovered'. The terms of the grant gave Pizarro the governorship of Peru, with the rights to explore and exploit the land on behalf of the Crown; and, in addition, a salary, to keep troops to protect each new colony, and to pay 'a mayor, a doctor and an apothecary'.

The die was cast. In the New Year of 1530, Pizarro sailed from Seville with a small fleet and an army whose core was drawn from his neighbours and kinsmen, including his half-brothers, Hernando, Juan and Gonzalo. It was the beginning of the family's almost Mafia-like grip on the affairs of Peru, a private entrepreneurial organization, which grew from the original small company to a vast financial and military enterprise, linking the private interests of the Pizarros to the political ambitions of the Spanish empire.

Pizarro's third voyage sailed from Panama on 27 December 1530, its overt aim the conquest of Peru. With him were 180 men, including twelve of the original thirteen from Isla del Gallo. The composition of the army is revealing: thirty-eight gentlemen, ninety of moderate rank, twenty of the lowest class. A third of these could read and write, a third sign their name, a third illiterate or unknown. The core of the group – seventeen warriors came from Pizarro's home town – were from Estremadura. These men demonstrated intense loyalty to Pizarro – surpassed only by the personal loyalties of his clan – which never failed, despite personal differences.

Pizarro landed his small expedition on the desolate Pacific coast, high up on the north part of Ecuador. He was either very cautious or very nervous, and spent seven months in the Puna region – a stay which led to grumbling among some of his force who began to wonder whether the promised riches had been just talk. Perhaps Pizarro wanted to acclimatize his men before moving south, or even to sever links with home, accustom them to living rough, and prepare them for the unknown.

Several more months followed as they moved along the coast; there were frequent skirmishes, and it soon became known that this time the bearded strangers had not come with peaceful intentions. Conscious of the translation difficulties which had dogged Cortes – the cumbersome transitions between Mayan, Nahuatl and Spanish – Pizarro had at least made sure that the Quechua-speaking Peruvian prisoners from his second voyage were now fluent Spanish-speakers, too; so he could speak clearly to the Peruvians, listen to them, and divine their intentions. Mastery of the Inca language would be a key to the campaign.

Pizarro finally came overland to Tumbes in April 1532. The rainy season had come by then, and although the weather is hot around the Tumbes river, there is less of a problem with the wind blowing in from the Sechura desert. This is where he had been in 1528, where Molina had been with the lovely women of the town, where the black man had washed his face for the locals, where Candia had eaten a meal surrounded by chattering temple virgins. But it was now a scene of desolation: the buildings were ruined, their thatched roofs burned, the population gone. Pizarro asked after the Spaniards, Molina and Gines, who had stayed there, but they had disappeared. Everything looked very different from the paradisiacal world he had glimpsed four years before.

The locals told him that the destruction had come about in a civil war which was still being fought between Wayna Capac's sons, Atahuallpa and Huascar. It was a dramatic moment for Pizarro, for it opened up the possibility – just as in Mexico – that he could exploit the dissension. A divided society is easier to break into. Seeing his chance, he made his move. In May 1532, he gave the order to cross the Tumbes river and march south into the heart of the Inca empire.

Journey into the Interior

THE NEXT STAGE OF OUR JOURNEY was to follow in Pizarro's footsteps. Ahead of us was 1000 miles of Inca road to Cuzco – and, beyond this, more travelling still across deserts, up glaciers and through trackless jungles in search of the conquest of the Incas. And this was just part of the astonishing series of journeys which led the Spanish, in a few years, into the forests of Colombia and Venezuela, over the High Andes of Peru into Amazonia, and as far south as the Rio Maule in Chile. Never in history has knowledge of the world expanded so fast, by sea and land.

So, on 16 May 1532, Pizarro left Tumbes. The diary by his secretary, Xerez, gives us an eye-witness account, and his route can still be followed, along the Inca road to the south – parallel lines of stones covered in windblown sand, which weave in and out of the old Pan-American Highway: 'We were astonished to see the extent of their road system,' says Xerez, 'well-paved footways crossing the whole country.'

Pizarro's route has never been accurately pinned down, but we now know that the main Inca Royal Road from Quito to Chile came down the coast, through Tumbes, and crossed the Chira river, close to where Pizarro founded the little town of San Miguel. The Spanish crossed the river at this point and slept on the south side. They marched for three days to the Piura valley, and then turned in towards the mountains, sending an exploratory foray up into the Andes. There, for the first time, they saw the Inca terrace-systems all the way up the mountainsides, wonderfully maintained. Coming from barren Estremadura, an austere land of swineherds, they were taken aback by 'the vast productivity of the land… We were amazed to see what an orderly state it was,' says Xerez, 'and also to see evidence of such rationality in the Indians.'

The news had spread that the bearded strangers no longer had peaceful intentions, and there was fighting – resistance from the local leaders. Meanwhile, all the way, 'every day, every hour' almost, the Inca Atahuallpa received reports about their progress; he knew exactly what they were doing, but the war with his brother Huascar occupied all his attention. Although he debated with his leaders whether they should divert to attack the foreigners, all judged Huascar the greater threat. The Spaniards, after all, were only 160 men. It is, indeed, astonishing to think how small Pizarro's army was: sixty-two horsemen and 102 foot, to attack an empire of at least five million, and perhaps as many as ten million. But he had deadly weapons – the latest technology: guns and mechanical crossbows. And he had that other priceless asset in war – fearlessness.

Through his interpreters, Pizarro interrogated the locals. He knew about the bitter civil war which had rocked the empire, and news now came that the new Inca, Atahuallpa, was only a few days away in northern Peru. For Pizarro, this was crucial news. Cortes had exploited internal dissensions to conquer the Aztecs; perhaps he could do the same. In fact, he, too, gathered Indian allies during this march because many of the regional peoples in Peru were hostile to Inca rule, especially in the north where it had been only recently imposed. So Pizarro was now marching with a force of Bronze Age warriors, their clubs and spears and feathered headdresses contrasting with Spanish lances and steel helmets.

About 300 miles south of Tumbes, they arrived at a place where the plain narrows, between sea and hills, and the Andes begin to loom up on the left. On 6 November, they stopped 'at the foot of the mountains' where the road divided. Here, a minor path left the main road and ascended into the mountains. Pizarro's local guides told him that this was the direct route to Cajamarca, some twenty leagues (sixty miles or so) away, but it crossed passes at a high altitude. There was some argument over what to do next, but Pizarro was adamant that they should go this way. He wanted to get to the Inca Atahuallpa as fast as he could.

On 8 November, Pizarro's small army left the plain and started its ascent of the Andes on a narrow made-up road. 'Sometimes the ground was so steep,' says Xerez, 'that the path was the only place where an ascent could be made.'

More and more breathless as the altitude affected them, they climbed up to Paucal, where there is a fantastic view down to the Pacific coast; just beyond the crest, they camped for the night at a large Inca-fortified *tambo,* an ancient staging post, which, although now in ruins, still stands in these beautiful hills. Next day, they continued along the Inca path, which still runs through San Miguel de Palaques, and found themselves marching over bare hills at over 10,000 feet. Still it rose, till they crossed the watershed of the Andes over freezing windswept uplands at 13,500 feet. But, to their surprise and relief, the Incas had left the passes undefended.

The altitude made some of Pizarro's men sick, and the place was also unexpectedly cold. Used to the equatorial heat of the plains, they were wearing the light, quilted, cotton armour developed in Panama, and found the conditions at altitude trying – especially after nightfall when the temperature drops sharply: 'The cold in these mountains is so intense after the heat of the valleys that we had to kindle fires at night, and we slept in cotton tents we brought with us.'

At night, their minds were whirling with stories about what lay ahead, and many of them were now very nervous. It was as if Atahuallpa were allowing them to go on...as if he had decided – like a spider in a web – to let the strangers come to him. But Pizarro spurred them on: 'It was not appropriate to show fear,' he said, 'and still less to think of turning back...'

Finally, late on 14 November 1532, after a seven-day hike over the mountains, the Spanish came out over the valley of Cajamarca and gazed down on the town below. Atahuallpa was still there. Beyond the town, they could see an immense camp and the smoke of thousands of fires – and the Inca army, with its vast assembly of servants, bearers and hangers-on.

As dusk fell, 'the camp fires of the enemy were a fearful sight...' Anxiously, the Spanish soldiers tried to guess the number of their enemies: 'There seemed to us to be upwards of 30,000 men in the camp outside the town,' they said. 'Few of us slept that night, we just talked about what we should do. All were full of fear, for we were so few, and so deep into the land, with no hope of rescue.'

Cajamarca: the Meeting of Two Worlds

TODAY, CAJAMARCA IS A PRETTY COUNTRY TOWN surrounded by green hills. The great square where the drama happened is still there – a lovely sunlit plaza, with flower beds and topiary, its perimeter lined with fine churches and several old-fashioned hostels backing on to picturesque courtyards with wooden staircases. The square

was bigger in Inca times: a vast parade ground for the performance of royal rituals.

In the middle of the plaza was a large square dais for the Inca throne. Here Atahuallpa was to hold his ceremony of royal entrance after the pacification of the region in the civil war. Among the Inca leaders there had been much debate about the strangers – an attempt to evaluate and classify them, just as there had been among the Aztecs. But they seem to have had no doubt from their intelligence reports that the Spaniards were humans – wherever they were from. Moreover, the Spaniards' destructive acts had not pleased Atahuallpa and, as we shall see, there is no doubt that he had decided to arrest and kill them. But perhaps he was also curious to meet them and had decided to allow them to come to him first, so he might study and question these creatures from another world.

He met the advance party at the Inca baths, which were situated in the flat land south of the town, surrounded by the most beautiful ranges of hills. There are still hot sulphur springs here today.

According to the Inca account dictated later by Atahuallpa's nephew Titu Cusi, there was an immediate failure of communication over the traditional guest rituals of Andean diplomacy: 'My uncle received them well according to our custom,' he said. 'He offered them the customary welcome of chicha, maize beer, in gold cups; but they poured it away on the floor. Which much angered my uncle.'

The Incas had never seen horses before, and the Spanish, realizing that many of the king's entourage were frightened of the animals, made a deliberately threatening gesture to unnerve them – just as they had done in the first exchanges with Montezuma. Hernando de Soto rode right up, spurring his horse so close to Atahuallpa's face that its breath tousled the crimson tassels on the Inca's royal headband. Atahuallpa, however, was unmoved and unblinking, and ordered those who had panicked to be killed. Such lack of courage was demeaning in the staff of a great king. Atahuallpa knew how to be a king.

Atahuallpa now told the Spaniards that he would meet them in the town and told them to wait for him there, where they would be given lodging in one of the royal enclosures facing the square. There is substantial agreement between the Spanish and Inca versions as to what happened next.

Before Atahuallpa came down from his camp, the Spaniards marched into the deserted town and took up hiding positions in the colonnades of one of the royal festival halls which looked out on to the great central square (where the Inca's throne dais stood). They had a long wait, standing for hours in battle gear, and, as Pedro Pizarro later recalled, the tension grew almost unbearable:

The Indians' spies were letting the Inca know that we were all inside the hall, full of fear, and that none of us was showing our face in the plaza. And it was true what they were saying, because I saw myself many of us who without noticing pissed ourselves out of sheer terror.

In the late afternoon, several thousand Incas came into the square, and then Atahuallpa himself was carried in on his palanquin. Waman Poma takes up the tale: 'Atahuallpa was carried on the *usno*, a golden throne with steps which was mounted on his open litter. He arrived in great state surrounded by his officers...' Great crowds of people were now crammed into the square, partly out of curiosity to see the strangers. Then Pizarro sent a message out through one of his priests, Friar Vicente Valverde, saying he was an ambassador from a great king overseas, a king who desired to be his friend. That is what the Spanish say, and pretty much what Waman Poma says too:

Pizarro explained through his interpreter that he was the messenger and ambassador of a great ruler who desired friendship with the Inca and that this was the only object of their mission to Peru. Atahuallpa listened with close attention to the words spoken by Pizarro and then by the interpreter. He then answered with great dignity that he had no reason to doubt the fact of the Spaniards' long journey, or their mission from an important ruler. However he had no need to make any pact of friendship with them because he too was a great ruler in his own country...

Friar Vicente now intervened, holding crucifix and breviary, and explained in rather hectoring tones that the Spanish ruler according to his account was a friend of God...and called upon the Inca to renounce all other gods as being a mockery of the truth.

The exchange now reaches a surreal plane, in which one can only sympathize with the Inca in the face of such 'primitive' ways of thinking:

Atahuallpa now replied that he could not change his belief in the immortal son and the other Inca deities. He asked Friar Vicente what authority he had for his own belief, and the friar told him it was all written in the book which he was holding. The Inca then said: 'Give me the book so that it can speak to me...'

It is a fateful moment in the encounter of two worlds. Is Atahuallpa playing with the Spanish – mocking them? The king's lively intelligence and capacity for self-mockery, which are revealed later, suggests that this was possibly the case.

The book was handed up to him, and he began to eye it carefully and listen to it page by page. At last he asked: 'Why doesn't the book say anything to me?'

▲ Atahuallpa – one of many idealized portraits of the Incas produced during and after the War of Independence. By then nostalgia for the Inca past had softened the memory of his disastrous handling of the Spanish invasion.

And still sitting on his throne, he threw it on to the ground with a haughty and disdainful petulant gesture…

This was the moment that Pizarro had been waiting for, the moment to which his entire life – all his plans, voyages and petitions, his sufferings on the Isle of the Gorgon – had led him. According to Waman Poma, Friar Vicente shouted that the Indians were against the Christian faith and gave the order to attack. The Spanish emerged with their guns from the porticoes around the square and fired in to the massed crowds of unarmed people. Waman Poma describes the massacre in a wonderfully gripping passage:

They killed the Indians like ants. At the sound of the explosions and the jingle of bells on the horses' harness, the shock of arms and the whole amazing novelty of their attackers' appearance, the Indians were terror stricken. The pressure of their numbers caused the walls of the square to crumble and fall. Desperate to escape from being trampled under the hooves of the horses, in their headlong flight so many were crushed to death. So many Indians were killed it was impracticable to count them. As for the Spaniards, only five of them lost their lives, and these few casualties were not caused by the Indians, who at no time dared to attack the formidable strangers. The Spaniards' corpses were found intertwined with their Indian victims, and it was assumed they had been mistakenly trampled to death by their own cavalry.

Atahuallpa Inca was pulled down from his throne without injury and became the prisoner of Pizarro. He was put in chains and placed under guard by Spanish soldiers in a room close to Francisco Pizarro's lodgings. Deprived of his throne, and all his majesty, he was left sadly and disconsolately sitting on the ground in his prison…

Titu Cusi's account is equally graphic and moving, and he gives us further detail from the family tradition of the royal Incas. He says that the square was enclosed by walls and the Indians were trapped inside:

They could not get out, nor did they have any weapons – they had not brought them because of the low opinion they held of the Spaniards; all they had were slings and ceremonial knives – and the Spanish killed them all just as one would slaughter llamas, for nobody could defend himself.

Although some suggest a slightly different order of events, the Spanish accounts say much the same. Cieza de Leon claims their first speaker was not Pizarro, but the priest, and adds important details: that Atahuallpa showed, as he listened to Friar Vicente's speech about God, that he thought it 'something of a mockery'.

And, most important, that after he had thrown down the breviary he told Friar Vicente to tell Pizarro that he 'would not move from the place where he was until they returned and restored to him all the gold, silver stones, cloth, Indian men and women, and everything else he had stolen'.

The scene at Cajamarca imagined by Sir John Everett Millais, *c.* 1846. Pizarro grasps the Inca Atahuallpa, who clings to the *usno*, the ceremonial throne platform. To the left is Pizarro's priest, Friar Vicente, in a suitably lurid light.

If this is true, it is fascinating that Atahuallpa saw the Spanish intruders as committing crimes in international relations: customary law was important in Inca society and these were crimes which should be compensated within a legalistic framework. It is plain from this that Atahuallpa thought the Spanish were creatures of this earth rather than gods. But, of course, the king of Tawantinsuyu, the great Inca, can hardly have imagined that these 160 bearded strangers had come with the intention of destroying him – let alone that they had the capacity to do it.

According to Cieza de Leon, it was when Atahuallpa demanded restitution from the Spanish that they attacked: 'With this answer, having collected the breviary, the skirts of his habit flying around him, Friar Vicente rushed back to Pizarro, telling him that the tyrant Atahuallpa was like a wounded dog, and that they should attack him…' In the moments remaining before disaster, more of Atahuallpa's words are recorded by Cieza de Leon, no doubt from his eye-witnesses:

When the friar left, according to what we are now told, in order to provoke his people's anger, Atahuallpa told them that the Christians were in contempt of him, and had raped so many women, killed so many men, pillaged whatever they could without shame or fear – and were now only asking for peace with the intention of gaining supremacy over them.

On hearing the Inca's words, says Cieza de Leon, the atmosphere turned against the Spaniards: 'The people now let out loud cries and sounded their instruments.' Many more people were pouring into the town, in part, no doubt, simply fascinated to see the strange new arrivals. But they could not enter the square because it was crammed with people. When Pizarro learned what had happened, 'realizing that he had no time to lose, he raised a towel, the signal to attack…'

On these details, Cieza de Leon agrees: that the panic-stricken crowd broke down walls to escape; that the Incas never defended themselves; most pointedly, that they simply could not believe what was happening ('they asked themselves if this was real or a dream?'). According to Cieza de Leon, more than 2000 Indians died. (Titu Cusi says 10,000.) Many more were wounded and, after the Spaniards pursued them to Atahuallpa's camp, more than 5000 unarmed people were collected up as captives. It was now pitch dark and had begun to rain heavily.

It was well into the evening when the Spanish came back to the town. After the nerve-jangling tension of the last few hours, they were in a state of almost hysterical excitement. Their pent-up tension had been released in their unrestrained savagery against the unarmed Incas and, flushed with the adrenalin rush of violence and killing, they were now roaring their heads off. The noise was such that Pizarro had to fire a shot to get silence and make himself heard. The ransacked Inca camp outside the town had yielded plunder rather like that of Darius the Persian's tent after the Battle of Issus: 'Great spoils of gold and silver vessels, a thousand different cups, precious cloths, jewels, stones.'

As for Atahuallpa, Titu Cusi adds: 'And they took my uncle to a cell where they kept him bound all night, with a chain around his neck.' Many of the royal family had also fallen into the invaders' hands. The noble female captives were herded into the Spanish presence: another perennial theme which occurs in all stories of the conquest, and a theme of women as loot which Cieza de Leon, who understood war and warriors, did not omit:

Many principal ladies of royal lineage or of the chiefs of the kingdom became captives – some of them very lovely and beautiful with long hair dressed according to their fashion, which is of a most elegant style. They also held many mamaconas, who are virgins of the temples...

Few, one imagines, escaped rape or abuse by the conquerors.

The scale of the loot was beyond belief. The treasure for 160 men was such, that if this was merely a foretaste, 'there would have been none in the world that could equal them. None had been in danger. They all believed it was a miracle...'

It was now nearing midnight on Saturday, 16 November 1532. 'A heavy rain was falling now,' says Cieza de Leon, 'a relief to the Indians.' In his prison, a couple of hundred yards away from the square, rain beating on the thatch, and dripping down the window shutters, Atahuallpa stared into the wall, the events of the past hours swimming before his mind. The empire of the Tawantinsuyu had begun to unravel.

Atahuallpa's Downfall

THERE ARE MANY THEORIES about why Atahuallpa had allowed such events to happen. Some say that the Inca was paralysed by superstition, by astronomical conjunctions and prophecies, or by the technological and cultural superiority of the Europeans. Cieza de Leon says that when the news reached Cuzco there were those among the line of the defeated Inca Huascar's family who thought the disaster a fulfilment of prophecy: revenge on the usurper Atahuallpa. But that is as far as it goes. It is a natural human instinct to make such catastrophes conform to religious conceptions, or to ideas about history and the cycles of time – especially as the catastrophe went across the board, with disease, physical and spiritual conquest, and the collapse of the dynasty.

But it is all a question of what our primary sources tell us. Spanish sources, written soon afterwards – Xerez, Cieza de Leon – and Inca ones within living memory – Titu Cusi, Waman Poma, Santa Cruz Pachacuti – leave us with little doubt that the Inca perceived the Spanish as earthly creatures, a kind of human being, who were to be dealt with as such.

It seems likely, then, that the Incas correctly diagnosed the strangers before they met them and that Atahuallpa intended to capture them, probably kill or enslave them, castrating a few as eunuchs for his court, keeping some of the specialists – the horse-breaker and the blacksmith, for example – who would be useful to him. If anything, the Incas looked down on the strangers as subhuman, rather than superhuman. Complacency, then, rather than superstition, was Atahuallpa's downfall.

Add to that the devastation wrought by smallpox, and the ravages of civil war, and we begin to get a realistic picture of the reasons for the Inca's fall. Had Wayna Capac still been on throne, had smallpox never come, it is debatable that Pizarro would have got to Cajamarca. Even his own side acknowledged that. From what Pedro Pizarro heard later, for example:

If Wayna Capac had been alive when we invaded Peru, we could not have won for he was greatly loved by his people; if the country had not been divided by the wars between his successors, we could neither have invaded, nor triumphed – not even if over a thousand Spanish troops had come at once.

Whether the Inca world could have survived the European expansion of the sixteenth century is still questionable. But it is worth noting that, by 1536, the Incas fought their battles around Cuzco using Spanish weapons, and were even able to defeat Spanish forces in pitched battle. Once again, the 'what ifs' of history remain.

'A Roomful of Gold'

THE RANSOM ROOM IS STILL THERE, off the square in Cajamarca, behind a great old family house, with faded murals on crumbling plaster, an inner court ringed by creaking balconies, and a rickety service-wing stretching back behind the yard as far as the open space where the town's last Inca building stands.

From the seventeenth century, the story has been told that it was here that Atahuallpa was held in chains; and here that he made his famous offer to ransom himself by filling the room full of gold as far as he could reach with his hand. (There is still a faint line cut into the stone about six feet or so above the old floor level. But who cut it is another matter. Even in the seventeenth century, Spanish tourists were being shown around the place.)

The Spanish visited the traumatized Atahuallpa in his cell, gave him food, and allowed his women to come to him. It was then that Atahuallpa – now understanding that the Spanish wanted gold – came up with his plan to ransom himself for it.

For the Incas, the Spanish desire for gold was both curious and fascinating. For them, gold had an aesthetic rather than a monetary value. They used it for decorating their shrines, for the images of their gods, but not for bartering. They found the Spanish obsession with gold as a commodity uncouth and even

◀ The Inca room in Cajamarca, where tradition holds that Atahuallpa was kept prisoner, and which he later filled with gold.

▼ Inca gold: detail of a gold collar from the Classic Inca period. Such was the Spanish greed for gold that only tiny pieces remain today; and nothing survives to give a hint of the lifesize figures, human and animal, that the Spanish looted from the sacred garden in Cuzco (pages 148–9).

uncivilized. Waman Poma included a cartoon in his book of the Inca asking the Spaniard (in Quechua): 'Do you actually eat this gold, then?' and the Spaniard replying, 'Yes, we certainly do!'

Atahuallpa's motive, says Waman Poma, 'was to free himself by paying them gold'. If he paid up, he believed they would go away. It never seems to have occurred to him that these few – less than 200 – might be the precursors of thousands who would come to settle permanently in his land, and that one payment of gold would not be enough.

'Shaker of the Earth'

SO, ATAHUALLPA SENT OUT HIS MESSENGERS to announce that the Spanish had been granted freedom to travel across his empire and were to be given the gold they desired. And Pizarro's henchmen soon followed, travelling deep into the heart of the Inca empire for the first time. Most celebrated was the journey of Hernando Pizarro that December, down the Pacific coast to the ancient shrine of Pachacamac, the 'Shaker of the Earth'.

To get to Pachacamac today, one must journey down the coast through the suburbs, to the south of Lima, a Spanish colonial capital founded by Pizarro in 1534.

The old road that was taken by Hernando Pizarro is now the Pan-American Highway. But the landscape is much changed. Francisco Pizarro's City of Kings is a mega-city today, and its suburbs spread all the way to the site of Pachacamac. Running along the shore, past high hills of mud, the suburbs are honeycombed with shanties and prefabs the colour of mud. All, in fact, is the colour of mud; and swirling dust-storms create darkness in the early afternoon. There are huge billboards by the road, one sporting a languorous blonde beach girl in a blue swimsuit. She is fair-skinned, the epitome of Western consumer desire, advertising INKA COLA, the home-grown lemon-grass drink of the Andes. Then, after a few miles, you see the sign to Pachacamac.

Although little visited, and relatively unknown compared with famous Inca sites, Pachacamac is one of the great archaeological wonders of the Americas. Occupied from the early years AD, it was a famous oracle, seat of the creator god Pachacamac, and so holy that, when the Incas came to dominate the region, they incorporated it into their own religious system. Even today, after centuries of plundering (which started in 1532), its landscape is dominated by the huge pyramids which were enlarged and extended for a thousand years or more before the Spanish came; and even today the native shamans perform their rituals here.

The site stands in a dramatic position on a ridge, 300 feet above the coastal plain, looking out over the rolling breakers of the Pacific to the islands of

Pachacamac. Beyond, there is nothing till Australia. It is a place where earth, ocean and sky come together in the most primal way – as suitable a place as any to imagine the epiphany of the prehistoric creator. The site lies near the mouth of the Lurin valley, one of the many narrow valleys which cut across the coastal plain below the Andes, and it sustained the successive civilizations of ancient Peru – Chavin, Nazca and Moche. Small scale such civilizations may have been compared with the Bronze Age Old World kingdoms but, as the staggering discoveries made recently in the royal tombs of Sipan prove, they were fabulously wealthy. (Surely one of the greatest single archaeological finds since Tutankhamun?)

Pachacamac arose as a sacred site early in the first millennium and was enlarged by successive rulers. By the time the Spanish came, Pachacamac was as big as a city, dominated by the huge Pyramid of the Sun erected – or imposed – on the site by the imperial Incas in the fifteenth century.

In modern excavations of the shrine of Pachacamac himself, fragments of the painted murals were found on the walls, and the shell-studded doors which the Spanish saw in 1532 were lying in the debris where they fell. Amazingly, excavations in the 1930s turned up the wooden idol itself, perhaps buried by the priests to avoid destruction at the hands of the conquistadors. So, today, it is possible to stand alone in the darkness and to gaze on the face of Pachacamac, just as the Spanish did at the end of 1532. A description survives of the Spanish visit to the shrine by a member of the force led by Hernando Pizarro to strip it of its riches:

The Captain ascertained that the Devil frequented this idol and spoke with his servants saying diabolical things. They look upon him as God and offer many sacrifices to him, and they come to this Devil from distances of three hundred leagues with gold and silver and cloth. The Spaniards gave the Indians to understand they were in great error, and that he who spoke from the inside of the idol was the Devil who deceived them. They were told that from henceforth they must not believe him, nor do what he said. The Captain ordered the chamber to be pulled down and the idol broken.

Pizarro's own account is a poignant parable of the meeting of the two worlds:

I had an old man tortured, who was one of the senior and intimate servants of their god. But he was so stubborn in his evil creed that I could never gather anything from him but that they really believed their devil to be a god. It would seem that the Indians do not worship this devil from any feelings of devotion, but from fear.

HERNANDO PIZARRO MAY NOT HAVE FOUND MUCH GOLD *The Death of Atahuallpa*
inside Pachacamac, but he and his men stripped the
other shrines around it – including the Inca Temple of the Sun – and they were
full of gold. There were also many more: Pariacaca (where the Indian shamans still
go for initiation), Raqchi, where the vast adobe nave of the shrine still towers like
a cathedral over maize fields; and, in Cuzco, the Coricancha, the great Temple of
the Sun whose walls were covered with sheets of hammered gold. From all these
places, Atahuallpa's governors obeyed his wishes and dispatched the gold to
Cajamarca – seven tons of it, along with thirteen tons of silver. Most of this was
melted down into ingots on the spot.

It was a devastating cultural loss, for – along with textiles – gold was one of
the chief mediums used by Inca artists. It took a month for Pizarro's men to melt
it down, and, although a few choice pieces were sent back to Spain, remarkably
few of these items survive today. Over the next year the Spanish obliterated a great
artistic tradition.

Atahuallpa, meanwhile, remained under close guard in captivity. He was clearly
fascinated by his captors and soon learned to speak some Spanish:

*In his imprisonment Atahuallpa held conversations with Pizarro, Almagro, and
others of the Spaniards. He learned to play chess with his captors and this game was
given the Indian name of 'taptana' or 'surprise attack'. The Inca's character appeared
mild and peaceable, for he did his best to keep on good terms with the Christians.
He gave away all his wealth to them, but still put himself out to please them.
Meanwhile he lost much of the allegiance of his own nobility...*

As with Cortes and Montezuma, we detect in this what modern psychologists call
the 'hostage syndrome' – that is, complicity between the victim and the hostage-
taker. Pizarro ruthlessly exploited Atahuallpa's growing dependence on him, and
Atahuallpa was coerced into murdering members of other branches of the royal
family: in particular, his brother and rival Huascar was captured, abused, mocked
and killed.

'The motive, though, lay in the inquiries the Christians had been making
about the legitimate ruler of Peru and his family,' says Waman Poma (who, by the
way, was all the more horrified because he regarded Huascar as the legitimate
ruler). 'By Atahuallpa's orders, sent from prison, all the princes and princesses
were murdered, and even unborn children were done to death in the womb...
At this time our Indians lost all sense of direction. They forgot their gods and
missed the authority of their rulers...'

But, of course, all this appeasement and cooperation was no use in the end.

◂◂ A gold statuette of a
female goddess from the
Classic Inca period.
In Cuzco, Spanish furnaces
worked through the night
melting such treasures
into bullion.

When it came to the time for Pizarro to fulfil his side of the bargain, he accused Atahuallpa of plotting against him, and put him on trial for treason. For Pizarro it was a simple precaution: he was in Cajamarca; the Inca capital was a thousand miles away, so he could not let Atahuallpa go free. Making a pretence of acting within the law as Spanish conquistadors had to do in the New World, Atahuallpa was found guilty and condemned to death – sentenced to be burned at the stake.

Many of the Spanish were horrified at the sentence: 'It was the most despicable thing we Spanish ever did in the Indes,' said Cieza de Leon, a soldier himself. To the Peruvians, it was an appalling sentence, not only because it was unjust and cruel, but because, like the Ancient Egyptians, their mortuary beliefs centred on the survival of the body. The Inca cult of the ancestors required the mummy to be carefully preserved in the house of its lineage, to be brought out at festivals, paraded in the streets and cosseted like a living person. To be burned was to be denied the afterlife. And so, in the end, fearing the loss of his soul, Atahuallpa agreed to be baptized in exchange for death by garrotting – the death that Montezuma had suffered.

The Inca Atahuallpa was murdered in the square in Cajamarca on 26 July 1533. He was not an impressive character, and he did not handle events like a great king. But the manner of his death left an imperishable aura which, after his death, transformed him into a symbol of resistance in the Andean world, and even today he is still remembered in songs, plays and laments as the 'father Inca', whom the whites treacherously killed.

▸ The execution of Atahuallpa, as depicted in a mural of the Cuzco school. Sentenced to be burned to death – and hence, in Inca belief, to lose his immortal soul – Atahuallpa agreed to accept baptism and be garrotted (not beheaded, as shown here).

PIZARRO NOW MARCHED ON CUZCO, along the main Inca *To the Navel of the Earth*
route south, through Jauja and Huamanga. There were
battles on the way, but Pizarro had been reinforced, the opposition was hopelessly
confused and divided, and he could not be stopped. On Saturday, 15 November
1533, the Spanish entered Cuzco: 'the head of the great empire of the Incas, where
their court was, their solemn Temple of the Sun and their greatest marvels…'

Cuzco is still a wonderful sight today. The name means 'navel' in Quechua,
and the city stands folded in on itself at the head of its valley, in a bowl of hills
overlooked by the higher peaks of the Andes. It lies at over 11,000 feet and has
a high-altitude climate, with crystalline light, dry, crisp air and, by day at least, a
scorching sun which brings out the dazzling colours of the red hills, the whitewashed adobe walls and the matt black stone of the Inca masonry, which still
forms the foundations of the city.

This was the heartland of the Incas – the 'navel of the earth', as they called it.
For although the founding myth of the Incas took them back to the Isle of the Sun
in Lake Titicaca and the ancient civilization of Tiahuanuco, Cuzco in reality was
the birthplace of the dynasty – to be precise the sacred rock, just outside the city
where the first Inca, Manco Capac, had sunk his golden rod and marked the site
of their Andean home. This was their real root, and the surrounding landscape
remained the most intensively mythologized part of the empire.

Although Cuzco had a population of over 50,000, many were part of the vast
service industries attached to the royal court and the households of the various
lineages. Each branch of the royal family maintained palaces in huge walled enclosures grouped around the grand plaza in the centre. (Some were truly vast – the
great festival hall of Wayna Capac was 200 yards long.) The city had been rebuilt
by Inca Pachacuti in the 1440s and 1450s, after his victory in war against the
Chancas, the Incas' old rivals. Over twenty years, a 50,000-strong workforce had
remade Cuzco in the shape of a puma, its head the gigantic fortress above the
city at Sacsahuaman ('Royal Hawk'), its tail near the great curving enclosure of
the Coricancha, the Temple of the Sun. And from this place, the sacred heart
of the city, lines of shrines, which marked out the sacred landscape, were spread
out to all four quarters.

Pizarro's arrival in the city, early in 1533, had been uncontested. Indeed, there
were many members of the Inca royal lineages who were prepared to welcome him
– especially those who had been opposed to Atahuallpa's rule. They regarded the
Spanish as deliverers from the horrors of the civil war, and were far from unhappy
to see Pizarro begin by observing the proprieties of the Inca state and crowning a
legitimate member of the royal family with the crimson fringe. Pizarro, on the
other hand, saw the appointment of a puppet king as the best way to normalize

◀ 'Cuzco, the capital of the Kingdom of Peru in the New World'. This etching dates from 1572, by which time the city had been extensively rebuilt by the Spanish. Although idealized, the picture conveys the rugged mountain setting of the 'navel of the earth'.

◀◀ A view of Cuzco today. Though now a magnet for the world's backpackers, the city still rests on its Inca foundations; its people speak Quechua and, in the surrounding mountains, the old sacred places are still maintained.

Spanish control in Cuzco and, after consultation, decided that the new Inca should be Manco, a young son of Wayna Capac and half-brother of Atahuallpa.

At first it all went well: Inca ceremonials and processions were allowed. There was the usual heavy drinking of chicha beer which went on for a month. (Then, as now, Andean people were great drinkers, and Inca law had stringent penalties against drunkenness.) The mummies of the dead kings were paraded through the streets on litters – the last time this was done openly (although, centuries later, some were found, it is said, inside the effigies of Catholic saints). Spanish intervention, then, was not yet seen as fatal to the continuance of the Inca world.

During their seven months in Cajamarca, the Spanish leaders had taken Inca women from among their captives. Atahuallpa gave the fifty-six-year-old bachelor Pizarro the eighteen-year-old Quispe Cusi, who was the daughter of Wayna Capac.

Pizarro seems to have grown genuinely fond of her and he gave her the nickname of 'Pizpita', after a bird in his native Estremadura. Baptized a Christian, she bore him a daughter in Cuzco in December 1534, and a son the following year. Other leaders, such as Diego de Almagro and Hernando de Soto, did the same, taking their pick of the royal women, as did the rank and file.

In the heady early days, these liaisons – unions of Spanish and Inca royal blood – do not seem to have aroused enmities but, rather, were a cause for celebration; some were marked by tournaments and festivities. In the end, as we shall see, it was Spanish mistreatment of Inca women which helped to bring the two sides to blows but, inevitably, the first cracks came about because of the Spaniards' unquenchable greed for gold. As Manco Inca himself observed, 'Even if all the snow in the Andes turned to gold, still they would not be satisfied.'

Most of the gold taken from Cajamarca would go to the king of Spain and the Pizarro brothers, with the remainder allocated on a share basis, as promised, to the men who had served in the original army. There had been more plundering on entry into Cuzco. But as more Spaniards came in, this share-out was soon not enough.

At his coronation, the new puppet king, Manco, swore an oath committing the Inca monarchy to be a client state of Spain. This supposedly meant that Manco would rule independently while acknowledging the Spanish crown, for 'the Inca should serve no one'. Manco understood his position as that of an ally of the Spanish, but the whole charade was soon exposed as a fraud. Soon after Manco's coronation, the Spanish systematically began to strip the assets of the royal clans. And a vast plunder it was; as Pedro Pizarro remembered, the Spanish could hardly believe what they saw:

There were so many warehouses of wonderful textiles…of gilded thrones, of food, of coca leaves… There were clothes made of sewn sequins of very delicate and exquisite workmanship… There were many storehouses of copper tools for the mines, and sacks and ropes; there were stores of cups and plates in silver…

The Spanish had already stripped the walls of the Coricancha to gather Atahuallpa's ransom; now they went through its shrines and storerooms to loot its most precious cult objects. These included 'a gold effigy whose discovery caused the Indians particular pain, for it was said to be a figure of the first Inca'. They also emptied the famous garden of its gold llamas, flowers and people: 'In one cave,' says Pedro Pizarro, 'were twelve llamas of silver and gold, lifelike and lifesize.'

A full inventory of the temple and its garden was never made, and no doubt a huge quantity of treasure was misappropriated. An idea of its riches, though, is given by the royal share of one-fifth taken from this one temple, which, even after looting, amounted to 'a large quantity of gold, four gold llamas and eleven gold women…along with so much silver that it is unbelievable, and so many precious stones which if brought together would be worth a city'.

A foundry was set up in Cuzco to melt the newly acquired gold into ingots, and once more the Inca nobility were forced to watch as, day and night, their religious and artistic wealth – gold ornaments, rings, statues, censers, cups, plates, wall decorations – was thrown into the flames, the treasures of the ages dissolved into gold bars for the bankers of Europe. 'No loot equalled this one,' said one of the conquistadors, 'nor in the Indies was there ever found such wealth.'

Inside the Holy of Holies

IT IS NIGHT: an almost full moon sits in a cloudless sky. Inside the church of Santo Domingo in Cuzco, the sound of Catholic prayers floats through the partition walls. The Coricancha is an eerie place: darkened cloisters and an empty courtyard from which you enter the roofless buildings of the key temple of the Inca world. It is astonishing to find them still standing. This, I think, is the very best place to feel the presence of the Inca world – especially at night.

In 1950, an earthquake exposed all that had been hidden by masonry and plaster since the sixteenth century. There was a debate at the time about whether the whole church should be removed and the Inca temple exposed, but this was not done. As a compromise, the Inca buildings were left inside the Christian church, so now six marvellous Inca structures surround the cloister (a seventh, which had originally projected beyond the court, has gone).

The buildings are all large rooms, made of the most finely cut dark stone, with beautiful niches; all were once covered by steeply pitched thatched roofs. On the inside walls, you can run your fingers over rows of holes where golden nails once secured the bands of gold plate which covered their surfaces. The niches, where the idols and the mummies of the dead Incas were kept, are still intact. We are standing in the holy of holies of the Inca world.

First on the left, as we go round the cloister, is the room for the rainbow – the sacrifice room. A trio of neat circular holes once took the liquid from the sacrifice – the blood of llamas, libations of maize beer – into the street. Next is the room for the god Ilapa. Mercurial and frightening, the thunder and lightning, the shooting star, Ilapa was one of the primal deities of the royals. His room is a magnificent, intact, cult room, with rows of blind niches and three doorways. It is a place that had fantastic resonance in the Inca thought-world. A century before the coming of the Spanish, a young prince, son of Viracocha Inca, saved Cuzco and the empire from deadly enemies. Before the final battle, the prince saw a supernatural

figure in a dream or vision – the sky god, Ilapa, who spoke to him affectionately, saying. 'My son, keep to the true religion, and you will be a great Inca and conquer many nations.' So he did, thus freeing the Incas and thenceforth calling himself Pachacuti: the revolution, the turner upside down of the world and time. From that moment, the world was remade – and Ilapa was the king's double, his alter ego. So this room, with its images, rituals and liturgies, was designed to embody the Year Zero of the Inca world.

▲ Inside part of the surviving Inca palace under Cotopaxi, Ecuador, which later belonged to the conquistador Diego de Sandoval, who married a wife of Atahuallpa. Like many Inca buildings, it was converted into a chapel after the conquest.

◄◄ The immense, finely jointed limestone blocks (above left) formed the foundations of the Inca palaces and temples in Cuzco. The church of Santo Domingo in Cuzco (below left), built around and over the remains of the Incas' holiest shrine, the Coricancha. The Temple of the Sun stood on the curved bastion in the foreground.

Today, it is a Christian cloister, but it has kept the shape of the Inca court. Open to the sky, it is still bounded by the great Inca walls; only the high-pitched thatched roofs are missing. On the opposite side of the court is the Temple of the Stars, who are the daughters of the moon – Venus in particular. This temple is intact and, with two massive twelve-foot-high doors, it is magnificent. It has a superb double-blind niche in the centre, and its walls – with twenty-three beautiful inset niches – are perfect all the way round.

Imagine the decoration of these sombre rooms: the flashing colours which relieved the hard matt dark stone, the gilded figures of gods and founders, the gold walls gleaming in the lamplight, the smoke and incense curling upwards to the high-beamed roof. And the music: 'the great puma skin drum, the trumpet, the spiral shell, calabash, flute and pipe'.

It is not difficult when standing here, with the kerosene lamplight flickering on the walls, to imagine the nocturnal ceremonies of Wayna Capac, when the 'black llamas were sacrificed to the gods in the third month'; or to picture Coya Raymi, the queen's feast, 'when the great festival of the Moon was held, and the Moon, the bride of the Sun, was the queen of all the planets and the stars in the sky'. At that time, crowding in here in their embroidered dresses, would have been the 'women of high rank, including the Inca's family, and the temple virgins, who issued the invitations to the men and took a leading part in the entertainment…'

As for the most magnificent, the 'most stately of all their temples', the Sun itself, this was demolished in the sixteenth century and a Christian church built in its place. It is, however, still possible to walk to the end of the church on to a curving terrace, which stands on the magnificent curved buttress of the temple. This terrace – the finest of all surviving pieces of Inca stonework – once looked over the magical garden with its lifesize gold and silver men, women and llamas, and its ears of wheat and flowers.

Waman Poma gives us a picture of what the Temple of the Sun was like inside: 'Here the walls were decorated with the purest gold from top to bottom, there were huge rock crystals set above the gate, and sculptured pumas on either side.' Here, Waman Poma tells us, 'the Inca would make presents of gold and silver to his father, the Sun, and offered up the lives of children of ten years old, selected from the whole of Peru, none of whom had any spot, blemish or mole on their bodies'. The temple was aligned so that 'as the sun set its rays fell on to the interior'.

From the terrace one can stand on the curving Inca rampart and look down over the site of the golden garden. Standing there under a starry sky, listening to vespers through the blocked door of the Temple of the Moon, I felt the strange co-existence of the past in the Andean lilt of the plainsong – and distantly heard the song to the creator, described by Waman Poma, who had himself briefly known that splendid archaic world:

…a slow rhythmic incantation in which the Inca himself joined in, imitating the bleat of the red llama, joined by the ladies in attendance starting on a high note, gradually descending in a lovely effect, the words 'aravi, aravi' alternated with improvisations delivered in the same tone of voice…the sad melancholy song…

The civilization destroyed by the Spanish was a non-literate society and, inevitably, only tiny fragments of words and impressions, recorded by those who came later, shards of a broken world, are left. Both civilizations, one might say, were deluded, but which one was the more so – the Incas or the Spanish?

Around the cloister today are strange paintings of Christian saints and martyrs dying their gruesome deaths, with the ever-present blood and tears, which seems somehow more alien than the golden llamas of the Coricancha, or the tears shed for lost love in Waman Poma's Inca song. At least, that is how it feels when you are standing under the translucent blue night of Cuzco, with its brilliant stars, and the far-off ethereal vision, floating mysteriously on the horizon, the moonlit snow ridges of the sacred mountain of Ausangate.

SO PERU FELL TO THE SPANISH, and the Incas' ancient *Lima: the City of Kings* culture began to be systematically demolished.

Here in Lima, in the old colonial archives, you can uncover the complex web of relationships which enabled the Pizarro clan – and especially the four brothers – to dominate the Andean world and almost create a private empire. They were sixteenth-century venture capitalists, the progenitors of today's globalizers. That was why Lima was created. Cuzco was capital of a mountain world, and the Incas looked to the mountains, clung to the navel where their ancestors had planted the golden rod. The Spanish outsiders had their eyes on a wider world, they needed a port to ship out the silver and gold they had extracted from the veins of Peru. And their ships left ballasted with gold.

Pizarro's first ship, *Santa Maria del Campo*, arrived in Seville on 9 January 1534. News of its imminent arrival had spread like wildfire once it had crossed the bar at Sanlucar de Barrameda at the mouth of the Guadalquivir river, and huge crowds had gathered on the quayside to watch the ship come in. Among them was fourteen-year-old Pedro de Cieza de Leon, the future chronicler of the Indies, who stared as the *Santa Maria del Campo* unloaded its unforgettable hoard of treasure under the watchful gaze of royal agents and officials from the House of Trade. Years later, he still could not get that scene out of his mind: 'I can never stop thinking about those things, when I remember the fabulously rich pieces that were seen in Seville that were brought from Cajamarca, where the treasure promised by Atahuallpa to the Spaniards was collected…'

It was the beginning of a gold rush. From then on, in Spain, 'the talk was of nothing but Peru'. But only time would tell if the Spanish would be able to hold on to their new world in the Andes – 'the richest and finest ever found on earth'.

4
THE GREAT WAR OF THE INCAS

BY THE BEGINNING OF 1535, eighteen months after Atahuallpa's death, the future seemed clear. The Spanish had consolidated their power in Peru; Manco Inca was their puppet, and many of his chief kinsmen and leaders had been murdered. With a vice-like grip on the Inca polity, Pizarro was able to confiscate Inca lands and treasures with impunity.

He sat at table with his brothers, his conquistadors, and his young Inca princess, Ines Yupangui – 'my little bird Pizpita' – dandling on his knee his little half-Inca daughter, Francisca. (Francisca would later marry her uncle, Hernando; her bust on the Pizarro mansion in Trujillo shows that she had a pretty, alert face.) Already pregnant with their second child, a son, Ines quickly learned Spanish; introducing her in public, Pizarro would say: 'This is my wife.'

The growing rupture, however, between Pizarro and his old financial partner, Almagro, would, in the end, bring about the violent death of both men, starting a feud which would extend across the generations. And growing resentment of Spanish rule would lead to a great Inca revolt which would convulse the entire Andean world.

Early in 1535, while Pizarro was involved in the founding of the new capital at Lima, first news came of a settlement of King Charles V that entrusted the northern part of the Inca empire to Pizarro, the southern part to Almagro. Full details were not yet known, but it seems that the Inca capital, Cuzco, was considered within Almagro's jurisdiction. Needless to say, this did not go down well with hell-raisers such as Juan and Gonzalo Pizarro and their followers, who regarded Cuzco as their own, and soon there was open violence between the factions.

You have the face of a dead man...
But you can't terrify us with your mask,
because it is only a mask.
When you take it off we shall see
you as you really are. When you drop
your mask, then we shall know you.

•

WAMAN POMA'S *Chronicle,* written *c.* 1585–1613

This as I know from experience was the most fearful and cruel war in the world. For between Christians and Moors there is some fellow feeling, and both sides, acting in their own interests, spare their prisoners for the sake of ransom. But in this Indian war there was no such feeling on either side; both killed as savagely as they could.

•

The Life and Deeds of Don Alonzo de Guzman, 1543

◀ Machu Picchu, built by Pachacuti Inca in the mid-fifteenth century.

In late May, Pizarro returned to Cuzco to deal with the matter, and negotiated an agreement with Almagro, whose supporters felt they had been cheated in the sharing out of loot after Cajamarca. Almagro was another rough-edged character, typical of the age. Like Pizarro he was illegitimate, but his parentage was unknown 'for it is said he was found at the church door'. And Almagro also had grand ambitions. He, too, had taken a royal Inca wife, daughter of Wayna Capac, and full sister of Manco Inca, and he wanted to strike out on his own. Now, by royal appointment, he was viceroy of Collao, the southernmost of the Four Quarters of the Inca empire, the vast lands which extended through Chile almost as far as the Antarctic Circle. Always dreaming of new lands of gold, the conquerors of Peru now heard rumours which painted Chile as even richer than Cuzco. Inevitably, this was the next goal of the conquistadors.

Encouraged by Pizarro, who wanted him out of the way, Almagro now planned a great expedition to Chile. Pizarro even provided some financial backing, hoping this would mollify him. On 3 July 1535, the expedition marched out of Cuzco, with over 200 seasoned troops, horse and foot (a force eventually reinforced to over 500 men). A great herd of llamas carried the baggage, and there were several thousand pigs for food on the hoof. Native auxiliaries also went with Almagro: his 'ally' Manco Inca is said to have provided a force of 12,000 troops, led by his brother Paullu and the high priest, Villac Umu. It was to be one of the greatest and most gruelling of all conquistador expeditions, covering no less than 6000 kilometres in all.

After some incredible adventures, Almagro arrived back in the valley of Cuzco in early 1537, eighteen months after he had set out, to find the heart of the Inca world in turmoil, and the Spanish presence in Peru under grave threat. The Incas under Manco had risen in revolt.

The Great Revolt

THE SURPRISE, PERHAPS, IS THAT IT HAD TAKEN SO LONG. The Andean people had come to recognize the newcomers as plunderers who abused women and were greedy for gold, and Spanish rule was causing grievance and resentment across the land. The Pizarro clan had split up, with Hernando returning to Spain, and Francisco busy building Lima. Cuzco was left under the control of the young firebrands, Juan and Gonzalo. In Cuzco, though, Manco Inca was still nominally the Spanish regent and their looting of Indian property was rife, and the abuse of Inca noble ladies flagrant.

Already at the end of 1535, Manco had tried to escape and raise resistance, but he was recaptured and brought back to his capital in chains. After that, any attempt by the Spanish to be conciliatory towards their Inca 'allies' vanished. The Inca's holiest shrines were desecrated. Manco himself was clapped in irons and publicly humiliated. The story is even told (admittedly by enemies of the Pizarros) that they urinated on him, and threatened to burn his eyes with a candle, actually singeing his eyelashes.

A similar tale is told by Manco's son, Titu Cusi, who reports his father's protests: 'I gave Juan Pizarro 1300 gold ingots and two thousand gold bracelets, cups and other objects, and they still said to me, "Dog, give us gold. If not, you will be burned".' Spanish witnesses agreed: 'The Inca was treated absolutely disgracefully, for they urinated on him and slept with his wives, and, on account of this, he was deeply distressed.'

Gonzalo Pizarro, in particular, had conceived a passion for Coya Ocllo, the sister-wife of Manco, and, as Titu Cusi tells it, his obsessive pursuit of the lady scandalized the native nobility. Rebuked by the Inca high priest and by one of their generals, he told them: 'How dare you talk like that to me, the officer of the king? Don't you know what kind of men we Spaniards are? If you don't shut up…I will slit you open alive and cut you into little pieces.' When Manco tried to placate him with treasure, Gonzalo Pizarro sarcastically insisted: 'Senor Manco Inca, let's have the lady Coya. All this silver is well and good, but she is what we really want.'

Titu Cusi tells how one of the women companions, Inguill, dressed up as the Coya, the royal wife, and subjected herself to the coarse, lustful attentions of Gonzalo:

▲ An idealized portrait of Manco Inca drawn by Waman Poma in a manuscript completed in 1612. A Spanish puppet king, Manco became their most dangerous enemy.

▶▶ Overleaf: The awesome vistas of the high Andes looking across Mount Licancabur into Bolivia. Spanish expeditions crossed these forbidding landscapes to reach as far south as central Chile.

'Give her to me right away, I can't stand it any longer,' he said, and he went up to her in front of everyone and kissed and pawed her as if she were his legitimate wife. My father and the rest were amazed…and she was horrified and frightened being embraced by someone she did not know. She screamed like a mad woman and said she would run away rather than face people like these.

In the end, she went with him, out of fear, but Gonzalo Pizarro saw through the trick, and still took Manco's wife.

As the historian Waman Poma remembered, along with the ill-treatment, mockery and abuse of wives and daughters, a crucial factor was the murder of

several loyal Inca leaders. 'The insurgents,' Waman Poma noted drily, 'acted in defence of their lawful rights.'

The rising was led by Manco Inca's generals, such as Quizquiz, and surviving members of the Inca council of the realm, including some of the highest nobility of Cuzco. They knew, of course, that the Spaniards had an overwhelming advantage in technology, guns, armour, swords and horses, but they understood clearly by now what kind of people the Spanish were and what they wanted. There was no choice, it seemed, but to submit, or to fight.

Manco's speech to the secret gathering of Inca leaders was reported by eye-witnesses (and recorded by both sides). In particular, Cieza de Leon was able, only a few years later, to interview an eye-witness from the Inca court: 'Manco Inca's attendant Alimache told me all this who has a good memory and sharp mind':

I have sent for you in order to tell you in the presence of our kinsmen and followers what I think about what these foreigners are trying to do with us, so that before it is too late, and before more join them, we can devise a plan of action which will be to everyone's good. Remember the Incas my ancestors ruled from Chile to Quito, treating their vassals so well they might have been their own children. They did not steal and they killed only when it served justice. They kept order and reason in the provinces as you know. The rich were not overproud; the poor were not destitute. Now the bearded ones have entered our land, their own country being so far away. They preach one thing and do another. They have no fear of God, and no shame; they treat us like dogs, calling us no other names. Their greed is such that there is no temple or palace left that they have not plundered. In fact if all the snow turned to gold and silver it would not satisfy them. They keep the daughters of my father and other women, your sisters and kin, as their concubines, behaving in this like animals. They want to divide up, as they have already begun to, all the provinces, giving one to each so that they can loot them. Their goal is to see us so downtrodden and enslaved that all we will be fit for is to find them precious metals and give them our women and livestock...

After listing other crimes, Manco spoke of the killing of Atahuallpa 'without cause' and the murder of other generals and leaders, including the horrible killings of Ruminavi and his associates in Quito, 'burned alive in the fire so their souls would not go on to enjoy heaven'. Manco concluded with these words: 'I believe it would not be just or honest for us to accept this. Rather we should attempt with every determination either to die or to kill these cruel enemies.'

Passed down orally, but recorded from an eye-witness not long afterwards, Cieza de Leon's text agrees in general with the version recounted by Titu Cusi to a Spanish notary some thirty-five years later, and we may take it substantially as what was said. He gives us some of the same phraseology: 'They have given me a thousand insults, they have imprisoned me, and chained me like a dog by the feet and by the neck, and worst of all they have done this after giving me their word that…we had become allies.'

But Titu Cusi is more specific about how the revolt was to be organized, and gives us the names of the leaders of the various contingents who were summoned from the Four Quarters of the Tawantinsuyu. According to him, the plan was a boldly conceived coordinated attack on both Cuzco and Lima:

Send your messengers throughout the land, so that in twenty days from now everybody shall arrive here in the city [of Cuzco]. Make sure the whites know nothing. I shall send a message to Lima to my general Queso Yupangui, who governs that region, and order him that on the same day we attack the Spaniards here [in Cuzco] he and his men shall fall on them there. Soon we shall annihilate them, until none remains: and then we will be able to awake from this nightmare and rejoice.

The revolt was deliberately planned to coincide with Easter. Manco escaped from custody on 18 April 1536, at the beginning of Holy Week, and fled north into the Sacred Valley. The Inca army's rendezvous was to be at Calca, a few miles down the Sacred Valley from Yucay where Manco's father had built a summer palace, and only fifteen miles beyond Cuzco as the crow flies. Given the Spanish skill at intelligence-gathering and the number of collaborators available to them, it was dangerously close, but at least here at Calca there was a country estate belonging to Manco's uncle, Huascar (where, today, one can still see the Inca buildings). Here, Manco ordered his forces to gather. Initially, the Spanish seem to have had no inkling of what was afoot. The Inca preparations had been long in hand: weapons had been manufactured in secret, and Manco had arranged large plantings of crops to have enough food to supply his armies during the revolt.

Wary of betrayal, Manco and his leaders decided on a more distant refuge – Lares, an obscure but talismanic place, which lies twenty-two miles into the mountains, surrounded by jungle. Here, Manco had his last meeting with his chiefs and, swearing their oaths with chicha drunk from golden cups, they promised the extermination of every Christian in the Tawantinsuyu. At this moment, not all their forces had arrived, and some of the Inca generals argued that they should none the less attack immediately so as not to lose the element of surprise. But a further nervous delay ensued while they awaited the arrival of the more far-flung contingents. Finally, at the beginning of May, the signal was given and they rose up against the Spanish and attacked Cuzco. The Great Revolt had begun.

IN CUZCO THE PIZARROS HAD 170 SPANISH FRONT-LINE troops, and 1000 Indian auxiliaries – *yanaconas* – Andean retainers who fought with the Spanish. Manco's forces, camped on the surrounding hillsides, may have numbered tens of thousands, and the Spanish soon found themselves cooped up in one of the great Inca palaces on the central square, hiding behind its gigantic perimeter walls.

The Battle for Sacsahuaman

Manco cut the city's water supplies and gave orders to burn all the buildings around. Soon the thatched roofs of the magnificent royal memorial halls, mortuary shrines and temples were afire, and a pall of smoke covered the once beautiful city. But the only building which failed to ignite was the one sheltering the Spaniards. Its survival was later held up by the Spanish as a miraculous intervention by Saint James himself, who some said was seen through the smoke riding in the sky waving his sword. Titu Cusi, though, has a more prosaic explanation: the Spanish still had wells within their compound and made

◄◄ The great walls of Sacsahuaman above Cuzco, which the Spanish attacked in 1536. From the air (below) the zigzag pattern of the defences can still be seen.

a human chain of bucket-carrying black slaves, who crouched on the roof under a hail of arrows, dousing the thatch with water day and night.

Defeat for the Spanish still seemed the most likely outcome, but as that meant certain death, they fought on with incredible tenacity, sending out forays to terrorize the civilians who maintained Manco's supply lines. They had no qualms about inflicting terrible atrocities on these people, including the women, who were horribly mutilated and sent back to Manco. Terror against a civilian population is by no means only a phenomenon of modern warfare.

In the end, the battle hinged on whether the Spanish could retake Sacsuaman, the vast Inca fortress, with its great towers, which looks down on the rooftops of Cuzco at the head of the valley. From here the Incas dominated the city. If they could hold on to it, while their reinforcements continued to come in, it would surely be only a matter of time before the Spaniards were worn down.

Elsewhere in Peru, too, the revolt was spreading and had met with success. Three separate relief forces, sent from Lima by Francisco Pizarro, had been ambushed on the road and wiped out with the loss of more than 300 men. It rapidly became imperative for the Spanish to break the siege of Cuzco, and the Pizarro brothers, Juan, Gonzalo and Hernando, led a do-or-die assault on the fortress.

An epic struggle followed, in which Juan Pizarro was killed in hand-to-hand fighting (he was buried in secret so the Incas would not be encouraged by the knowledge that he had perished). Just as the Aztec accounts of the fall of Mexico remember the heroes of the final battle, both sides tell the tale of the Inca general who led the defence of the fortress. His name was probably Titu Cusi Guallpa, and he had a force variously estimated at 1500 or 3000 warriors.

Armed with a Spanish sword, he had vowed to fight to the death and, according to Spanish soldiers, performed acts of bravery 'worthy of any Roman'. (This was the highest compliment that could be paid to Spanish knights of the sixteenth century, with its overtones of stoic dignity and unswerving physical and moral courage.)

'The captain paced about like a lion,' says Pedro Pizarro, 'striding from one side of the tower to the other on its top floor. He beat off any Spaniards who tried to get on top with their scaling ladders. And he killed any Indians who tried to surrender. He smashed their heads with his battleaxe and hurled them from the top of the tower.'

In hand-to-hand fighting he was a match for the Europeans because he had learned to fight with their weapons:

He had a shield on his arm, a steel sword, a Spanish axe in his shield hand and a Spanish morion helmet on his head...Whenever his men told him a Spaniard was climbing up somewhere he rushed on him like a lion, sword in hand... He received two arrow wounds but ignored them as if he had not been touched.

Unfortunately for the Incas, they had too few European weapons, and too few warriors who could use them effectively. In the end, the Spanish ordered an attack with scaling ladders at four separate points, with the heavily armoured Spanish conquistadors backed up by their native allies. Finally, the pressure told and the Spanish mounted the parapet from both sides of the tower. Although Hernando Pizarro had ordered the Inca captain captured alive, the hero would not submit. He threw his weapons at his attackers, cast dust into his mouth, scoured his face, and, covering his head with his cloak, threw himself, with a howl of grief and frustration, to his death from the top of the tower in fulfilment of his vow.

With their captain's death, the Inca resistance crumbled. The Spanish broke into the fortress and massacred all of the garrison. It was the beginning of the end. Attacks and counter-attacks continued for several more days, but the Spaniards' hold on the fort was secure: they had saved themselves. In the end, Spanish technology – as much as their undoubted bravery and tenacity – had won the day.

Over the hills in the Sacred Valley, the news was received with disbelief by the Inca high command. According to Titu Cusi, Manco and his generals were dismayed by their failure when success had seemed so near:

'I am very disappointed,' said the Inca. 'There were so many of you, and so few of them, yet they have slipped through our grasp.'
'We are so ashamed we dare not look you in the face... We do not know the reason, save that it was our mistake not to have attacked in time, and yours for not giving us permission to do so.'

Perhaps the delay between Manco's escape and the final mobilization, while they waited for the more far-flung troops, had lost them the element of surprise.

The fall of Sacsahuaman took place at the end of May 1536, but the siege of Cuzco continued for many more months. While this was going on, Manco's generals were attacking the Spanish forces elsewhere in Peru. Beleaguered in his new town of Lima, Francisco Pizarro was so alarmed that he sent emergency messages by sea to Cortes in Mexico, and to the Spanish authorities in Hispaniola, Guatemala and Panama, asking for help. Four separate parties, under the leadership of captains, were sent into the interior to keep communications open with Cuzco, but they were all killed except for eight or nine men whom Manco kept as

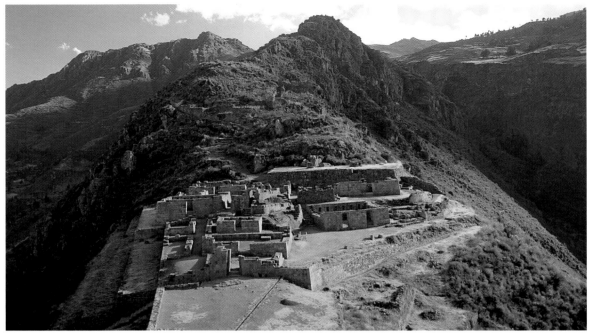

slaves to teach the Indians how to use Spanish horses, weapons and muskets. The fighting had gone on for ten months, and several hundred Spanish troops had been killed. Francisco Pizarro, though, was able to hold out in Lima. Then, in April 1537, Almagro came back from Chile with his battered forces and raised the siege of Cuzco.

In the Sacred Valley, Manco had his back to the wall. He now retreated more than twenty miles down the valley, further away from Cuzco. Now the Spanish could take the offensive, and Hernando Pizarro decided to attack Manco there, deep in the valley at the royal estate of Ollantaytambo.

In the Sacred Valley

'IN THE YEAR AND ONE HALF my father was at Tampu,' Titu Cusi said, 'they made this one of the greatest fortresses that exist in Peru.'

Tampu, or Ollantaytambo, was the heart of the Inca resistance. Today, immense terraces still rise up to Manco's huge palace fortress on its dramatic spur overlooking the valley. It lies at nearly 10,000 feet. Below, the steel-blue Urubamba river rushes along its stony bed; in the gorge to the east, an Inca road clings to the cliff, and ancient granaries stand roofless, beetling high above the town. These must have stored Manco's precious supplies of maize, chillies, and freeze-dried potatoes when this was the front line in the war.

Here, at Ollantaytambo, Waman Poma says, Manco built new terraces to support the extra population of warriors and refugees, and today on the rugged brown mountain slopes around us the man-made terraces rise to well over 13,000 feet. Every inch was cultivated in Manco's day. As Cieza de Leon remarked in 1545: 'In the days of the Incas there was very little cultivatable land, arable land that was not under cultivation. Now there are few natives, their former number diminished to what we see now.' Waman Poma also says that Manco built new houses here, and today, below Manco's fortress, there is still a perfectly preserved and inhabited Inca town. Laid out in the early sixteenth century, its blocks (canchas) show the original layout, the houses each with their communal living rooms and animal yards, each fed by open channels that still carry water down the streets.

This last period of Inca rule in the Sacred Valley lasted a mere eighteen months. Manco would have felt at home here. This is where the Inca kings had built their palaces and shrines in the fifteenth century during the height of their empire. The hilltop sites, like Pisac and Machu Picchu, with their ritual precincts and finely fitted masonry, are magnificent. Less well known are the riverside palaces of Manco's father, Wayna Capac, at Yucay and Quispiguanca.

◄◄ Pisac (above), an Inca palace on a dramatic spur over the Sacred Valley. The valley (below), looking down the Urubamba river towards Amazonia. This was the heartland of the last Incas, and was intensively cultivated, especially so during the great war of resistance of 1536.

Machu Picchu, the most famous of all Inca sites, lies further down the Sacred Valley. Whether the Spanish ever saw it, is a matter of conjecture, although sixteenth-century documents have recently come to light which name the place. Machu Picchu was probably built by the great conqueror and builder, Pachacuti Inca, in the mid-fifteenth century as a retreat for his *panaca*, his lineage; it was a place where their mummies could be kept and brought out to greet the sun at the festivals. Whether Manco and his high priest, Villac Umu, went there during their last months at Ollantaytambo to conduct the last rituals for the ancestors, we simply do not know, although it is possible. Machu Picchu is, after all, only twenty miles down the Urubamba river. But to go there now helps us to imagine those last days of the Inca state: Villac Umu with his priests and astronomers, performing the traditional ceremonials for the royal dead; Manco Inca watching the sun sink over the sacred stone in the cold blue light of that June solstice of 1536 (in the middle of the Peruvian winter). Did he, perhaps, look out from the 'hitching stone of the sun', over those wonderful vistas out to the south-west, towards the sacred mountain of Pumasillo, the marker for the solstices and equinoxes at Machu Picchu.

Today, as I write, Pumasillo's jagged snow-peaks are wreathed in cloud, with a translucent blue sky behind, the receding banks of cloud gradually suffused with pinks, golds and molten oranges as the setting sun lights them from below. Then, just before sunset, the full peak emerges, one of the most sacred in the ancient Andean universe. Looking at this, it is easy to imagine Villac Umu, with his long hair and long nails, twisting the black and white threads to make his spells, burning red llama and white rabbit, blowing the ash of sacrifice before speaking with the spirits: 'to know the secrets of the past and the future, and all that is happening across the world'. And all the while up the valley the Spanish were closing in.

The Battle of Ollantaytambo

WHILE MANCO'S TROOPS CONTINUED TO BLOCKADE Cuzco, Hernando Pizarro left garrisons in the fortress and in the town and, with seventy Spaniards and a large force of Indian auxiliaries, broke out to attack Manco. At Ollantaytambo, Manco had several thousand troops with a quantity of captured Spanish weapons, and several horses. (He had forced his Spanish prisoners to make gunpowder for the arquebuses.) The approach to Ollantaytambo had been defended with forts in the narrow entrance to this part of the valley; and a massive terrace, with rubble walls, blocked the immediate approach to the town. Manco had also prepared a nasty surprise for the Spanish: a dam to divert the stream that comes down between the fortress and the town so that he could flood them out.

The battle was fierce. The Spanish forced their way through the town right to the foot of the fortress, while Manco rode a Spanish horse high up on the terraces, waving a Spanish sword and urging his men on. An attempt by Spanish commanders to outflank the position was beaten off, and Hernando Pizarro was finally forced to admit defeat and retreated to Cuzco. It was the first time the Spanish had been worsted in open battle. But it was only a temporary reprieve for the Incas.

Manco had hoped to make a new Cuzco at Ollantaytambo, but he seems to have realized now that, in the long term, he had no chance of stopping the Spanish. His people had been devastated by disease, and although he may have been able to hold on to his mountain hideouts, the sea was controlled by the Spanish, who were now being strengthened every day. As Titu Cusi says, 'At this time an infinite number of people arrived from Spain, having seen the great riches taken to Spain from Cajamarca…every day ships from Panama, Mexico and Nicaragua put into Lima.' So Manco decided to retreat over the mountains into the cloud forest bordering Amazonia, where he hoped to keep an Inca state going out of the Spaniards' reach.

Before he left, he made a speech telling his followers not to forget what the ancient rulers had done for them and, most importantly, not to forget their rituals. Manco's words were recorded by Titu Cusi:

Reflect on how long my grandparents and great grandparents and I myself have looked after you, protected you, cared for you and governed…making provision that you had plenty…so do not forget us, not in your lifetimes, not in the time of your descendants.

Outwardly you can give the impression of complying with their demands. Give them small tribute, whatever you can spare from your lands – for these people are so savage and so different from us that if you don't they will take it from you by force…I know that some day, by force or deceit, they will make you worship what they worship. When that time comes, when you can no longer resist, do it in front of them, but on the other hand do not forget our ceremonies. And if they tell you to break your shrines, and force you to do so, reveal only what you have to, and keep the rest hidden, close to your hearts…

Today, on the citadel at Ollantaytambo, perhaps where Manco made his speech, the huge unfinished monoliths for his temple and palace lie where his architects left them. Carved with cosmic diagrams and royal pumas, they are weathered now, faint outlines of a vanished universe.

▸▸ Ollantaytambo (overleaf), looking down Manco's terraces to the site of the Inca ceremonial plaza, with the Inca town beyond.

Manco's Retreat Beyond the Andes

IN JULY 1537, Manco retreated northwards from the Sacred Valley to a far more inaccessible area of his empire – to Antisuyo, the jungle land, the last of the Four Quarters which had not yet been overrun by the Spanish. Although he still had troops with him, he was on the run, a hunted man, and the Spanish closed in for the kill. 'He has few men with him, and is totally disorganized at that. He is virtually finished now,' wrote Francisco Pizarro. He still feared the Inca's capacity, though, to 'send messengers out across the entire land so it might revolt once again'.

The Spanish assessment of the situation was that the Andean people had had enough of war; that they were demoralized by the terrible reprisals; and that, as Manco and his high priest were the only important leaders left at large, they would soon be handed over: 'The Indians are now so weary of war... By summer we will have him in our hands, either dead or as a prisoner.'

Manco's first move was to his palace at Vitcos, in the rugged mountains between the Urubamba and Apurimac rivers. Then he moved further into the forest, out of reach of the Spanish cavalry, to a remote place called Vilcabamba, which was about fifty miles north-west across exceptionally rugged wooded terrain. This place, as Titu Cusi described it, 'has a warmer climate than Vitcos, and my father stayed there for some time resting, and he built houses and palaces there, intending to make it his principal residence'.

For twenty months or so, Manco maintained himself there while the Spanish factions began to fall out and fight each other. In 1538, the feud between the Pizarros and Almagro came to a head in all-out war. In April of that year, at the Battle of Las Salinas, Hernando Pizarro defeated and captured Almagro; and in July the old conquistador, who had been the original partner in the discovery of Peru, was executed in Cuzco. Meanwhile, Manco's resistance continued with guerilla warfare across wide tracts of the central Andes as far as Lake Titicaca. In one battle, a force of thirty experienced conquistadors were wiped out. So, in April 1539, Gonzalo Pizarro set out with an expedition from Cuzco to pursue Manco into the wilds of Vilcabamba. He took with him 300 conquistadors and a large native contingent: 'We have the Inca cornered now: we cannot fail to kill or capture him.'

The Hunting of Manco Inca

THE FINAL – AND MOST GRUELLING – stage of our Peruvian journeys in the footsteps of the conquistadors was to follow the line of Manco Inca's retreat into the little-explored mountain and jungle fastnesses beyond – and the line taken by Gonzalo Pizarro's 1539 expedition. It was a memorable journey.

The road down the Urubamba valley, on that chill grey dawn, led us past Manco's fortress on its hill, and then rose to spectacular vistas of the Veronica range, and its snow-covered peaks. Soon it was very cold. We stopped at 14,000 feet by a rough, dry, stone-walled sheep corral and thatched hut. There – much as the conquistadors must have done – we took breakfast of flat bread and olives while Andean kites wheeled overhead, waiting for scraps. Over the pass, the road – hung with ferns, creepers and dotted with bright red wild begonias – rapidly descended into cloud forest. We were now on the other side of the Andes, subtropical in climate, with distant vistas of the Vilcabamba range where Manco built his last refuge, following the failure of the Great Revolt.

A few hours later, we come down to Chaullay at 3000 feet. Here, there was once a long Inca rope-bridge, but Manco destroyed it before Gonzalo Pizarro's advance. Today, there is just an open cable car, which you pull across yourself on an oily metal cable, and then swing over the raging torrent of the Urubamba river. Our truck had to go the long way round – a journey of several hours. Having crossed over, we climbed up a hundred yards or so through thickets of fern and white-flowered vine, and waited by a track where a datura tree, laden with pale bell-like flowers, drenched us with scent. We made the last stage through deep canyons and thick vegetation, and after thirteen hours on the road arrived at Huancacalle in darkness.

Next day, soon after dawn, we walked across the river and up the hill to old Vitcos. Just as the Spanish eye-witnesses had reported, Manco's palace stood on a high hill between the Vilcabamba river and the Las Andenes stream – a place which had already been an Inca residence in Pachacuti's day. There are wonderful views up and down the valley to the snow peaks. The palace site is approached over a narrow neck of land which leads on to the hilltop. There a huge grassy plaza is surrounded by the remains of palatial buildings, with 'finely joined stones and lintels', as the Spanish later described it. No palace could be more beautifully situated, but the site was too vulnerable for Manco, and he continued northwards into the jungle.

Journey to the Lost City

FIVE MILES BEYOND VITCOS, on the route to Manco's Vilcabamba, the vehicle road gives out, and it was here that we had arranged a rendezvous with our guides and animals – a dozen horses and mules – for our expedition. This is San Francisco Vilcabamba – 'the new'. The town has sixty damp-stained houses, half of them still stone bases, rough cob and sagging thatch, a great barn of a church built in the 1570s, dirt streets and an air of dereliction. Built only a generation after the conquest, it is as washed-up a place as one could imagine, its people drawn here by a silver mine, which was long ago

◄◄ The huge monoliths of Manco Inca's council chamber (above) inside the fortress at Ollantaytambo; from here Manco oversaw the battles of 1536. Vitcos (below), Manco's citadel above the Urubamba river. He was murdered here in 1544.

◄ On our three-day trek to Espiritu Pampa – Manco's lost city of Vilcabamba. Ahead, the path snakes across the face of a steep ridge where the Spanish expeditions of 1539 and 1572 had to fight battles against the Inca resistance.

exhausted and left behind by time. But this was once the brave new world of Spanish colonialism, the starting point for the final expedition of 1572. When Gonzalo Pizarro came through with his huge force in 1539, it was probably just a small Inca village. Today, it is the jumping-off point for our march to Vilcabamba.

The terrain ahead is very different in character from the Inca heartland around Cuzco. An immense area of high peaks, cold uplands and cloud forest, bounded by the two great gorges of the Apurimac and the Urubamba, Vilcabamba is rugged, poorly mapped, sparsely inhabited and seldom visited. Only a few primitive roads penetrate the region, and travel is still by mule or on foot with machetes, along steep and often muddy paths, climbing up to high altitude and down thousands of feet into tropical lowlands covered with thick forest. This is the area we were now about to enter in the footsteps of Manco Inca and his deadly enemy, Gonzalo Pizarro.

We were up before dawn and we made a steady ascent on foot, while our three horses and seven mules carried our gear, plus tents, cooking stuff, and food for several days. We reached the pass (nearly 13,000 feet, according to our altimeter) at eleven o'clock. Just below the crest, there is an old Spanish chapel on an Inca platform. The wind was blowing steadily, an intermittent sun glimpsed through the clouds.

Over the next few hours, we made a steady descent from the pass into cloud, then had a chilly, damp lunch on a rocky outcrop with cloud swirling around us. Then onwards, down the hillside – at times precipitous – hung with bushes and creepers, we zigzagged along the rugged pathway that is identifiable even now as an ancient Inca trail. Indeed, in places, there is a stepped stairway, but it is all badly worn and displaced, eroded rather like a river bed, and the horses picked their way gingerly down them. At the bottom, we crossed the river on a log bridge, then marched up and down muddy tracks all afternoon, under low cloud, in a fine drizzle, the temperature always too sweaty or too cold. On our left were thickly jungled heights, their tops always under cloud. It was easy to imagine the long column of Spanish troops in their padded cotton tropical kit, stretching back several miles. 'Innumerable Spaniards,' as Titu Cusi remembered, 'just how many I cannot say, for the forests were dense and it was impossible to count them.'

Towards dusk, we stopped on flat, grassy, open ground by the river, with the cloud right down around us. Our legs were aching from all the upping and downing, and we were grateful to stagger into the tents. The conditions, very different from the dry, crisp, sunny uplands, were cold and damp. The nearest habitation, a tiny place consisting of a couple of houses, is called Pampaconas. It was here, according to Titu Cusi, that Manco's sister-wife Coya Ocllo, who had been forced to go with the expedition, was assaulted by Spanish troops:

*They intended to rape my aunt. She would not allow [this], but defended herself
fiercely and finally covered herself with filthy matter [animal dung?] so the men
who were trying to rape her would be nauseated. And she had to protect herself in
this way many times on that journey.*

At 4.30 a.m. our guide, Don Juvenal, worried that we would not complete the
march in three days, was already saddling the horses. When I pointed out that the
conquistadors took ten, he smiled: 'They had to fight.' We set off, crossing the
Pampaconas river and marching on down the right bank through thick, semi-
tropical jungle. Soon we saw the remains of Inca roads and stairways, roughly-
placed blocks – part of the remarkable network which linked the 3000-mile-long
empire – and could hardly believe we were walking on it. We wound our way
down and recrossed the river on a rickety bridge of split logs which shook alarm-
ingly under our feet. Gonzalo Pizarro – the first Spaniard to come this way – was
struck by the route's 'appalling hardships and lack of food'. Thirty years later, the
Toledo expedition said much the same: 'We traversed the mountainsides and
ravines along this turbulent river only with the greatest difficulty for all.' Our Don
Juvenal, though, was harder to depress.

Just before midday – after a long, gruelling, up-and-down ascent of a hillside
covered with thick forest – we came out in sight of a long steep ridge rising above
the path on our left, the ground plunging steeply away to the river far below us. I
reckoned this must be the place where Gonzalo Pizarro fought his battle with
Manco: 'One morning they had to pass in single file across a rocky hillside called
Chuquillusca, which is very steep and dangerous, covered in jungle and undergrowth.' At this point, when the unwary Spaniards were crossing a clearing with
open hillside above, 'a great quantity of huge boulders' came crashing down on
them: three were killed by the rocks, two more by arrows. After severe fighting,
the column fell back to make camp and Pizarro was sufficiently alarmed to send
messages back to Cuzco calling for reinforcements.

The Inca keepers of the *quipus*, the knotted cords on which they recorded
information, said thirty-six Spaniards were killed in the battle; the Spanish admitted to the loss of thirteen men and six horses. Next day, Pedro Pizarro and a hundred of the best troops climbed on foot to the top of ridge – which I imagine was
here at Tambo, the most defensible site on the route.

The second Spanish expedition to the lost city also had to fight here in 1572,
at what they called the 'New Fort', and they reported circular stone defence
works along the crest: 'The fort was built at the far end of a knife-edge ridge with
a wall and low towers and many piles of stones ready to hurl and shoot.' Juvenal
says these are still up there, piles of rocks waiting to be rolled down on the

Crossing the Concevidayac river on a bridge of tree trunks weighted with boulders. It was close by that Manco Inca taunted Gonzalo Pizarro from the other side of the river.

'bearded ones' at the narrowest place where their column was most exposed to attack. This surely is the place where the Spanish say, 'Our path had high rocky outcrops on one side and the river plunging away below the path, dangerous and frightening.'

From the New Fort, a wonderful path cuts through the forest along the side of the mountain, high over the river, through thickets of blue lupins. Looking back on our track, we could see it stretching all the way back up the river into the cloud from which we had emerged that morning. After five miles, around one o'clock, we came to the end of the ridge on our left, where the two rivers meet, and descended a steep path down to a wooden bridge. Towards dusk, Juvenal rushed on ahead to look for a campsite, and soon reappeared to take us to a small clearing in the forest which he had made bigger with a machete. It is a lovely spot, about fifty feet above the river, and we made our night camp to the sound of the river's roar, surrounded by thick jungle, in a clearing only just big enough for our tents. We were all exhausted, reckoning we had done around eight miles as the crow flies, but allowing for all the bends, it must have been thirteen or more. It didn't seem much, given the effort it had taken. Tomorrow, we reckoned, it would be another ten miles, in a straight line, but 'the terrain is much harder', said Juvenal.

We decided to start early to try to get to the site of the lost city before dusk. As night fell, it was a lovely scene in our tiny forest clearing, perched above the river. From where we were, there was a trackless wilderness all the way to the Amazon basin. We were about as far away from civilization as it is possible to be. (Was that how Manco felt, one wondered?)

Early the next day, we began the last leg to Espiritu Pampa – the Plain of Ghosts – the lost city of the Incas. Manco's refuge was attacked by Gonzalo Pizarro in 1539, then abandoned in 1572, after it was destroyed, as the Spanish closed in. It was not seen again by the outside world until Hiram Bingham, the discoverer of Machu Picchu, glimpsed a distant corner of it in 1911 (without realizing what it was). The city was finally found again by the American explorer Gene Savoy in the late 1960s.

From the early hours the rain was torrential. When we rose at five o'clock, the ground and forest were sodden, trees dripping all around us. We had around ten hours walking ahead, not including rest stops. The first two hours took us up lung-busting paths, through thick mud and frequent landslides, the water cascading over the path. Then we pushed on at a forced march pace, which became almost a run when the path was firm. For the last few hours, we went at a truly ferocious rate, which allowed Juvenal to revise his estimate and say that we could make it before sunset if we didn't stop.

Finally, we ascended a ridge on our left, walked through the trees on the top of it, and passed a ruined building with ancient stonework (an Inca shrine, or a watchtower?). Soon after four o'clock, we came out into the open to see the valley stretched before us: a wonderful vista – the lost valley of the Incas.

To our left, towards Amazonia, the setting sun was lighting up the cloud cover, the taller peaks beyond disappearing then emerging again as wisps of cloud enveloped them; the silver ribbon of the river far below wound through the green of the valley, and dotted throughout the forest, on the valley floor, were a few small clearings with an occasional house. A metal roof glinted incongruously in the late sun. Apart from some patches of cultivation, it was all forest. A smaller valley led off left; a longer one, to the right, disappeared into the clouds. Juvenal pointed ahead up the river: 'That's where the ruins are, under the forest, that is the Plain of Ghosts.'

It is a wonderful spot – a hidden valley. No wonder the Incas came here in the hope of continuing a small corner of the Tawantinsuyu; no wonder it was not found and identified until our own day.

By the time we began the descent, the sun was gone. Within an hour, we reached the clearing by the river where we had spotted the hut with the tin roof. There we pitched camp less than an hour's walk from the ruins. We had made it to Espiritu Pampa, the Plain of Ghosts, the lost city of the Incas.

Inside the Lost City

WE SET OFF JUST AFTER DAWN. Everywhere was under low cloud cover, still soaking – all the jungle paths deep in squelchy mud. We plunged into the forest and soon entered the vast ruinfield of the lost city, under a towering canopy of dripping forest.

Juvenal had sent some of the men ahead with machetes and in no time they had cleared the vegetation, creepers and ferns from a massive triple-terraced platform about 200 feet square. This is part of the 'plaza principal' of the city. Under our feet was a deep mulch of rotting trees, bark and leaves. A hundred yards or so away, we came across a huge standing stone, a natural rock, fifteen feet high and thirty feet long. This was very much like the *huaca* (big stone) at Machu Picchu – the sacred stone within the precinct which mimics the shape of the mountain peaks behind. To judge by its position in the centre of the ceremonial area, this rock *was* the *huaca*, the sacred place of the lost city. At the lower end of the stone, where the ground falls sharply away into a ravine, the earth had been dug away to leave a space – an offering place – under the overhang, and fires had been lit there fairly recently. 'But no one does the traditional ceremonies here any more,' said Juvenal.

We walked on, passing large buildings with Inca-style windows and door jambs, along huge terraces built of massive Inca boulders, and now covered with a thick cloak of emerald green moss. There are stairways, bridges, a canal – all overlaid with decaying vegetation, all in the process of being taken back by the forest.

In the debris of the buildings east of the rock are Spanish-style terracotta roof tiles (as was mentioned by Spanish visitors to the city before it finally fell in 1572). And, in the centre of the plaza area, abutting the rock, but almost invisible now, there is a huge building, about seventy-five paces long, with a dozen doors along the main wall. Was this, perhaps, the main shrine, the Temple of the Sun, which was the seat of the principal idol, the Punchao, and the storehouse of the royal mummies?

The scene is one of utter desolation. It is hard to imagine the fields of sugar cane, cassava, cotton, that once existed here, the parrots, macaws and thousands of other species of birds of different colours, the fruit trees and the Inca palace with its terracotta roof tiles: 'Its interior painted with a great variety of murals in their native style, its doors of fragrant pine…'

For a moment, we were all hushed – only the sound of howler monkeys in the distance. All in all, I have to say that walking through this vast ruinfield, out of which huge hardwoods rear their tops, over whose grand masonry ferns and creepers spread their tendrils, is a most powerful demonstration of the transience of human civilization.

Gonzalo Pizarro arrived there in May 1539, and for two months hunted Manco in the jungles of Vilcabamba, tracking him from place to place on the trails through the forest. But, as close as he came, the Inca escaped him. According to Titu Cusi, in one memorable exchange, Manco taunted him across a river: 'I am Manco Inca! I am Manco Inca!' And, according to one of the conquistadors in Gonzalo Pizarro's army, Mansio Serra de Leguizamon (who crops up again in this story on page 273) Manco also shouted that he and his Indians 'had killed two thousand Spaniards during the great uprising, and that he intended to kill them all, too, and regain possession of the land that belonged to his forefathers'. Such hopes.

The People's Hearts Are with the Inca

GONZALO PIZARRO RANSACKED THE CITY, but, having failed to capture Manco, was forced to retreat because of lack of supplies. Francisco Pizarro, though, was not a man to take such failures lightly. Furious that Manco had not surrendered, he secretly murdered the high priest, Villac Umu, and many other Inca nobles, says Titu Cusi, 'so they could not rejoin my father'. And, even more revolting as an act of gratuitous violence, he had Manco's favourite sister-wife, Coya Ocllo, beaten and shot to death with arrows by his Indian auxiliaries, then floated her body in a basket down the Urubamba river so it would be found by Manco's men. Manco 'was grief-stricken at the death of his wife and wept greatly and lamented long – for he had loved her much'.

By the skin of his teeth, Manco survived and maintained himself in Vilcabamba. His hated enemy Francisco Pizarro died before him, murdered in revenge in his house in Lima by the son of his old business partner, Almagro, in 1541. Manco himself was assassinated at Vitcos in 1544, the killing witnessed by his son, Titu Cusi:

One day with much good fellowship they were playing at quoits with him: only them, my father, and me, who was then a little boy. We were without any suspicion… Then just as my father was raising the quoit to throw, they all rushed upon him with knives, daggers and some swords. My father feeling himself to be wounded, strove to defend himself, but he was alone, and unarmed, and they were seven fully armed; he fell to the ground covered with wounds, and they left him for dead. I being a little boy, and seeing my father treated in this manner, wanted to rush over to help him. But they turned furiously on me and threw a lance which only just failed to kill me too. I was terrified and escaped into the bushes. They looked for me but could not find me. The Spaniards, seeing that my father had ceased to breathe, went out of the gate in high spirits saying, 'Now we have killed the Inca, we have nothing to fear.'

▼ The remains of Vilcabamba, the lost city of the Incas at Espiritu Pampa. Here you can see the grand terrace of the central plaza.

Manco's murder was a disaster for the Incas. He was the one leader with the lineage, courage and tenacity to keep things going, the one who enjoyed the widest respect. Still only in his thirties, he might, had he lived, have negotiated a return as regent; he might have kept an independent Inca state, like an Inca Abyssinia, in the jungles of Vilcabamba. Imagine this, in the United Nations, New York, today: 'And now a speech from the Ambassador of the Tawantinsuyu…'

Manco's successors ruled an uneasy rump state on the fringe of the Spanish world – a tiny enclave but, as one Spaniard said, 'the hearts of the people are still with the Inca there and will be till they die'. Titu Cusi – the little boy who had seen his father stabbed to death – became Inca in 1560, and later made formal submission to Spain, and was baptized.

In Titu Cusi's day, the city of Vilcabamba was visited by Spanish missionaries. He died in early 1571, after dictating the remarkable account of his father's life and times which I have used in this book. The new Spanish viceroy in Lima, however, was not prepared to let an independent Inca state survive any longer. In 1572, he declared war and mounted a huge expedition to crush it once and for all. Because of the difficulties of the journey, retired conquistadors, such as Mansio Serra de Leguizamon, were required to go along as on-the-ground advisers to the Spanish captains.

Finally, on 24 June 1572, they entered the city and the standard was planted by Pedro Sarmiento de Gamboa (the author, later, of *A History of the Incas*, whose astonishing career led him across the Pacific, to imprisonment in the Tower of London, and even to erudite conversations – in Latin – with Queen Elizabeth I).

Only 1000 Inca warriors had been left to defend this final corner of the Land of the Four Quarters and, along with most of the population, they had fled into the forest: 'We found the city deserted, with some four hundred houses intact, but the residences of the Incas burning.' The only people who remained were the old, women and children. The last Inca, Tupac Amaru, the twenty-five-year-old son of Manco, was captured in the forest nearby and taken back to Cuzco where he was executed with other members of his family on 24 September 1572. It was the end

▲ An eighteenth-century painting of a nobleman of Inca descent who holds a Christian cross, but with the red Inca royal tassel on his forehead. There are many descendants of the Inca royal lineage still alive today.

of nearly forty years of resistance by the Incas. And the end of the line. Or so it was thought.

As for the lost city itself, it was abandoned and forgotten until it was rediscovered in our own time. And, standing on the spot, it was impossible not to feel the poignancy of its story. As the Spanish chronicler Murua wrote:

The Incas enjoyed scarcely less of the luxuries, greatness and splendour of Cuzco in that distant land of exile. For the Indians brought with them whatever they could get from outside for their contentment and pleasure. And so for that time they enjoyed the good life there.

For us, these were thoughts to conjure with as we went to bed in that beautiful lonely spot, the rain drumming on our tents.

Reflections on a Lost World THIS STAGE OF OUR SEARCH WAS OVER but as the weather deteriorated and the surrounding mountain ranges disappeared into a thick blanket of cloud, we found ourselves marooned for several days in the forest at Espiritu Pampa. Later that week, we were lifted out by helicopter over mist-shrouded peaks, passing by dark, brooding, mysterious Salcantay. As big droplets of rain beat against the windows, I found myself staring out over the landscape of Vilcabamba, mulling over the old chestnuts of history.

The Inca high civilization did not survive the *Conquista* – their palaces, *tambos*, roads, civil servants, customs men, royal cults, all went. But, as is often the case in history, something survived. For, at a level just below civilizations, there is a long-lasting, deep-rooted, tenacious continuance. The life lived by local peoples, sometimes over millennia – their encoded identities, customs, ways of being and thinking – survives the surface ephemera of events, and even the rise and fall of civilizations. And so it was in the Andes.

It is often said by European historians that the Incas never really fought back, that they allowed their empire to collapse without putting up any resistance. The implication, of course, is that Native American peoples had no courage or ability to improvise; that they were trapped in an archaic view of history, and so constrained that they were incapable of decisive action when confronted by scientific-minded, rational Europeans.

It is true that the Inca world-view was based on sacred conceptions of time, and that their rulers were hedged in by many taboos which the Europeans categorized as 'primitive'. But, nevertheless, the Incas lived in a rational, ordered state, governed by workable concepts of justice. And, as we have seen, although they were confounded by the initial successes of the Europeans – and lacked the Spaniards' technology – they resisted with an heroic tenacity.

In truth, the Inca Revolt of 1536/7 – along with the Aztecs' defence of Tenochtitlan, and the successive Mayan struggles from the 1520s to the Great Caste War which ended in 1901 – was one of the greatest wars of resistance waged by natives against colonial powers in the Americas. Likewise, the Great Inca Revolt of 1780 was one of the first great modern revolutions against the European empires. As Waman Poma wrote to the king of Spain in 1613:

Our Indians should not be thought of as a backward people who yielded easily to superior force. Just imagine, Your Majesty, being an Indian in your own country and being loaded up as if you were a horse, or driven along with blows from a stick. Imagine being called a dirty dog or a pig. Imagine having your women and your property taken away from you without a shred of legality. What would you and your Spanish compatriots do in such circumstances? My own belief is that you would eat your tormentors alive and thoroughly enjoy the experience...
To conclude, it is not the Spanish administrators and employers who are the rightful owners of Peru. According to the laws of both God and man, we Indians are the proprietors. It is our country because God has given it to us. We are the true masters.

A ...... Yndio Yun
        de las ímmed
        de Quito con s
        de Plumas y Co
        Animales de Caz
        quando estan de
B ...... Platano, Arvol e
        los de la Casta de
        su Fruto, y son los
C ...... Platano Arvol q̃ l
        mados Dominicos
        tan delicado savo
        meros.
D ...... Arvol que Pro
        y su Fruta e
        saludable.
E ...... La Piña con
        tera Se Fruz

5
EL DORADO
THE JOURNEY OF FRANCISCO ORELLANA

CLIMB UP THE WOODEN LADDER inside the crumbling eighteenth-century clock-tower, past a dusty pile of old pendulum weights, and a broken organ, and you will find yourself out on the roof of the Franciscan monastery of La Merced. Walk over the undulating expanse of green and brown tiles, over the humped cupolas and oriels, and you suddenly come to the towering corner of the nave roof. There are few better places to view the Spanish presence in the New World – in front of you is a magnificent vista of the old city of Quito in Ecuador.

The most charming and atmospheric of all the capital cities of the Americas, Quito lies in a rugged valley, flanked by majestic mountains, and on a clear day the view from the Merced roof takes in breathtaking vistas of snow-capped volcanoes. To the east, the high Andes rise, shading into the clouds, their blue-grey shoulders and gleaming white peaks emerging and disappearing into the haze.

Centred almost dead on the Equator, Quito has a wonderful spring-like climate outside the rainy season and, at 9000 feet, the air is exhilarating – especially in the early morning before the clouds come in.

In the cloisters right below us, white-clad monks are hurrying to matins. Just over the precinct wall, the old town is waking up: a warren of old streets, whitewashed houses with terracotta roofs, a little hotel with an ornate red and white façade, an open-air market, its covered stalls jamming the alleys where Indian traders are unloading their bundles of weavings.

Further away, over the rooftops, are the great squares of the old city, with their colonial arcades, the grand buttresses of convents and monasteries, and the spires

Many nations have excelled others and overcome them, and the few have conquered the many. They say Alexander the Great with thirty-three thousand Macedonians undertook to conquer the world. So with the Romans too. But no nation has with such resolution passed through such labours, or such periods of starvation, or covered such immense distances as the Spanish have done. In a period of seventy years they have overcome and opened up a new world, greater than the one of which we had knowledge, exploring what was unknown and never before seen. And this exploration of Gonzalo Pizarro, we are bound to say, was the most laborious journey ever undertaken in these Indies.

·

PEDRO DE CIEZA DE LEON *The War of Chupas,* 1545

◀ An eighteenth-century Yumbo Indian from Ecuador. Orellana's men were impressed by the 'intelligence and capacity' of the Indians, but did not question the right of Europeans to rule them.

and towers of San Francisco, La Compania, San Augustin. And, perched over the old town, often shrouded in the mist which rolls in from the Andes, is the great statue of the winged Virgin of Quito, with her crown of stars and her eagle's wings. Beneath her feet is the chained dragon of the *Book of Revelations*, coiled on top of the globe, a prophecy and a riddle.

To me, no town so conveys the flavour of that astonishing era of the conquest: the three centuries of Spanish adventure in the New World. To walk the narrow streets of the colonial city of Quito is to enter an older world, in which a Spanish empire existed, linked by galleons which sailed from Lima and Panama to Manila, and from the Spanish Main to the Guadalquivir.

The church of San Francisco is the city's oldest church – construction began only weeks after the founding of Quito at the end of 1534 by the conquistador Benalcazar. Inside, it takes a moment for the eyes to become accustomed to the gloom. The nave is dark and smoky, with a fug of incense, oil-lamps and candles. It is a mysterious interior, glittering with gilt, its polished wooden floors worn uneven by use, the high altar a dim waterfall of gold. But behind the images of sunbursts and boy-childs, it is still easy to see the Inca ghosts. And, in the Indian faces of the worshippers who crowd the pews and aisles in the lunch-hour, lighting their candles at bleeding mannequins of the Saviour, you can still see their living descendants.

These days, the conquest is a matter of shame in Mexico, and controversy in Peru. But in Quito that heroic past is still commemorated. For example, just down from San Francisco, in the old town, you will find this great public inscription:

The Glory of Quito is the discovery of the River Amazon. Much as one may glorify Babylon for its walls, Nineveh for grandeur, Athens for letters, Constantinople for its empire, so Quito is honoured for the founding of Christianity here; for the Conquest of the New World, and also to this city belongs the great river of the Amazons.

That is not strictly true, of course. As we have seen, the Amazon was, in fact, discovered in January 1500 by the Spanish navigator Vicente Pinzon – or, at least, he saw the mouth of the river, which he named Saint Mary of the Sweet Water because of the staggering spectacle of fresh water so far out into the salt ocean. In that same year, Pinzon was followed by the Portuguese Pedro Alvarez Cabral, whose India fleet was blown off its course to the Cape of Good Hope. From then on, it was clear that a vast river came from somewhere in the interior, even if the shape of the continent was unknown.

For the next two or three decades, there was no further exploration of the

Atlantic coast of Brazil. It was not until the early 1520s, when the Spanish began feeling their way down the Pacific coast from Panama (as mentioned in Chapter 3) that a picture of the other side of the continent began to take shape. Then, in the 1530s, with the conquest of Peru, and expeditions as far as central Chile, knowledge grew of a great mountain range running 3000 miles from the Caribbean to Chile. But what lay east of the passes across the Quito Andes was still unknown.

The discovery of the interior of Amazonia, the existence and course of the longest and greatest river on earth, as the great sixteenth-century historian Oviedo said, was entered into by accident. The tale takes us back to Quito in the 1530s and 1540s. It was from here that the Spanish mounted a series of expeditions into the interior of South America, over the Andes into Ecuador, Colombia and Venezuela, journeys that surpass most other land explorations in history. These began even before the conquest of Peru in the early 1530s, and led to the discovery of the gold-rich tribes of southern Colombia.

By the end of the 1530s, rumours of new lands of gold were rife. Somewhere, the explorers thought, in an as yet unlocated kingdom, the astonishing treasure trove of Peru would be repeatable. These tales now crystallized around a beautiful and haunting legend – El Dorado: the Golden Man.

The Legend of El Dorado

THE LEGEND WAS BORN HERE IN QUITO, at the beginning of 1541, after the last expeditions had come back from Venezuela and Colombia. Oviedo was intrigued by the tale and later questioned veterans who had been there, to try to pin down its genesis:

I interviewed Spaniards who have been in Quito…and asked them why they call that prince 'The Golden Lord or King'. They tell me that what they have learned from the Indians is that the great lord or prince goes about continually covered in gold dust as fine as ground salt. He feels that it would be less beautiful to wear any other ornament: It would be crude and common to put on armour plates or hammered or stamped gold, for other rich lords wear these when they wish. But to powder oneself with gold is something exotic and unusually novel, and more costly, for he washes away at night what he puts on each morning, so that it is discarded and lost, and he does this every day of the year…

The prince, so Oviedo was told:

…was very great and very rich. Every morning he anoints himself with a kind of resin or gum to which the gold dust easily adheres, until his entire body is covered,

from the soles of his feet to his head. So his looks are as resplendent as a gold object worked by the hands of a great artist.

From this literally fabulous account, Oviedo concludes: 'I would rather have the sweepings of the chamber of this prince than the great meltings of gold which have taken place in Peru… I believe that if a chief does do this, then he must have very rich mines of the finest gold indeed.'

It was Gonzalo Pizarro who, in 1541, organized the most famous and fateful expedition to find El Dorado, and we had come to Quito to do something which had never been done before – to follow in his footsteps. I hoped our adventure might reveal more about what happened then, and why. It might also tell us about the climate, geography and conditions the conquistadors went through, and about the indigenous peoples of the Amazon, recorded by Gonzalo Pizarro and Francisco Orellana for the first time: what they have gone through since, and the pattern of their lost history in the intervening centuries.

With the help of Ecuadorian friends, we equipped ourselves in Quito. We bought machetes in a cavernous old ironmongers round the back of the Cine Atahuallpa; found a cheap supply of waterproofs in the Ipiales market; and, in the Ecuadorian Army Geographical Institute, searched out excellent large-scale maps of the river systems that lead from the watershed of the Quito Andes down to the jungles of Amazonia.

But this adventure was also a historical quest, so we armed ourselves with a cluster of primary texts. Chief among these were the first-hand witness accounts of the two main protagonists in this amazing tale: the diary made by Orellana's party as it took its epic first journey down the Amazon, and the baleful letter of Gonzalo Pizarro, telling his side of the story on his return to Quito.

▲ Lake Guatavita in Colombia, the scene of sacred rituals of the Muisca Indians, became identified as the 'Lake of El Dorado'. The cut on the far shore was dug by the Spanish in an attempt to drain the lake and recover the gold hidden in its depths.

◀◀ El Dorado, the golden man: 'every day he looks as resplendent as an image in gold made by a great artist'.

The Expedition Prepares

GONZALO PIZARRO PREPARED HIS TROOPS in Quito early in 1541. The half-brother of Francisco Pizarro, the conqueror of Peru, and some thirty years younger, he was the first son of the fourth main liaison of his father. He was a dark-haired, strongly built man, a formidable soldier whom the historian Garcilaso Inca described as 'the greatest warrior who ever fought in the New World'. He was not, one imagines, a man of deep thought but, like others of his clan, he had a finely calculating mind and was a 'coarse but effective speaker'. A born fighter, he was a leader with limitless stamina and self-belief, and was unconcerned by the humanitarian concerns bruited about by the likes of Las Casas. Now in his mid-thirties, and already vastly wealthy, Gonzalo

Pizarro was looking for new worlds to conquer and new fields of glory. 'He saw in the city of Quito many unemployed men, either youths or veterans,' says Cieza de Leon, 'and became eager for the discovery of the valley of El Dorado.'

Gonzalo Pizarro used his name, his fame and his new-found wealth to gather and equip a powerful expedition. His goal was threefold. First, he hoped to find La Canela, the Land of Cinnamon, which was believed to lie beyond the Andes. As we have seen, the Pizarros were above all entrepreneurs and traders, and cinnamon was a spice much coveted by Spanish merchants. Second, he wanted to assess this territory for colonization. And third, he hoped to find El Dorado: the Land of Gold.

Of course, no army marches into the unknown, and Gonzalo Pizarro made much of his intelligence reports: 'We were relying on many sources of information,' he said later, 'accounts received in Quito and outside the city from prominent and aged Indian chiefs, as well as from Spaniards, all of whose accounts agree with one another, to the effect that the province of La Canela, and the region round Lake El Dorado were a very populous and very rich land.'

Cieza de Leon adds that the same story had also come from captains who had been on advance forays across the Andes, into 'the land of Quijos and the Cinnamon valley' – apparently over the Andes passes to Papallacta:

They had returned without a full exploration of a region of which they had heard such great things…for the Indians said that further on, if they advanced, they would come to a widespreading flat country teeming with Indians who possess great riches, for they all wear gold ornaments, and where there were no forests or mountains. When this news spread in Quito, everyone who was there wanted to take part in the expedition.

Gonzalo Pizarro explicitly confirms this in his later letter to the king of Spain:

I became fascinated, and I decided to go and conquer and explore it, both to serve Your Majesty and in order to broaden and increase Your Majesty's realms and royal patrimony. I had been made to believe from these provinces would be obtained great treasures whereby Your Majesty would be served and aided in meeting the great expenses with which Your Majesty is faced every day in his realms. In my zeal and eagerness to do this, I spent more than fifty thousand castellanos which I paid out in advances to the men whom I took with me, both on foot and on horse.

His force was bigger than the one his brother Francisco had taken to Peru to confront the Inca Atahuallpa. Deputed by his brother to rule in the north, he was wealthy enough to contemplate organizing such an enterprise on his own. As Cieza de Leon remarks: 'At that time Gonzalo Pizarro was so powerful and influential in Peru because his brother was the Marquis Don Francisco Pizarro, colonizer and discoverer of the land…'

Like a Mafia clan, the family had accrued vast wealth in a few years. A schedule of the 1540s tells us that Gonzalo Pizarro's estates included houses and shops around Cuzco, with coca plantations and estates of Indian workers, anything from a dozen or two up to 150 strong. He had 8000 tribute-payers in 140 towns and villages in Peru; cattle and houses in Quito; ranches in southern Peru; other coca plantations, *encomiendas*, houses in Bolivia, and silver mines at Potosi and Porco.

The system was all-embracing: not only did his overseers work Indians to death in the mines, but Gonzalo Pizarro and his clan enjoyed the monopoly of the coca leaves that the Indians needed to do their work. Disbursing lavish patronage, paying hefty advances out of his own purse, was how he managed to fund such a massive expedition with thousands of native bearers, some of whom were perhaps captives of war, others maybe drawn from his own estates.

By February 1541, they were ready to go. Among the new colonists of Quito, rumours were everywhere: 'the people of the town declaring that they would find great riches, praising the lands of which news had been brought, while the Spaniards already imagined the plunder before their eyes and believed it to be theirs'. Little did they know.

The Expedition Crosses the Andes

'IN ORDER OF EVENTS, THIS IS WHAT HAPPENED on the expedition,' Gonzalo Pizarro begins. It was March when he and his troops left Quito, pennons flying, 'a magnificent array' heading east towards the Andes. His account survives in a letter written to the king of Spain from Tomebamba (the old Inca town of Cuenca, 150 miles south of Quito, where he owned an *encomienda*), after his return in the September of the following year.

'I started off with over 200 Spanish troops, thousands of native servants and great quantities of gear and munitions of war…' The precise figure seems to have been 230 plus 200 horses, later reinforced to over 250 men, and maybe in the end as many as 280 men with 260 horses. These were conquistadors of the highest calibre: 'a large number of the noblest and most prominent people of the realm'. It was an impressive force, given how few Spaniards there were in Ecuador at that early stage of the conquest.

Gonzalo Pizarro had paid many upfront, and this quality of troops did not come cheap: 'The price of the lowest, 500 pesos of 22 carat gold, the best, double

that' (so we are talking of 150,000 or even 200,000 gold pesos just for the men). Among them were specialists in building bridges and boats – construction workers, pioneers, carpenters. The troops carried arquebuses, cannon, crossbows, spare horseshoes, tools, rope, tents, all of which had to be carried by hundreds of llamas or by native bearers. For food, along with basic supplies of grain, salt, biscuits and wine, there were over 2000 hogs to be slaughtered and eaten on the hoof. In addition, there were hundreds of hunting dogs, customarily used by the Spaniards as a terror tactic against the Indians.

Finally, there were 4000 Indians to serve as guides, porters and labourers. These probably included women to prepare and cook food, including tortillas, and also to serve the Spanish soldiers' sexual needs. All in all, says Toribio de Ortiguera, writing a generation later, it was 'a great supply of munitions and implements of war…a very magnificent body of men and one well prepared for any adventure which might lie ahead'.

The old road into the Andes is still called 'the way of the conquistadors'. It is an old cobbled back road which slips down from Quito into the great ravine of the Machangara river, then rises by a slow steep ascent up towards the Andes. (If one is not acclimatized to the altitude, it can be an exhausting trek just to reach the foot of the mountains.)

The problem for Gonzalo Pizarro was that, whereas they had been operating inside a well-ordered and well-governed state in Peru, they were now heading beyond the frontier of the Inca world. The Andes foothills of Quito marked the eastern edge of the Tawantinsuyu. The Incas had dealings with the peoples of the forests beyond (there is some evidence of long-distance trade into the Amazon), but they had no desire to extend their lordship over peripheral areas of the Four Quarters. So, in the Andes and beyond, this meant that there were no roads, no way stations – and no knowledge. Local guides knew only their own areas, although, even after torturing some of them to death, Gonzalo Pizarro refused to believe that this was the case.

His troubles began as soon as he entered the mountains: 'Only seven leagues out of Quito we came to very rugged wooded country and great mountain ranges through which we were obliged to open up new roads, not only for the men but for the horses…'

From Quito, the road goes up to a pass at 14,000

▼ Seventeenth-century image of an Amazonian cannibal. Such myths served to dehumanize native peoples, making it easier for the conquistadors to treat them as 'barbarous beings, justly conquered by a humane nation which excels in every kind of virtue'.

feet that leads over to Baeza, leaving the great cone of the Antisana volcano off to the south. To the right of the modern road is the old cart-track, the eighteenth-century royal road, which is roughly Gonzalo Pizarro's route. The mountains were thickly forested and, after opening up a new road, he says:

We were exhausted simply getting over the other side. We continued our journey till we reached the province of Zumaco, a good sixty leagues away [in fact, thirty, as Cieza de Leon rightly points out] and within which it was reported there was a big population, but it was impossible to travel about there on horseback, and there I halted the expeditionary force in order to get it rested, both the Spaniards and the horses, for all were quite worn out in consequence of the great hardships which they had gone through in climbing up and going down the great mountains [the Andes] and because of the many bridges which had to be built for the crossing of the rivers.

Not a good omen. But, as it turned out, they had hardly begun.

They had left in the wet season and, along with the altitude, the incessant rain made things doubly difficult. The Spanish had developed light quilted cotton armour for the tropics, but even if the men were acclimatized to Quito, conditions soon became irksome in the extreme: 'For two months solid it just rained: it never stopped long enough to dry the shirts on our backs…'

In the Land of Cinnamon

BEYOND THE PEAKS, they entered the equatorial cloud forest of the Andes, a drenched green world, abounding in streams and waterfalls which eventually become the Amazon. We traced their route into the Quijos valley, past Papallacta, under the Reventador volcano: the 'spewer', or ' blower'.

Although delightfully green and fecund, this is very rugged terrain indeed, through which a metalled road has been gouged and dynamited in recent years. Criss-crossed by deep gorges and river valleys, it was – and still is – covered by a thick mantle of forest. As the rains continued to fall, Gonzalo Pizarro attempted to press on through trackless forests, sending pioneers ahead with native detachments to cut a track and make a passable road.

Finally, they came to the fertile, well-provisioned valley of Sumaco (possibly where the later Spanish colony of Baeza was created, west of the Sumaco volcano). The rains were now heavy. The area is plagued by wet weather, and in the rainiest season, from May to August, the trails turn to mudbaths and the mountains rarely emerge from cloud, often removing any sense of direction for days on end.

Gonzalo Pizarro tried as best he could to gather information about the Land of Cinnamon and decided to camp the main part of the expedition in the fertile

countryside at Sumaco. Here, their numbers were boosted by the arrival of another detachment of twenty-three conquistadors who had come up from the coast at Guayaquil and made their own crossing of the mountains. Their leader was Francisco Orellana – a relative of the Pizarros, who had made a name for himself in the later wars against Manco Inca. The one-eyed Orellana would turn out to be both hero and villain in the amazing adventure which followed.

Gonzalo Pizarro now decided to leave the main force in the camp and push on ahead looking for the land of cinnamon trees. Taking with him seventy or eighty foot-soldiers with crossbows and guns, he 'headed for the direction of the sunrise'. He was gone for an astonishing seventy days.

Exactly where he went is still a mystery. We can only guess that he travelled east and south from the area of the Sumaco volcano, and in a great circle south-east along the Andes foothills as far as a river, which was probably the Napo, which was later known to the Spanish as La Canela, the River of Cinnamon. He and his men experienced hunger and much hardship through the terrible terrain, but found few signs of future profit. The cinnamon trees were disappointingly small and scattered: 'It is a land and a commodity by which Your Majesty cannot be rendered any service or be benefited in any attempt to exploit the business, because the cinnamon is in small quantities and would yield even smaller profit.'

All the while, Gonzalo Pizarro was reliant on information drawn from natives who – terrified by his brutality and the knowledge that they would be tortured if they did not cooperate – gave false information. Gonzalo Pizarro was certainly a tough customer. Angry that the Indians did not tell him what he wanted to hear, he tortured them – sometimes burning them alive on wooden frames, or casting them to be eaten alive by dogs – including some women, notes Cieza de Leon with horror.

Finally, the expedition reached a large river in an area where 'ranges of forest clad and rugged mountains stretched in all directions'. My guess is that this was a stretch of the upper river Napo below Tena, where the ice-blue, sparkling river flows over shingle and sand beaches, framed by majestic forest-clad mountains in all directions, save downriver. This fabulous place lies below what is known today as the 'gate of the Napo'.

Here, on a beach of level sand, a sharp rise in the river caught them in camp one night and swept away some of their baggage. Gonzalo Pizarro was now on the edge – profoundly depressed, according to Cieza de Leon. In an intimate passage, which could only come from a survivor, he tells us Gonzalo Pizarro was 'much distressed at finding he could not reach any fertile and abundant province...and deplored many times that he had undertaken the expedition. Although he did not let his followers understand this, on the contrary giving them every possible encouragement'. After discussions among the experienced captains, the decision was put to the troops, who agreed with their officers, that they should withdraw from the path they had taken and rejoin the main force in the valley of Sumaco.

In fact, they bypassed the main force and went straight on north till they hit a big river. This was the Coca, which they then descended, looking for a good crossing place. Here we picked up Gonzalo Pizarro's trail again. Having trucked over the mountains and journeyed down to the Napo, we now left our vehicle behind and followed him on foot with pack animals down to the Coca river.

What it might have been like for him, we ourselves experienced on a day's trek down a forested mountainside to reach the Coca. At one point, on a narrow dirt path traversing a very steep slope in the jungle at about a forty-five degree angle, we found that a huge landslide had come through the forest and swept the path away, leaving giant trees upturned amid tangled debris of roots and undergrowth, and a great red scree of mud, slippery with rain. We tried to climb over the wreckage, then realized it would be better to make our way below the fall and to hack a way through the untouched forest for the pack animals. Just getting round the avalanche took two hours of cutting. Admittedly, we had only four machetes with which to do this, but it was easy to imagine that, at this rate, we would scarcely progress more than a mile or two a day. We began to understand why Gonzalo Pizarro and his men achieved so little in so many months.

Gonzalo Pizarro had pushed on with his advance guard, looking for a place to cross the river. Following him, we came to two landmarks mentioned in the Spanish accounts. First, a great waterfall where 'the sound of the falling water was audible several miles off'. It is a wonderful sight, falling about 200 feet, jets of water shooting out to the side of the main fall and churning at the bottom in a cauldron of spray. Here, later legend said, the gold of the Inca Atahuallpa was hidden but, according to our guides, the belief among local Indians today is that behind the falls there is 'a gateway to another world, an entrance to the world of spirits'.

Gonzalo Pizarro moved on, still looking for a place to cross safely, and soon came to the second landmark, close by: a gorge 'so narrow it was not twenty feet across, yet as far down to the river as the water falls'. (This we found to be true: it is, indeed, a terrifying drop down a vertiginous canyon.) Here, they had to fight off natives before they could span the gorge with fallen trees and make a wooden bridge. Only then did Gonzalo Pizarro send messengers back to the Sumaco valley to summon Orellana and the main expeditionary force to meet him there, on the right bank of the river, below the San Rafael gorge.

Having crossed the river, they now had a route down into the plains, descending the Coca on its left bank, surrounded everywhere by forest. It was late in the

▸ 'We heard the sound from ten miles off.' The San Rafael Falls on the Coca river in Ecuador: Gonzalo Pizarro came this way on his descent of the river.

▸▸ The forest interior of Amazonia, depicted here in a painting (detail) by Tirzah Ravilious, has haunted the European imagination since Pizarro and Orellana first saw it in 1542.

year, and hardship and starvation had been so severe that most of the native bearers had already died. It is often said that the cause of death was simply that people of the High Andes could not survive in the tropical lowlands, but medically this makes little sense. Without question, the Indian servants died from maltreatment: from brutal pressure, starvation, and probably from European diseases. Commandeered by force in Quito, incarcerated before the expedition started, chained together day and night, they spent many months with the Europeans, among whom malaria, smallpox, venereal diseases and other pathogens were rife. They hardly stood a chance.

In the Emerald Forest

THE COCA IS A BEAUTIFUL RIVER. It turns east and south in a great curve as it threads the gorges and rushes from the Andes foothills. From the last of these you can see an immense flat horizon, green forest stretching like an ocean, shading in the far distance into a blue haze. Even with their limited geographical knowledge, the Spaniards understood at once that this stretched all the way to the Atlantic, that the Coca was, as Cieza de Leon says, 'an arm of the Sweet Sea' (*Mar Dulce,* the Amazon). But what lay in between? And how far was it? No one knew, as they had few good instruments and no means of calculating longitude. The sun and stars gave them rough directions, but essentially they had only the vaguest idea where they were.

For the next two weeks, they marched down along the left bank of the Coca, 'pushing on down river', Gonzalo Pizarro says, 'through thick forest, hacking with axes and machetes, and often it was impossible to get the horses through…' The river widened out: 'a beautiful and abundantly flowing river', over a hundred yards wide, with long sandbars and a glittering strand of whitened boulders along the northern shore where the current races down from the mountains, surging over rapids, ice-blue and cold.

Today, the landscape is sparsely inhabited, just a few isolated Runa, Quechua speakers. The chief sensation on the early part of the journey is provided by the wonderful green forest, blue river, and immense skies – pale china-blue in the mornings, daffodil yellow in the heat of afternoon, with towering piles of dazzling white cloud. It was all very exhilarating for us, especially at first light and in the early hours before the sun rose over the forest tops and the heat of the day began. But for Gonzalo Pizarro there were no compensations in the view. Fording creeks and swamps, never getting dry, his progress was painfully slow. And there was still no sign of El Dorado…

By early October, seven months after they had left Quito, they were demoralized. The weather had improved a little (the best months here, although not free of rain, are from October to December), but by now nearly all of Gonzalo Pizarro's 4000 native bearers were dead, and many of his men were too sick to move. Decision time had come. Should he go back or go on? By now, they had passed the last rapids along the Upper Coca, and the river was 'wide, gentle and deep flowing'. So he stopped, made camp on a high bluff, safe from sudden rises in the river, and decided to build a boat.

With a boat he could carry the tools and heavy gear, ferry the sick and wounded, and fight off the Indian canoeists who were now beginning to trouble his men with their hit-and-run attacks, shooting arrows from the safety of the river. These were probably ancestors of the Cofanes tribes who were once widespread along the foothills of the Andes. Implacable resisters of conquistadors, gold-hunters and missionaries alike, there are now only a few hundred survivors to the north of here on the Aguarico river. But they are a people who, in the twenty-first century, have preserved shreds of their noble culture in their language, textiles and traditions.

So, through October, the Spanish stayed at their camp on that high bluff, surviving on fish, by killing and eating the last of their hogs and any sick horses, and by making forays into the jungle to plunder fruit and roots from isolated native settlements. Meanwhile, using wood from the forest, Gonzalo Pizarro's carpenters set about making a brigantine (or pinnace). The boat was about twenty-six feet long, with an eight-foot beam, and a two-foot draught. It would have carried twenty men comfortably, even more at a pinch.

They named the place where it was built El Barco (The Boat), and luckily this is recorded in a 1570s' document as Barco: 'the place where Gonzalo Pizarro built his boat'. It is now San Sebastian, which is situated just below a gorge where the Coca river flows through a narrow passage between cliffs of brown rock, only ten or twelve miles above the junction of the Coca with the Napo.

When the boat was ready, Gonzalo Pizarro put twenty-five of his sick men on board, plus the heavy gear and tools. The boat was christened *San Pedro*, and they set sail on the Coca on 9 November 1541.

Down the Coca River

WE USED INDIAN TOOLS to make our Indian-style raft of balsa logs, nails of hard wood, and bark ropes. We tackled all the rapids, and followed the river for the next fifty miles. The raft proved amazingly stable and durable – and we had three wonderful days on the river under a turquoise sky, with the forest towering above us.

We camped on the bank each night, plagued by torrential rain pouring on to our tents and leaking into every cranny. Tremendous flashes of lightning would approach us ominously across the forest, as the treetops shook in the rain; then, just as mysteriously, the lightning would turn away, lighting up the horizon towards Colombia. By dawn the air cleared, and in the early hours we would sail along under an overhanging cliff of green forest, shooting past great levees of pebbles, littered with the wrecks of fallen trees.

The forest was now well over 100 feet, even 200 feet high, with occasional splashes of red leaf in a riot of different shades of vermilion. There were palm trees with towering shaggy heads, rosewood, brazil, orchids, clumps of tree ferns, and groves filled with canes festooned with pale-spiked leaves.

During our descent of the Coca we saw few people, although we knew from occasional sightings of banana and yucca plantations that families were living out there – Quechua speakers who have migrated over the Andes into these parts in every century since the Spanish took Peru. Sometimes, through the trees, we would glimpse their isolated houses built on stilts. Now and then, we would land and pay a visit to eat fruit, drink chicha and swap news of the outside world.

The river would have been much more populous in Gonzalo Pizarro's day. Since then, the indigenous people have been driven away from the river by prospectors, missionaries and soldiers and, as we discovered, it is the same sad tale all the way down the Amazon.

Provided we steered carefully round some of the giant boulders in the stream, our balsa raft took the big rapids with no trouble. Once we were past these, the lower Coca broadened out to a flat shallow river, a quarter of a mile wide, and was easy sailing. But, as Pizarro continued down the Coca, he was still limited,

On our balsa raft, taking rapids on the Coca river; a larger version of such a craft might have served Pizarro better than his laboriously constructed brigantine.

remember, by the speed of his men tramping on foot through the swamps and creeks along the bank.

According to the Spanish, they did forty-three day marches, or fifty leagues, between the boat setting sail on 9 November and the Christmas camp. Even if this is an over-estimate of the progress of the army along the river bank, this would still take us nearly 150 miles down the Napo. They were deep into Amazonia when disaster struck.

This, I think, is what happened: from the Coca, they turned on to the Napo and marched eastwards. In all directions, there is immense forest. To the south, as far as the Curaray river, stretches the territory of the Huarani, many of whom still shun contact with Europeans and who have only recently killed uninvited intruders.

Then, long since out of sight of the Andes, exhausted, sick and demoralized after six weeks marching through incessant forest, they stopped – to celebrate Christmas. They had priests with them, of course, and regular celebration of the Christian liturgy was one of the things that marked all the Spanish expeditions. They almost never omitted to mark the main festivals of the Christian calendar and

the celebration of mass on Sundays – and, even when starving, they kept a small supply of communion wine and bread for the host. Reading their accounts, it almost feels that this was one way they structured life and kept up their morale in such an alien world.

▲ Our expedition trekking through the forests of the Coca river below the Reventador volcano. 'The terrain was very difficult,' wrote Pizarro, 'and we had to hack our way through with machetes.'

It was, however, a gloomy Christmas, and there was (one infers) much murmuring against the leadership. Next day, Boxing Day, matters came to a head. Starvation had now set in. Unaware of what was edible in the forest, the force of 200 to 300 men, with their remaining camp-followers, was like a plague of hungry locusts; for all Gonzalo Pizarro's famed expertise as a soldier, they had rapidly whittled away all their supplies and started to kill and eat their dogs and horses. And El Dorado was nowhere to be seen.

Christmas was made even more miserable by news from their native guides that a vast uninhabited region lay ahead – where no food whatsoever would be found. It was Gonzalo Pizarro's nightmare come true. What to do next? This is when the one-eyed Francisco Orellana enters the tale.

The Expedition Splits

ORELLANA'S STATUE CAN BE SEEN all down the Amazon – in Quito, at Coca Town, in Peru, even in Leticia, on the Colombian border with Brazil. But what he looked like, we really do not know. He was a typical conquistador, thirtyish, born in Trujillo (where he has a statue) and related to the Pizarros. He had participated in the fighting for Lima in 1536, and had a spark of humanity, and a capacity for leadership, which are amply demonstrated in what followed. Orellana offered to take the boat and go on downriver to try to find food, and save the expedition. It was the beginning of one of the most famous dramas in the story of the conquest. As told by Gonzalo Pizarro, the conversation went like this:

Orellana told me he had questioned the guides I had placed in his charge so that he might get better information about the country beyond (as he had nothing to do since I looked after all matters to do with fighting) and he told me that the guides had said that the uninhabited region was a vast one and that no food whatsoever was to be had this side of a spot where another great river joined up with the one down which we were proceeding; and that from this junction, one days's journey up the other river, there was an abundant supply of food.

Orellana now offered to take the brigantine and go on ahead, using oars and sails – that is, at good speed – to reconnoitre the land ahead, and see if there were inhabited areas with supplies. Gonzalo Pizarro says he agreed with this:

I was confident Captain Orellana would do as he said because he was my lieutenant. I told him I was pleased at the idea and that he should see to it that he got back within twelve days, and in no case go beyond the junction of the rivers, but bring the food and give attention to nothing else. He answered that he would by no means go beyond what I had told him… So with this confidence I had in him, I gave him the boat and sixty men…and so he departed.

Orellana's version, recorded by the expedition diarist, Father Carvajal, is subtly but significantly different. Reading it, one hardly needs to look between the lines to see in his version many explicit criticisms of Gonzalo Pizarro's leadership, which make it clear that there was already dissatisfaction – even outright dispute – between Gonzalo Pizarro and his lieutenant: 'There were many opinions which disagreed with Pizarro,' says Orellana, namely in his decision to leave the savannah country, near Popayan. But Gonzalo Pizarro had 'insisted' (note the hint of obstinacy) on leaving a safe territory and following the river. Orellana had then disagreed with him again, this time over the decision to build the boat, and 'for several good reasons', favoured returning on their track to the savannah country, where there was a sizeable settled population and food.

But, once more, Gonzalo Pizarro 'would consent to nothing, save that work on the boat should begin' (again the suggestion of pig-headedness). Now, after fifty leagues of fruitless trekking, the army was suffering great privations as a result of this decision, and lacked food: 'because of which all the companions were greatly dissatisfied and the talk was of turning back and going no further'. Mutiny no less – if we believe Orellana's account.

At this juncture, says Father Carvajal, with things falling apart:

▲ A statue of Francisco Orellana in Quito: there are monuments to him and his amazing journey in all the countries along the Amazon.

Captain Orellana seeing what was happening and seeing the great privations every-
one was suffering…went to Pizarro and told him he would go on down the river
and, if luck favoured him, he would find an inhabited region and foodstuffs which
might sustain everyone. But if he, Pizarro, should find that Orellana was delayed,
he should not be concerned about him, and in the meantime he should turn back to
where food was to be had, and wait for Orellana there for three or four days, or for
as long as he should see fit. And in case Orellana did not come back, he should not
be concerned about him. Thereupon the said Governor [Pizarro] told him to do
whatever he thought best.

It is a drama worthy of Hollywood. If Gonzalo Pizarro really said those last words – 'do whatever you think best' – then, at that moment, his authority over the expedition had clearly collapsed. But that this was not the case is suggested by the events that followed. We will never know the whole truth, of course, for both versions are special pleading after the event.

Father Carvajal is trying to convey a breakdown of leadership, with a string of bad decisions contributing to the situation which prompted the split. Gonzalo Pizarro, needless to say, is anxious in retrospect to show that he was still in control. What Orellana had proposed was tantamount to splitting up the army, and surely Pizarro would never have agreed to the arrangement that Father Carvajal describes; he would never have given over the boat, with irreplaceable munitions, powder, arquebuses, crossbows and tools, on a vague promise that Orellana might come back. Behind the tale, surely, lies a breakdown of command – and the breakdown of a relationship.

Orellana left on Boxing Day with fifty-seven Spaniards, two African slaves, four or five crossbows, three arquebuses, a supply of powder, spare ammunition and some native canoes. Gonzalo Pizarro had thought that 'within ten or twelve days he would rejoin the expeditionary force'. But very soon, within three days, according to Orellana, it was obvious from the speed of the river that he could

never get back as he had promised. As it happens, Orellana had a diary kept of what followed, written up by the expedition priest Father Carvajal (it is one of the most gripping eye-witness narratives from the New World) and, in it, we can read how he justified his decision:

We soon realized it was impossible to go back. We talked over our situation (seeing we were already nearly dead from hunger) and we chose what seemed to us the lesser of two evils…trusting to God to get us out, to go on and follow the river: we would either die or get to see what lay along it.

It seems clear that from the start, Orellana's group were concerned that their actions could be construed as mutiny, and eventually they held a meeting and had a scrivener record their actions and decisions on paper, to be witnessed by the members of their 'armada'. An amazing series of documents, preserved in the Archive of the Indies in Seville, charts this process. The key ones are signed by most of the expedition. They even allege that Orellana himself, out of loyalty to Gonzalo Pizarro, wanted to go back, but had been dissuaded. Interestingly enough, though, we know from other sources that there was not a united front in Orellana's group. According to the contemporary historian Ortiguera: 'These were all arguments to bolster their case, for they could easily have gone back up the river in the brigantine according to information I obtained from some of those who took part, who were persons of reputation and good faith.'

Ortiguera goes on to name five witnesses who told him this. What we will never know is whether by then hatred of Gonzalo Pizarro was such that Orellana decided not to return to him. Gonzalo Pizarro, however, expected Orellana to come back – and, later, even before he heard that Orellana had survived, he cast him as a dyed-in-the-wool traitor:

So he displayed towards the whole expeditionary force the greatest cruelty that ever faithless men have shown, aware that it was left so unprovided with food, and caught in such a vast uninhabited region and among such great rivers, carrying off all the arquebuses and crossbows and munitions and iron materials of the whole expeditionary force…

On the Napo

ORELLANA WAS NOW AFLOAT on one of the main tributaries of the Amazon, the Napo, heading eastwards on its great brown flow through a vast green wilderness, the horizon bounded by a great forest which stretches in every direction. During those first few days, they passed through the silent deserted landscape between the Yururi and Tiputini

rivers, and then the mouth of the Aguarico, where they camped and built shelters. Finding the native people open and sympathetic, Orellana decided to stay with

▲ A local ferry on the Napo river, a tributary of the Amazon near the township named after Francisco Orellana.

them and allow his men to recuperate. So the Spanish made camp at the Indian village and rested there for a month, from 3 January to 2 February, eating native food prepared by the women, and slowly recovering their health. By now, Orellana knew that their salvation lay in keeping the brigantine seaworthy and, thinking ahead, he used the time to make a forge and manufacture iron nails from the supply of horseshoes carried in the belly of the boat.

Orellana called this place Imara, after its people. It was ten days' sailing above the junction with the Maranon, and probably lay above the junction of the Napo with the Curaray – that most beautiful river which flows down through the lands of the Huarani.

Orellana also realized that their survival would depend on their ability to talk to the native peoples, and he made a determined effort to learn their language, keeping a notebook primer in which he recorded their speech. 'Next to God, the captain's ability to speak the languages of the natives was the thing that saved our lives,' says his diarist Father Carvajal.

At this stage, though, Orellana was still thinking like a conquistador. In the name of the king of Spain, he took possession of the village of Imara, and gave

the Indians a lecture on Christianity: 'We told them we were Christians who worshipped a single God: not trees and stones,' says Father Carvajal. None the less, a change was beginning to take place in the mind of the Spaniard, for, by the time Orellana left the people of Imara, he understood that the 'kind treatment of the Indians was the proper procedure to be followed…' The people who taught him this fact of life – who fed him, and saved his men's lives – were probably ancestors of today's indigenous people, the Huarani.

The Legend of the Amazons

MUCH REFRESHED BY THE HOSPITALITY they had received, but fearing to impose on their hosts any longer, Orellana and his men set off again on 2 February. They had debated whether to try to get a message back upriver to Gonzalo Pizarro, using volunteers and Indian guides, but in the end dismissed the idea as hopelessly dangerous: 'They all feared the death that was sure to come if they tried.' After all, it was pointed out, they were now 150 or even 200 leagues (over 500 miles) further on. They had simply come too far. There was nothing to do but push on, trust to God, and see what wonders lay ahead.

Ten days later, Orellana and his men came to a gigantic confluence, which he named Santa Eulalia, after the date, 12 February. This was the meeting of the Napo and the Maranon, the beginning of the Amazon proper.

Following in his track, we were now inside Peru, at a point where there is another place named after the conquistador, the delightful little town of Francisco Orellana – one of those tiny places on the face of the planet which is somehow truly memorable, though it is still, just as the Spanish remembered, a place 'plagued by great swarms of mosquitoes'.

The river here has shifted its course over time, and the old channel by which the village stands is now only a shallow tributary. The little ferry comes down the Napo and lands its passengers in the golden light of dusk on the edge of a damp green wilderness. There is a tiny wooden jetty, some dug-outs, and an old houseboat from which children wave cheerily. From here, you walk for half an hour through tall grass to reach a landing-stage for small boats, situated below a huge monument to Orellana, which was built in 1942, on the four hundredth anniversary of his epic journey.

A subtle shift occurs now in the tone of the expedition diary. This may have been with the benefit of hindsight, but Father Carvajal appears to be already aware that the journey was turning into an epic voyage of exploration: 'It seemed to us by our survival that our Lord Jesus Christ was pleased with such a great venture into the unknown – for such a feat of discovery might not otherwise have taken place for many centuries in the future…'

It was hereabouts that Orellana first heard tantalizing stories of the existence of a fierce tribe of female warriors, like the Amazons in Greek myth. It was an old tale, of course, even in the New World, let alone the Old. Columbus had told something similar, and many others since him. But Orellana's men had no doubt that the tale was true. And, lower down the river, towards what is now Belem, in Brazil, Father Carvajal assures us they actually met – and fought with – these extraordinary warriors. To this day, no one knows whether they ever really existed, but the tale gave the river the name it still has today: Rio Amazonas – the River of the Amazons.

Closing Father Carvajal's diary, I went to sleep imagining Orellana and his men out there on the river, in the velvet night, their look-out keeping his eyes peeled for fallen trees which could have smashed their boat to smithereens and killed them in an instant. Strengthened and cheered by the hospitality of the Imarans, their leaking boat repaired, they sail on, a tiny skiff on the huge dark river; they are silent now, some asleep, squashed against each other in the bottom of the boat, feeling on their faces the lovely cool breeze that comes up in the middle of the night. Like ghosts, they pass the immense confluence with the Maranon – so wide that only a distant dark line along the horizon marks the other bank. They know now that to survive they must somehow find their way to the sea.

The Journey of Gonzalo Pizarro

WITH ORELLANA HAVING DISAPPEARED down the broad sheet of Napo that Boxing Day, we left Gonzalo Pizarro marooned in the forest. But where exactly was he? And what happened to him? This part of the tale has never been traced on the ground, but we can make a good guess. Orellana and Gonzalo Pizarro say they had done fifty leagues, or forty-three days' march, from Barco before they reached the Christmas camp where they split up. These accounts roughly agree on a marching rate of not much more than a league, or three miles or so, each day, through thick forest, crossing innumerable creeks and tributaries.

Even if this is only approximately right, it places the Christmas camp somewhere on Middle Napo. Although the rivers in Amazonia have changed course over time, this is less likely to be the case the nearer they are to the Andes; and the main features of the Napo are the same today as they are on early Spanish maps. This is also confirmed by recent archaeological excavations of Indian habitation sites, dating from the eleventh to fifteenth centuries, which then lined its course.

So, my hunch is that the Christmas camp was not far above the junction with the Tiputini river, where a string of pre-conquest native village sites have been discovered by archaeologists of the Napo culture – among which, Sinchi Chicta, Ocaya and San Vicente have yielded fine ceramics. These cultures fished and

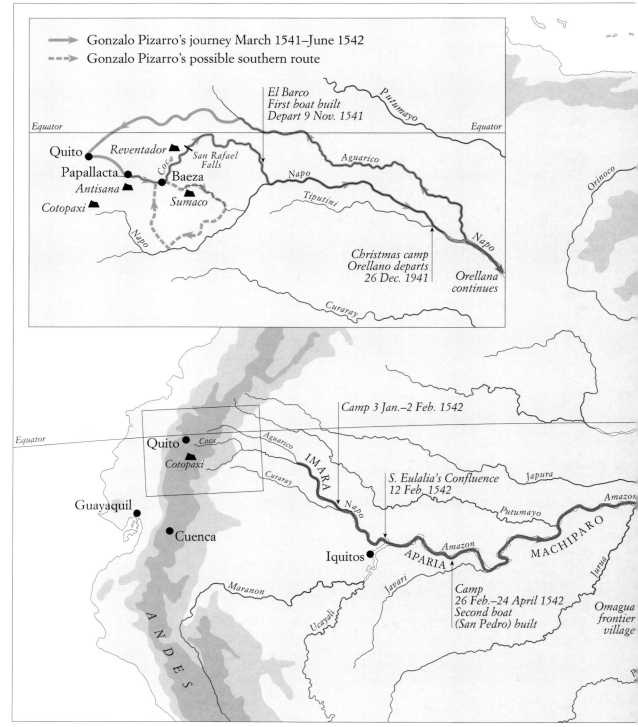

Gonzalo Pizarro's journey March 1541–June 1542

Gonzalo Pizarro's possible southern route

El Barco
First boat built
Depart 9 Nov. 1541

Putumayo

Equator   *Equator*

Quito   *Reventador*   *San Rafael Falls*

Aguarico

Papallacta   Baeza

Antisana   *Napo*

Sumaco

Cotopaxi

Tiputini

Napo

Orinoco

Napo

Christmas camp
Orellano departs
26 Dec. 1941

Orellana continues

Curaray

Camp 3 Jan.–2 Feb. 1542

Equator

Quito *Coca*

Aguarico

Cotopaxi

Curaray

IMARA

S. Eulalia's Confluence
12 Feb. 1542

Japura

Amazon

Guayaquil

Napo

Putumayo

Cuenca

Amazon

Maranon

Iquitos

APARIA

MACHIPARO

Javari

Jurua

Ucayali

Camp
26 Feb.–24 April 1542
Second boat
(San Pedro) built

Omagua
frontier
village

A N D E S

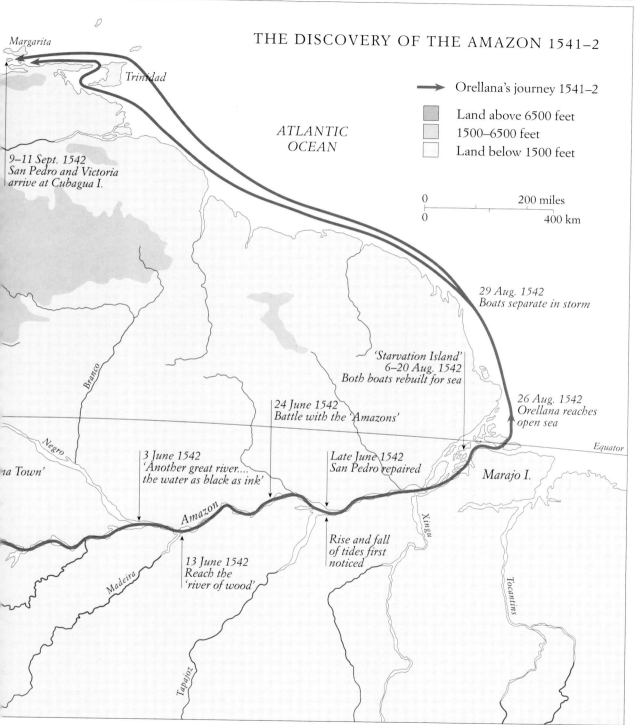

THE DISCOVERY OF THE AMAZON 1541-2

Orellana's journey 1541-2

Land above 6500 feet

1500–6500 feet

Land below 1500 feet

Margarita

Trinidad

ATLANTIC OCEAN

9–11 Sept. 1542
*San Pedro and Victoria
arrive at Cubagua I.*

0   200 miles
0   400 km

29 Aug. 1542
Boats separate in storm

'Starvation Island'
6–20 Aug. 1542
Both boats rebuilt for sea

24 June 1542
Battle with the 'Amazons'

26 Aug. 1542
*Orellana reaches
open sea*

Branco

Negro

na Town'

3 June 1542
*'Another great river....
the water as black as ink'*

Late June 1542
San Pedro repaired

Marajo I.

Equator

Amazon

Xingu

Madeira

13 June 1542
*Reach the
'river of wood'*

Rise and fall
of tides first
noticed

Tocantins

Tapajoz

cultivated, using slash-and-burn tactics, and lived in small communities like those which still exist today deeper in the forest.

Believing Orellana would come back within a fortnight, Gonzalo Pizarro decided to press on along the bank. With his troops in such a bad shape, and whispers of dissent around the camp fires, inaction would have been fatal at this stage. Better to move on. So, he formed up his men and horses – he probably had about 200 men left – and choosing the youngest and toughest to wield the machetes, he continued on down the Napo. Famished, exhausted, and soaked by the incessant rain, after a few days the army found its way blocked by a great swamp.

Nearby was an island in the Napo, and my guess is that they were now just short of the mouth of the Tiputini river – one of the most important tributaries on Middle Napo. Here, today, there is a large island well above the flood level of river, with a small settlement (also called Tiputini), and an abandoned jungle airstrip.

Pre-conquest settlements have been excavated in this vicinity, with beautiful ceramics – including magnificent figured funerary urns and superb plates painted with the animals of the forest. The forgotten peoples who made these were once densely settled along the Napo, and created a magnificent regional culture here. Gonzalo Pizarro tells us that this place was eight days' march from a very big river, which cannot be other than the Aguarico, about thirty miles downriver from Tiputini. This is where I imagine them making camp, on an immense curve of the river, thick jungle right up to its banks, on one side a great marshy creek.

At his wits' end, Gonzalo Pizarro now weighed up the possibility of building another boat. But making the first one had been a very long job – cutting the wood, making charcoal, forging nails – and doing it again would have been a tremendous effort for now desperate men who were beside themselves with hunger. Besides, Orellana had gone off with the tools and the spare iron horse-shoes, which they would need to make the nails. Their most urgent need was food.

Individuals who know the ways of the forest can always survive there, collecting rainwater, gathering edible herbs, and getting salt from certain buds; there are also fruits and tubers cultivated by the locals. But such options were not open to Gonzalo Pizarro who in any case must have been unaware of what could be eaten in the forest. To avoid killing his remaining horses and dogs, his men were now feeding on lizards and snakes, and any other animal they could catch. In the end, Gonzalo Pizarro says, 'We were forced to eat the little buds of a plant, like a vine stalk.' They had now reached the point of no return. Without food, it was only a matter of time before they started dying in numbers.

In fear of the white men, the native people in the area had abandoned their villages and fled into the jungle. But then, 'by a miracle', one of Gonzalo Pizarro's foraging parties captured five canoes, and with these Pizarro sent a captain, Mercadillo, downstream with a dozen men to search for food, and to look for any trace of Orellana. After nearly a week's absence, they struggled wearily back with no news, and no food. It was a body blow.

As a final throw, Gonzalo Pizarro sent another party, led by Gonzalo Pineda, a very experienced conquistador, who, in the late 1530s, had led the first expedition over the Andes from Quito into the Land of Cinnamon. Pineda was their last hope, and was told bluntly that he had to find supplies of food, or they were all doomed.

Pineda paddled downstream until he came to the mouth of a very big river – the one known today as Aguarico, 'the gold-bearer', because of the flecks of gold in its sands. Here he landed and found the place on the bank where Orellana had camped. There were cuts on the trees and the remains of temporary shelters. This was where the rendezvous was supposed to have been made, and Pineda immediately put two and two together and realized that Orellana was either dead or had gone on. Either way, he now knew they were on their own:

They realized that there was to be no relief there in way of food, because Orellana had gone on, and there was no way of finding food, and they became desperately discouraged, because for many days they had eaten nothing but palm shoots and fallen fruit stones.

Reasoning that Orellana must have continued down the main stream – and not found food anywhere within reasonable distance, or he would have long since returned with it – Pineda decided to turn up the tributary and search for food there, as their native guides had suggested. This way, they would also have the current with them on their return to the Napo. So, they sailed up the Aguarico, paddling against the current, hoping against hope that they would find a major cultivated native settlement.

Pineda later estimated that they had journeyed upriver for ten leagues (over thirty miles) before finding thick plantations of cassava. They came ashore and 'fell to their knees and gave thanks to God'. Having cooked for themselves and eaten, they then loaded their canoes and sailed back downriver to the junction with the Napo, and then slowly paddled their way back up the Napo against the current to reach Gonzalo Pizarro's camp. There, they were greeted with unrestrained joy by their demoralized and starving comrades 'who had all [with the exception of Pizarro himself] given up hope of ever seeing them again'.

Unbelievably, Pineda's expedition had taken twenty-seven days, during which time, the main force had been camped by the swamp, Gonzalo Pizarro says:

…eating nothing but saddles and stirrup leather, sliced, boiled, and toasted over embers, with palm shoots and fruit stems fallen from the trees, together with toads and snakes. For we had by now eaten in this wild country over one thousand dogs and more than one hundred horses, and many of us were sick, and others weak, while some had actually died there of hunger.

The mind boggles at the hellish scene of the camp: the howls of the famished dogs at night, the moans of the sick, the roar of forest insects, the perennial rain, and the flashes of electrical storms which go around the horizon at night in the Napo region, briefly lighting up the darkness. And all for a fantasy – El Dorado.

Heart of Darkness: the Return of Gonzalo Pizarro

AFTER THEY HAD EATEN, Gonzalo Pizarro marshalled his forces, lashed the canoes together, crossed the swamp, and in eight days marched down the Napo to the confluence with the Aguarico. Next came a laborious crossing of the river to the opposite bank, which took a week, ferrying the troops and animals in canoes, during which several horses were drowned. Then, after a ten-day march up the Aguarico, they reached the cassava plantations where they camped for over a week and rested ('after a fashion', Gonzalo Pizarro notes laconically). Again, no relations with natives are reported, but the plantations probably belonged to the ancestors of the Siona-Secoya peoples, who once populated the lands all way down the river. Today, a remnant of these tribes lives higher up the Aguarico.

As we have seen, Gonzalo Pizarro was nothing if not a resourceful leader, but by now he must have been wondering why on earth he had forsaken the riches of Peru for this. Here, after all, was a man who had seen it all. He had seen the golden rooms of the Coricancha in Cuzco, and had trekked to the last city of the Incas in Vilcabamba. These were adventures enough for more than one lifetime, but all that was meaningless now. At stake was simple survival. Unfortunately, the eating binge of the starving men had had a violent reaction upon them. Cassava root, unless cooked properly, is poisonous. Two men died from eating too much of it, and many others became so ill they could not walk, their stomachs agonizingly swollen. Even the healthiest were sick and sore.

After nine days of this, Gonzalo Pizarro realized he had to move on or die. The search for El Dorado was forgotten; the question now was: did they have the strength to keep going? In this totally desperate situation, Gonzalo Pizarro showed his quality of leadership. Those who were too sick to move were lashed to the saddles of the surviving horses, their feet roped together under the horses' bellies, and they rode in agony while their companions hacked a path through the forest on foot.

They then marched for forty leagues (over 120 miles or more), passing signs of cultivation all the way. (The length of the river from its junction with the Napo back to the Andes foothills is about 300 miles, allowing for twists and turns.) Nerves were now so raw that anger flared towards the sick by almost equally tormented men who were well enough to walk and do the hard work. Gonzalo Pizarro tried to encourage them, marching with the rearguard, urging the stragglers on, and giving a hand to the sick.

After eight days, they came to a straggle of small villages, probably populated by the Secoya people, of whom 300 still survive in Ecuador. Remains of their pre-conquest cultures have been excavated on the Aguarico at Zancudo, and it may have been here that Gonzalo Pizarro stopped. Using sign language, the Indians told him that there were no people ahead. He had little idea of which direction to follow – the river takes a much more twisting course than the Napo, but its general direction is to the north-west. He must surely have known that it would eventually lead back to the Andes. They pushed on, sending the resourceful Pineda ahead of them with two canoes, while Gonzalo Pizarro continued upriver on foot.

On this next stage of the march, they guessed they covered fifty-six leagues – nearly 200 miles – and in the pages of Cieza de Leon one can feel the utter desperation of this 'worst march ever in the Indies'. Gonzalo Pizarro himself was now 'very depressed…for he did not know in what land he was, nor what direction to take to reach Peru, or any other part where Christians might be'. The constant diet of cassava continued to make everyone ill with the 'flux' (dysentery). The rain poured down on men clad in rags, and most of them barefoot, as their footwear had long since been worn away or eaten.

The 'magnificent armada' for El Dorado had been reduced to the most basic struggle: a march against death itself, where human beings are stripped of everything but the will to live. In the end, they were cutting pieces of meat from the last living horses and then plastering their wounds with river clay, and letting the horses' blood to make a soup in their helmets with wild herbs and peppers. Gonzalo Pizarro's account is livid with anger:

In the course of this uninhabited stretch of river all the remaining horses, more than eighty of them, were eaten. There were many rivers and creeks of considerable size to be crossed, and there were days on this march when to get two leagues forward a dozen or more bridges had to be built. And there were days when we waded through swamps up to our knees in water, for many stretches up to our waists, and even higher…

▲ Native Indians along the Napo, as portrayed by an early nineteenth-century ethnographer.

Meanwhile, Pineda's party continued upstream, using Indian paddlers. Finally, they were forced to stop and fight off fierce Indian attacks. This skirmish must have taken place in the area of the present-day Cofanes people, on the upper Aguarico, around its junction with the Dureno. The Cofanes, once densely settled around the Andes foothills and into the forest, were badly hit in later times by gold prospectors and, latterly, oilmen. Eventually, using their crossbows and swords, the Spanish drove off their attackers. Pineda cut crosses in the trees to mark the spot, then carried on, rowing through the night rather than risking a halt.

Dawn came without rain – the sky for once bright and clear. And, in the far distance, over to the south-west, Pineda and his weary men saw the faint blue outline of 'a great range of mountains'. The distinctive volcanoes of the 'cordillera of Quito,' Pineda said later, 'or what lies near Popayan and Cali'. They had come out to the north of the Coca river, where the Aguarico comes down from the Andes. They set off once more, and soon came to rapids where, for the 'first time in 300 leagues' (1000 miles), they saw stones. They were not far short of Lumbaqui, about thirty miles before the Andes foothills begin to rise to the Reventador volcano.

Before the crossing of the final pass over the Andes, a comet was seen in the night sky. The next morning Gonzalo Pizarro said that in his dreams he had been attacked by a dragon which had torn out his heart. Jeronimo de Villegas, who was respected in the army as an interpreter of dreams, said it meant 'Pizarro would soon learn of the death of the person nearest to his heart.' What that meant, Gonzalo Pizarro would soon discover.

In June 1542, sixteen months after they had set out, the army staggered back over the Andes. They were emaciated, half-naked skeletons in animal skins, each only with his sword and a walking stick to help him stand. There were eighty men left – less than half of those who had waved Orellana goodbye. It was a miracle that so many had survived 'the worst journey in all Indies'. They had endured as much, perhaps, as it is possible for human beings to take, and still live.

News of their return preceded them and the citizens of Quito came out of the town, hurrying down the steep gorge where the old road winds – 'the way of the conquistadors' – bringing soup, blankets and horses. Keeping up appearances until the bitter end, Gonzalo Pizarro refused the horse, and walked all the way to the gates of Quito.

The Murder of Francisco Pizarro

FOR GONZALO PIZARRO, the expedition had been a disaster: a fortune spent; hopes of El Dorado dashed. But with family riches awaiting him in Peru, the catastrophe was not in itself the end of his ambitions. Potentially fatal, though, was the news he heard when he arrived. Another leader, Castro, had seized Quito and proclaimed himself governor. Worse, 'Don Diego de Almagro, and other persons had murdered the Marquis, my brother, and taken possession of Peru.'

So Francisco Pizarro, the conqueror of Peru, was dead. The interpretation of Gonzalo's nightmare had come true. The man who had survived the Isle of the Gorgon and Cajamarca had been killed by Almagro, the son of his former friend and most important business partner, co-founder of the 'Company of the Levant', which had mounted the early explorations from Panama.

Almagro's father had been a confederate in the conquest of Peru, but Francisco Pizarro had fallen out with him, and eventually captured and executed him. Like a sixteenth-century version of *The Godfather*, the tale had dissolved into a labyrinthine search for revenge which had now crossed the generations.

The Pizarro clan's unrivalled private empire in the New World, which linked their estates in Estremadura and their bankers in Germany and Italy with the silver mines of Bolivia and their *encomiendas* across the Andes from Ecuador to Chile, was about to unravel.

Gonzalo Pizarro rested his aching bones in Quito and tried to recover his shattered health. But his mind was already racing with plans to win back Peru, which had been the family fiefdom, 'in the name of the king'. And, indeed, he did so briefly, in defiance of the king, taking back Peru and ruling there until he was overthrown and beheaded in Cuzco by his enemies. Masterful and cruel, lustful and ruthless, he was, by common consent, the greatest and most charismatic soldier of them all. And of his Amazonian adventure, his contemporary Cieza de Leon wrote:

No other race or nation in history has with such resolution passed through such labours, or such long periods of starvation or traversed such long distances as they have. And in this expedition of Gonzalo Pizarro assuredly very great hardships were endured, for this exploration and conquest by Gonzalo Pizarro, I am bound to say, was the most laborious expedition that has ever been undertaken in these Indies, and in it the Spaniards endured hardships, famine and miseries, which truly tried the virtues of their nation.

MEANWHILE, AS GONZALO PIZARRO STRUGGLED in the swamps of the Napo, Orellana and his fifty men sailed

Orellana Sails On

on in the *San Pedro*. They were now on the main flow of the Amazon, heading eastwards though a vast fluid wilderness. Even today from the air, it is a bewildering maze. The satellite charts used by air pilots are no use here, for the land is so flat, the river so low-lying, that it is forever breaking its banks and shifting its course. The jungle stretches in every direction: huge oxbows, big as rivers, lead nowhere; giant tributaries flow in, bearing the debris of the forest; islands of wreckage swirl past; new lakes glint in the low sun; great floods leave their long brown scars gouged through the green forest.

Nature is unconfined here. Occasionally, you can see tiny clearings dotted with houses on stilts in little plantations of cassava and banana, and the odd boat, like a waterfly, the tiniest dot on a great chocolate-coloured stream. That is how Orellana and his men must have felt. They simply had to follow the main flow, looking on the scene, partly in wonder, partly in terror.

All the way through what is now Peru, the local people responded with kindness to these strangers from another world. Having passed the confluence of the Napo and the Maranon in mid-February 1542, Orellana was now on the Maranon – an immense glassy waterway that sometimes stretched to the horizon, with great islands masking both banks from view. Placid as it might sometimes appear, it is always a perilous river. Fallen trees race by like floating rams, and sometimes, when they become jammed into the river bed, they make deadly obstacles which can smash a boat apart in an instant.

Talking to the native people, Orellana discovered that he was travelling through the lands of a major Indian polity, a confederation of tribes called Aparia. As they were friendly, the Spaniards were able to stop in this region, just below Iquitos, for two months.

The Aparians, it turned out, engaged in long-distance trade and were able to give Orellana useful intelligence about the journey downstream. Their lands, they told him, extended downriver for eighty leagues (250 miles or more), as far as a kingdom called Machiparo. The Machiparos were hostile to the Aparians and it was regarded as certain that they would attack the Spaniards. If that were not disturbing enough, beyond Machiparo was an even bigger federation called Omagua. This news doubtless explains why Orellana gave orders to repair and modify the *San Pedro*, and to build a new bigger ship. Travelling in just the *San Pedro*, an open boat with low freeboard and accompanied by small canoes, they would have stood little chance of resisting serious attacks.

The Aparians, who seem to have been fascinated by their strange visitors, provided them with wood for hull and masts, creepers for rigging, and gum and wild cotton for caulking. Orellana's men made sails from 'Peruvian blankets', and a small hut of palm leaves midship protected the sick from the sun, and the precious supply of gunpowder from the rain. This second major stop on the journey lasted fifty-seven days, from 26 February to 24 April, throughout which the Aparian women provided Orellana and his men with a wide range of local food: fish, fresh-water turtle and forest animals, cooked in the local style with hot peppers.

The second bigger ship was built from the start as a sea-going vessel. Its waterline length was nineteen 'goas', or nearly twenty-four feet, but wide in the beam and with nine thwarts to take eighteen oarsmen. It was named, optimistically, *Victoria*. When all was ready, Orellana abandoned his canoes, left gifts for his hosts, including a Spanish sword for the king of Aparia, and finally set sail with both vessels on 24 April.

OUR OWN JOURNEY HAD TAKEN US by small boats to Francisco Orellana, and then by a little single-decker ferry

The Journey into Brazil

through a tranquil opal dawn into Iquitos. From here, because the Amazon is now a great waterway full of traffic day and night, we would be able to travel on by more regular transport. Iquitos is an astonishing 2000 miles from the sea, but it is the terminus for ocean-going ships, and from the port travellers can pick up a whole variety of boats down to Brazil or up the Maranon into central Peru.

Standing there on the pontoons, I found myself wondering how much long-distance trade existed in the pre-conquest world, at a time when tribal federations along the river knew of each other's existence halfway across Amazonia. Then I recalled Orellana's' surprise at seeing 'Peruvian deer' (llamas) on the lower Amazon. How did they get there, if not by trade? It is easy to believe that – ever since human beings first migrated to the virgin forests here 11,000 years ago –

▼ View from Iquitos, looking over the old course of the Amazon. Orellana spent two months near here with the Aparians.

the river has always been a means of contact. Only after the Europeans came were the native peoples driven from it, by war, exploitation and disease.

What has happened here, in Amazonia, since Orellana's time is a holocaust – and one which has gone almost unrecorded. Today, we think of these societies as primitive, but it would be more accurate to say they are post-holocaust – and part of the tragic power of Orellana's narrative is that he saw them before the fall.

We followed Orellana from Iquitos to the Brazilian border on the good ship *Natalia Carolina*, a small open-decked steamer bringing passengers, supplies and cattle downriver, servicing the small ports of the Maranon – Pevas, Pablo de Loreto, Caballococha. And for me, travelling in Orellana's tracks, the voyage had begun to gather, like static, the history of the intervening 500 years.

During those nights on the *Natalia Carolina,* we sailed with our searchlight flashing over the river, our hammocks swinging on the open deck alongside a hundred or so fellow passengers. Great rafts, like islands, passed in the night – ghostly shapes bearing cattle, wood and produce, which suddenly appeared and disappeared from the beam of our flashlight.

Glimpsing them, it was easy to imagine the Spanish on their precarious boat, travelling through the night, afraid to risk a landing. 'What hardships, what bodily suffering, what extraordinary dangers we passed through,' wrote Father Carvajal. They were now in Machiparo territory – a country 200 to 300 miles long, densely populated, with hardly a gap between the settlements. The biggest, according to Father Carvajal, was huge – consisting of over eighteen miles of houses. On this stretch, they suffered violent attacks. The Indians were openly hostile, and Father Carvajal lost an eye in one attack ('and I suffered agonies from that wound from then on').

For three days and nights, they had to defend themselves with no sleep. As for Orellana himself, he rose to every challenge with cool composure and resourcefulness: 'Too kind-hearted a soul by far', according to his critics, he had learned to speak the river speech, to read the signs, and to negotiate fear – perhaps most of all in himself.

A Forgotten Empire in the Amazon

ON 12 MAY 1542, ORELLANA passed the frontier between the Machiparo and the Omagua empires, and he describes a formal crossing place like any modern border. 'At the entrance of this land,' he says, 'was a garrison village on an elevated spot' – a customs post of the kingdom of Omagua. By now, nerves were frayed. Orellana had launched a pre-emptive attack, and had to fight his way through. Curiously enough, the present-day border of Peru and Brazil is precisely at this spot – perhaps preserving the memory of much more ancient territorial boundaries.

From this region onwards, the Spaniards saw wonderful ceramics in the villages. One place they christened Pueblo de la Loza – 'China Town' or 'Porcelainville' – because of its fine pottery, including hundred-gallon storage jars of fabulous quality and artistry, 'rivalling the best in Spain'. They also describe an organized religious cult: in one shrine house were idols of palm leaves with silver discs on the arms and legs.

Here, Orellana found a wide road going off into the interior, and explored some way inland. But to venture too far away from the reassuring safety of the *San Pedro* and the *Victoria* proved too nerve-racking, and they were soon back on the river, so wide now that they could see only one bank at a time.

The Spanish travelled for several hundred miles through the territory of the federation of the Omagua; and the more they journeyed, the greater was their impression of the scale of the land and the river – a river fed by tributaries which were themselves far larger than anything they had previously imagined. On 29 May, they passed another immense river, coming in from the right, the Jurua. They estimated their position now to be well over 1000 miles from their original camp among the Imara.

All along the river, they saw roads leading off into the interior, and from their account it is clear that this entire part of central Amazonia was densely peopled. The native Indian people are gone. A population estimated at three or four million in 1542 now stands at 240,000 surviving indigenous people, and you have to go well away from the river, into the hinterland, to find them – the last remnants of our old selves.

On Saturday the eve of Holy Trinity [says Orellana's diary] we saw the mouth of another great river on the left, the water black as ink; for which reason we called it the River Negro… The current so big and strong that for sixty miles it forms a long black streak through the other river and the waters do not mix.

It was 3 June 1542. The black sediment-rich water of this river, one of the most remarkable spectacles in nature, still separates itself from the brown flow of the Amazon; and it is still called the Negro.

DURING EARLY JUNE, Orellana moved down the main stream, eastwards from the junction with the Negro. Allowing for the river's twists and turns, they guessed they had gone about 1000 leagues (over 3000 miles) from El Barco (a pardonable over-estimate).

On 13 June, Orellana passed the mouth of another

To the Sea

▸ Overleaf: On the ill-starred return to 'his' river, Orellana 'couldn't find his way into the main channel…and became infallibly lost'. This aerial view of part of the Amazon mouth shows why.

huge river which he called Madeira – 'river of wood' – after the immense islands of floating timber that kept passing them by. Then they entered a more temperate region, where the landscape began to change from the interminable jungle they had observed so far. To the left, low heights began to open out, then hills, and reddish cliffs. Where this starts to happen – fifty miles beyond the Madeira – is still over 500 miles from the sea, but they began to get their first intimations of the presence of Europeans. The native people hereabouts said they had heard of white-skinned ones living in the hinterland – and this may have been true. They could have been survivors of the expedition of Diego Ordaz, who had investigated the mouths of the Amazon ten years before and lost one of his ships with a large number of people, including women, on board.

In the lower Amazon were countless villages whose populations grew maize, cassava and cane. These peoples knew of the depredations of the Europeans on the coast, and Orellana's men had to fight all the way – sometimes nightmarish battles against poisoned arrows. Among these battles was one on 24 June, which everyone had cause to remember. They were attacked by natives, including a dozen pale-skinned women with braided hair, who were experts with long bows and copper-tipped arrows. Real-life Amazons, if we are to believe the diary of the expedition.

Badly shaken, they made camp close to the Tapajoz river to make repairs to the *San Pedro* and heighten its bulwarks as a protection against arrows. They were living now on herons, iguanas, monkeys, sloths and fish. And here, for the first time, they noticed the rise and fall of the tide, although – amazingly – they were still 300 miles from the sea. Their hopes raised, they sailed on. Then, on the left bank, they saw a line of flat-topped blue hills. This was the Serra de Almeirim, which rises about 800 feet above the river and runs for ninety miles along its north bank.

By now, they had lost all sense of the distance they had covered, reckoning they had gone 1600 leagues (about 5000 miles) since the split with Gonzalo Pizarro. At last, they passed into the labyrinth of islands in the Amazon mouth. The sea was near now, and they had to give thought to what they would do when they reached it. They may have got all the way down the great river – but how could they get home?

Starvation Island

ORELLANA'S HOPES OF SURVIVAL now centred on getting to the nearest Spanish settlements in the Caribbean, on the islands of Cubagua and Margarita, near Trinidad – a daunting 1200-mile journey across open sea. So their first task was to completely rebuild and replank the *San Pedro*, which was coming apart at the seams.

To do this, they forged a new set of iron nails from surviving bits of metal, using an improvised forge and charcoal. One never ceases to be amazed by their resourcefulness. It took them eighteen days to replank the boat, make the new metal fittings and rig them. Using grease and tattered bits of cloth, they made their own caulking, too, working on past the sunset when the fireflies come out on the sandbanks, and the scent of the trees wafts on the breeze.

It was early August, and, knowing the sea to be near, they searched for a place to beach the bigger brigantine. On the shore of a large island, they found a place where they could haul the *Victoria* out of the water. Both vessels needed to be completely re-rigged for the long sea voyage and to withstand the heavy weather they were likely to encounter.

This they did between 6 and 20 August, using tree vines and palm-fibre rope for the rigging; making proper masts, sails, rudders and spars; stripping off the arrow-proof bulwarks; planking in decks, and recaulking. Anchors were improvised out of hardwood, with stone and metal tips. Two bilge pumps were made out of hollowed sections of tree trunk, with plungers sealed with grease and old leather. During this fortnight, they were in desperate straits, eating only edible snails and the reddish crabs which live at tide level. They called the place Starvation Island.

So they readied themselves for the open sea, with no real knowledge of how to succeed in the journey. As Father Carvajal said:

I am leaving out many other things we lacked, such as pilots and sailors and a compass, which are necessary things, for without any one of them there is no one, however devoid of common sense, that would dare to set sail on the open sea, except ourselves – to whom this long and winding voyage came by accident and not by our will.

AT LONG LAST, ON SATURDAY, 26 AUGUST 1542, they left the river, probably to the north of the big island of ## The Journey Home

Marajo. After eight months on the river, Orellana and his men finally reached the open sea. Their adventures, however, were not over. They now had a 1200-mile sea journey in homemade boats. Three days later, they ran into bad weather and heavy seas, and the vessels were separated. Both crews assumed the others had perished.

In fact, the *San Pedro*, having been washed further out to sea, rounded Trinidad, and made it to Cubagua on 9 September. Relief at their survival was mixed with grief that, after all they had gone through, the other boat had been lost. But on 11 September, Orellana and the *Victoria* limped into the port of New

Cadiz, having been drawn into the Gulf of Paria behind Trinidad. Forty-seven members of the original expedition were still alive.

'So great was the joy we felt, the ones at the sight of the others, that I shall not be able to express it, because they believed us lost, and we thought the same of them.' It had been 'less of a journey,' said one of them, 'more of a miracle…'

Aftermath

SO ENDED 'AN EXPERIENCE which had been entered on unintentionally, but which turned out to be so extraordinary that it is one of the greatest things that ever happened to men…' So said Oviedo, who spoke to many of the survivors. But it is strange to reflect that when Orellana returned to Spain, he was by no means feted as a hero. For a start, there were those who disputed the usefulness of his discovery. The mouth of the river was in Portuguese territory – the wrong side of the line marked by the Pope at the Treaty of Tordesillas. What good, then, would this discovery of the great river do for Spain?

Also, Orellana still had Gonzalo Pizarro to contend with, and he was a man with wide and powerful connections. In Pizarro's eyes, Orellana was the man who had deserted his commander and left him to die on the great river, 'the worst traitor that ever lived'.

Even before he received the news that Orellana had survived, Gonzalo Pizarro had no doubts that Orellana had deserted him. Orellana had passed out of the Amazon into the Atlantic at the end of August, his boats making amazing speed to reach Cubagua in little over two weeks by 11 September. But Gonzalo Pizarro wrote his account to the king (which we have followed in this story) from Cuenca, in Ecuador, on 3 September 1542, while Orellana was still at sea. So he cannot yet have known that Orellana had pulled through.

During the next few months, the news of Orellana's survival went to Spain, and also from Cubagua to Panama and down to Peru. Before the end of the year, Gonzalo Pizarro knew for sure that Orellana was alive. But, despite his extreme bitterness towards Orellana, he had bigger fish to fry – his mind racing with plans to win back Peru. After all, had it not been his family, his brother Francisco, who, with his own labours and money, had opened up Peru for the Spanish crown?

▼ The sum of knowledge after Orellana's epic voyage. Part of a world map of 1584 showing the river and marking boldly the presence of 'Amazons'.

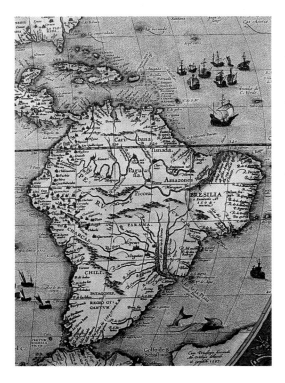

▲ Seventeenth-century painting of the Tapuya people of north-eastern Brazil: they were among the tribes who attacked Orellana near the mouth of the river during the summer of 1542, well aware by then of what the coming of the white man would mean.

Gonzlo Pizarro invaded Peru and expelled the first royal viceroy in October 1544. This civil war continued until he defeated and killed the viceroy in October 1547, only to be overthrown himself in 1548 and executed by his enemies.

Few people since have had much sympathy for Gonzalo Pizarro but, like Orellana, with whom his name will always be linked, he is still remembered along the Amazon – although Orellana, it has to be said, has come off best. Indeed, for a time, the river itself was named the Orellana river – until the myth of the warrior women overshadowed the more prosaic facts of Captain Orellana's voyage, and it became known as the River of the Amazons, as it still is today.

The Fate of Orellana

SO ORELLANA CAME HOME TO TRUJILLO, back to the house which still stands in the Street of Doves, close to the church of Santa Maria where his neighbours, the Pizarros, worshipped and are buried. You go through a medieval doorway, through the hallway, with its fireplace carved with knights, and out into the garden. From the terrace, there is a wonderful view to the west over the city's watchtowers. There is an old vine on the garden wall, roses and sweet-smelling gardenias, an orange tree and a cypress – and, under the old date palm, there is a piece of Roman stone. How good it must have felt to be back.

But, three years later, after all he had gone through (and having cleared his name), Orellana returned to his river, now accompanied by his young wife, Ana, a

teenage girl from a well-to-do family, whom he married before setting out on his last journey. Why did he go back? Did the Spaniards not think him a hero? In a town like Trujillo, endurance and survival were perhaps not enough. One had to be a conquistador – not just a discoverer but a conqueror.

Orellana's second Amazon expedition was as dogged by disaster as his first was marked by courage and skill. Even before he left Seville, it was whispered that Orellana was no leader; that he did not know how to organize such an expedition; that he had no real capacity for command. In response to all the rumours, the government's Office of the Indies set a spy on him, who reported administrative chaos, and a man, in his memorable phrase – 'too kind-hearted by far'.

Eventually, Orellana set sail to the Canaries with 400 men and a royal licence to be governor of the Amazon. On the coast of Brazil, disaster struck. One of his ships was wrecked and others ran aground. The starving survivors ended up pumping day and night to save themselves. Orellana had hoped to lead them back to the main channel through which he had passed after leaving the rich and fertile lands of the lower river, the lands of the Amazons. But, irony of ironies, approaching it from a different direction, he could not find his river.

After months of confusion, he became 'infallibly lost' in the innumerable islands and channels of the river mouth, 'without hope of any news of us ever being heard by the outside world'. Most of the expedition were never seen again, and there, abandoned and alone, Orellana died. The story, such as we have it, came from survivors who met Orellana's young wife on Margarita Island, Venezuela:

She it was who told us that her husband had not succeeded in getting into the main branch of the river which he was looking for, and that as a result of this, and especially as he was ill, he had made up his mind to withdraw to Spanish territory; and that during this time when he was out looking for food the Indians shot seventeen of his men with arrows. For grief over this, and from his illness, Orellana had died somewhere up the river.

Fitting, perhaps, that Orellana should have found a nameless grave, under some great tree by the banks of the river, which for a time bore his name.

The Meaning of Orellana's Journey

YEARS LATER, ORELLANA'S WIDOW, ANA DE AYALA, recalled the nightmare of the expedition's disintegration. In particular, she remembered the constant 'heavy rainfall', at one point adding in explanation to the court that 'in that country, you see, there are a great many heavy rainfalls'. In that reiteration of the rain, one senses the ache of an old bruise – the memory of the torrential downpour on the forest canopy, the lashing of the river so fierce that land, sky and water turn into the same uniform brown; the drenching of clothes which never dry. She continues:

*Everyone had endured great suffering because of our hunger and the illnesses...
we reached the point when we had eaten all the horses and dogs, and for a period
of eleven months 'we wandered about like lost men in the region of the said river,
during which time the greater part of the expedition had died...among them my
husband.*

So, what was it that drew Orellana back? Was it the myth of El Dorado, with its promise of untold wealth? How did he finally understand the world he had passed through? With such questions we seek meanings from these tales. Mexicans in their art, literature, film and theatre have argued about Cortes for 400 years. In Peru, people of Indian descent still act out the meeting of the Inca Atahuallpa and Francisco Pizarro every year in their folk plays – gingerly touching the scar which still aches below the surface. Cabeza de Vaca's journey has become a metaphor for our response to the Other. So what is the meaning of Orellana's journey?

Orellana's journey has always been portrayed as an epic of exploration, and as a triumph of indomitable human will. But now, nearly 500 years on, his odyssey has begun to take on the burden of a symbolic journey: the entry of a white European conquistador into the primal wilderness of the imagination, into the vast green heartland of the last naked unaccommodated humans.

Through Father Carvajal's diary, at a dreamlike pace, we watch the first act of the tragedy of Natural Man, who is portrayed in all his mythic facets, from most savage to most kind, from cannibal to Amazon, to a denizen of an Amerindian Eden. All meanings are there, on both sides, for colonialists and for indigenous people alike. The setting is the theatre of untrammelled nature. At stake is the destruction of primal nature and the final extermination of the first people.

As the holocaust of the Amazonian people draws to its end, and the catastrophe in nature moves to its climax, this is perhaps what gives Orellana's journey of 1542 its peculiar imaginative power. The one-eyed captain is an ancient mariner; an Ahab whose Pacific is the emerald forest. We would like to see him as our conscience, and regard Gonzalo Pizarro as his destructive *alter ego*, but our sources do not allow such simple comforting solutions. Orellana, one suspects, was – and remained – a conquistador.

And yet, something drew him back. In the end, did he perhaps realize that in the landscapes he passed through, in the teeming fecundity of the forests, in the people he had stayed with, whose languages he had learned, he had, after all, touched El Dorado?

6
THE ADVENTURE
OF CABEZA DE VACA

THE STORIES OF THE CONQUEST told in this book –
Cortes, the Pizarros, Orellana – are tales of heroism and
endurance, but also of immeasurable greed and staggering brutality. This final tale of the Conquest, although
another epic journey, is a narrative of a very different
character, and its protagonist, Cabeza de Vaca, is a
different kind of hero.

The story of Cabeza de Vaca made little impact in
the sixteenth century – although his book the *Relacion*
(later retitled by an eighteenth-century editor as
Naufragios – Shipwrecks), was read by a number of
famous writers and polemicists. But today his tale has
become a parable. The earliest great work of literature
about America, this is also the first historical text for the
peoples of the southern United States and northern
Mexico. It is a tale with all the power of a myth – *The
Tempest* and *King Lear* rolled into one – a tale of
redemption in which the conquistador becomes a
'naked unaccommodated man' and discovers something
about himself, and about the Other. Above all, it is
simply an astonishing story.

*Tired out and in tears, I fell
asleep and heard a very compassionate
voice saying, 'O fool, slow to believe
and serve your God, the God of all.
What more did He do for Moses,
or David his servant, than He has
done for you? He gave you the
Indies which are so rich a part of
the world...and to all the barriers
of the Ocean seas, which were
closed with such a strong chain,
He gave you the key...'*

•

CHRISTOPHER COLUMBUS *Letter to the King and
Queen of Spain*, 7 July 1503

On the Isle of Misfortune

IT IS NOVEMBER 1528: a wide, flat shore, lashed by gales
and sleeting rain, a great ink-dark bank of cloud masks
the dawn. The sea is grey and bitterly cold. In the swell, a group of shipwrecked
sailors try to relaunch their boat – soaking, freezing, naked men, no strength left
in their limbs, struggling even to stand. They have already survived a terrible
journey in open boats all the way from Florida. Unbeknown to them, most
members of their expedition have already drowned: of 300 men, only four in the
end will survive.

At this moment, the handful left are all but dead and their landfall here is their
last hope. During the night they heard the roar of breaking surf and dropped a

◄ The encounter with the Other: Europeans in Florida in the sixteenth century.

plumb line, which gave them seven fathoms. They guessed they were about five or six miles from land, but, fearing to try to land in the dark, they kept offshore all night, numb with hunger, shuddering with cold, scarcely able to hold on to their oars. And so, grimly hanging on to their lives, they waited for dawn.

As the light lifted, they came in, but their boat overturned in the violence of the tide. Washed up on a desolate shore never before seen by Europeans, they were ready to abandon all hope, but in the morning human beings appeared, Indians of the island, who took pity on them. Although among the poorest inhabitants of the Americas – people who lived on roots, oysters and fish – the Indians made a fire and shared their food with the shipwrecked men. With a little strength restored, the lost men then tried to sail on:

We were in such a sorry plight that any effort exhausted us, but we launched a boat, and we were two crossbow shots out when there came a huge wave, so huge it soaked us all, and as we were naked and the cold was so great, we could not hold onto the oars, and a second wave overturned the boat. Three men clung onto it to escape death, but quite the opposite happened for they were carried under and drowned …The rest of us escaped as naked as the day we were born and lost all we had with us, which though not much was everything to us at that moment. By then it was November, and the cold was very great, and we were in such a plight that you could have counted our bones with no difficulty. And we looked the very image of death… And the north wind began to blow and we were closer to death than life… But as we searched the embers of the fire we had made, we were able to start a fire and make a great bonfire, and each of us shed many tears, bewailing his own plight and his companions. And at the hour of dusk the Indians came looking for us…and when they saw the disaster which had come upon us, and the depths we were in of trouble and misery, they sat down among us, and with the grief and great pity they felt for us, all of them began to cry… And to see those uncivilized and savage men, like brutes, were so sorry for us, caused me and others in our company to feel even deeper grief, and to fully understand the nature of our misfortune…

It is the opening of a parable and the beginning of an odyssey which ended on the shore of the Pacific eight years later. The narrator is a Spanish conquistador, Alvar Nunez Cabeza de Vaca. The scene is probably Galveston Island off the shore of Texas ('which we called the Isle of Misfortune').

That autumn, as they sailed south from Florida, the prevailing winds and currents round the Gulf had taken them down towards the Texas coast. But, at that time of year, northerlies can come off the land without warning – November storms which are well known to all old salts on the windy Atlantic shore of the

island ('Blue Westers', as they call them). Wild gales suddenly pile their dark thunderheads over the Gulf of Mexico and break along the strands with unpredictable violence. This was what engulfed the remnants of Cabeza de Vaca's expedition.

Even now, on a bleak November day, it needs little imagination to see the scene: the amusement arcades are closed, the rain lashing the ferry to the mainland, surf surging along the old breakwaters and thrashing the old legs of the piers. On the wide sandy beach, surfers struggle on their boards in all weathers, recalling the Spaniards who staggered out of the sea all those years before.

In the middle of the island, past the rainswept golf courses and weathered clapboard holiday houses, you can still see two little copses of live oaks shaking in the gale. They are one of those wonderfully precise topographical clues that we so often stumble on in these tales, for these copses are marked on the earliest maps of the island, 200 years ago – one of them at a lonely spot called Ekhert's Bayou. Here, archaeologists have found scant remains of the Indian camp where the Spanish must have stayed, and where one of Cabeza de Vaca's friends climbed into a tall oak to discover that where they had landed was indeed an island.

We are on the edge of the United States here, and this journey will skirt the world of modern America, keeping out of sight of its skyscrapers and shopping malls, away from the ordered mainstream reality of today, and entering an older world, physically and mentally, which was seen for the first time by Cabeza de Vaca.

The Expedition to Florida

THE EXPEDITION HAD BEGUN with a landfall the previous April, 1528, in Florida. It is story of greed, arrogance and incompetence. Its leader, Panfilo de Narvaez, was the one-eyed leader outwitted by Cortes at Zempoala eight years before (see page 69). Narvaez had recovered from his humiliation, and eventually got himself a royal commission, a licence to explore 'Florida' (a name that then covered the whole south-eastern part of the modern USA). His hope was to find another civilization, another source of gold and silver as rich as Mexico or Peru. That spring he led 400 conquistadors ashore on the coast near Tampa Bay.

From the start, Cabeza de Vaca – who was treasurer or accountant of the forces – did not see eye to eye with Narvaez, and the expedition became compromised by failures of leadership. After a dispute between them, Narvaez divided the army and led about 300 men up the peninsula, moving northwards, parallel to the Florida coast, but some way inland. It is a harsh landscape, full of swamps and plagued with poisonous snakes and mosquitoes. Progress was slow and difficult and Narvaez failed to make his rendezvous with the remainder of his force, which sailed up the coast and, eventually giving him up for lost, headed back to Cuba.

▲ The west coast of Florida, where the Spanish hoped that the forbidding mangrove swamps concealed places as rich as Peru.

During the stifling Florida summer, they made their way up from Tampa Bay towards northern Florida, near the present city of Tallahassee, where remains of a large Spanish camp have been excavated. By now, they were thoroughly demoralized and worn down by disease. Narvaez came down to the sea at Pensacola Bay. There he decided to build five barges to try to escape to Mexico.

After terrible suffering, Narvaez's men launched their flimsy boats in late September and set off south, but they had no charts, no instruments, and no means of fighting the northerlies blowing off the Mississippi coast. The five boats were separated by bad weather and strong currents, and most of the 300 – along with Narvaez himself – were never seen again. Fewer than a hundred survivors were washed up on the Texas shore, on the Isle of Misfortune.

CABEZA DE VACA SAYS THE ISLAND was five leagues long ## *The People of the Island*
by half a league wide – that is, fifteen to twenty miles
long by nearly two miles wide – just right for Galveston Island. Here, Cabeza de
Vaca spent his first winter. The survivors, who passed the winter in two or three
groups, were soon reduced to fifteen men. One party lived on the beach, but the
weather was so bad that they began to starve to death, 'and the five Christians
encamped on the beach,' says Cabeza de Vaca, 'came to such straits that they ate
one another until only one was left. This one only survived because there was no
one left to eat him.'

This is one of those rare moment in Spanish narratives when cannibalism is
admitted. Crucially, Cabeza de Vaca also tells us that 'the Indians were so indig-
nant about this, there was such outrage among them, that had they seen it when it
happened they would surely have killed the men and the rest of us would have
been in dire peril'. The Indians would rather die of starvation than eat a fellow
human being.

The tale is typical of the almost novelistic technique of Cabeza de Vaca's narrative. In it, the conventional roles are reversed – and Indian values are allowed to
comment on those of the Europeans. The first point, though, as related at the start
of this chapter, was the crucial one: 'barbarians felt for me' – the natives had taken
pity on him. It was Cabeza de Vaca's first lesson about the Other.

So, he settled down to live in conditions of (to a European) extreme adversity,
with a community or extended kin of 400 to 500 people. He tells us a lot about
them in passing: their burial rites, for example (they had a one-year mourning
period and ordinary people were buried, only the shamans cremated); their marriage customs; and their beliefs about raising children. On marriage, in particular,
he has much to say, and one wonders whether he had an Indian wife but omitted
to mention this for his Spanish audience.

The Indians, he tells us, were transhumant. They lived on the island seasonally
from October to the end of February. The weather is not good then, but this is the
oyster season along the coast and, although exposed to gales, they could survive
the winter better here than in the barren interior. The people, he says, were 'tall
and handsome', and skilled at bows and arrows. And 'it is the women who do the
hard work'. (He is careful to observe women's work, customs, appearance, throughout his journey – another possible pointer to his intimacy with Indian women.)

Cabeza de Vaca began to share the Indians' lives and to learn important things
about their beliefs and attitudes:

*Of all the people on earth, they are the ones who love their children most and
give them the best treatment; and when it happens that they lose a child, the*

parents and kinsfolk and the whole tribe weep for him, and their lamentation lasts for one year…

Who were they? There are no Native Americans on the coast of Texas today, or anywhere nearby. Their name, though, we know. They were Karankawas, a people last recorded in the late eighteenth and early nineteenth centuries, after which they were finally wiped out by disease and maltreatment. They left no survivors but, in the later nineteenth century, an old lady of Galveston, of part-Karankawa descent, was able to record a word-list of the Karankawa language (some of which match the words that Cabeza de Vaca gives us) – a tenuous link down almost to our day.

In 1992, a Karankawa cemetery was found on the island in the path of a real-estate development. The excavation of their graves and a camp nearby has enabled us finally to discover something about their lost history, not only through Cabeza de Vaca's text but through their own intimate material remains.

Archaeologists from the University of Texas found the settlement at a place called Mitchell Ridge. It had been intensively occupied by a seasonal population, from about AD 800, on a low ridge only 12 feet above the sea. Interestingly enough, of the two ancient clumps of oaks recorded in the early nineteenth century, one at Oak Bayou was near the camp, and perhaps this is where Cabeza de Vaca's companion climbed up to discover the shape of the island.

The camp where Cabeza de Vaca lived stood close to the sheltered salt lagoon on the landward side of the island at the little creek of Ekhert's Bayou. Here, the people lived a very basic life, hunting, killing white-tailed deer, fishing and gathering oysters. Cabeza de Vaca mentions that they also harvested the nutty tubers of a hardy reed that grew with its roots in the water: 'some roots resembling nuts, some larger, some smaller, which they eat that are gathered under water and with much effort'. (These are known locally as 'swamp potatoes' – which may not sound particularly appetizing, but they are a source of protein and are not bad tasting, although, as Cabeza de Vaca clearly remembered, their sharp spikes can lacerate your hands as you feel for them under water.)

So Cabeza de Vaca began to learn the Karankawa language and now, separated from all his companions, settled down to the routine of his adopted clan of hunter-gathers. They would come to the island in the October oyster season, and pass the winter on the island in simple huts covered with reed mats. At the end of February, they would cross the lagoon in canoes, and go inland to gather berries and nuts, and to hunt.

Their grave goods show us the sum of their material culture in intimate detail: glass beads, shell-bead necklaces, a bird-bone whistle, pebble rattles, conch-shell bracelets, sharks' teeth – all of these treasured objects. Such was the poor level of

culture that Cabeza de Vaca experienced. Their life was a far cry from the courtly magnificence of Cuzco or Tenochtitlan, and almost incomprehensibly harsh to a Christian gentleman from Spain. But, as he says: 'They were a very generous people, sharing whatever they own with others…'

WHAT CABEZA DE VACA CHOOSES TO RECORD of his adventures – and what he does not say – constitutes the

The Spanish Become Healers

great riddle of his text. But in one area, though, he allows us a detailed glance. It was first of all on the island 'that the Indians tried to make us into medicine men or healers'. This moment is one of the inciting incidents in his inner journey: a key part of the process by which Cabeza de Vaca came to see things the Indian way, although it was obviously understood by him in Christian terms as he shaped his remarkable story into a book eight years later:

It was on that island that they tried to make us into medicine men, without examin-ing us or asking for our credentials: for they cure illnesses by blowing on the sick person, and by blowing, and use of their hands, they cast the illness out of him; and they ordered us to do the same and to be of some use. We laughed at it, saying it was a joke, and that we did not know how to heal, and because of this they stopped giving us food, until we did as they had told us. And seeing our resistance, one Indian said to me that I did not know what I was talking about when I said that his knowledge would be no use to me – for [he said] stones and other things that grow in the fields have virtue, and by using a hot stone and passing it over the stomach he could take away pain; and we, who were superior men, surely had greater virtue and power than that.

It is, of course, a fantastic moment in this encounter with the Other. Like those first exchanges on the shore of Peru (told on page 119), this is another conversa-tion in which the 500 years separating us are simply erased: 'At last we were under such pressure that we had to do it, without fear that we would be held up to scorn for it …' (Remember that Cabeza de Vaca is excusing himself here to his readers in Spain, many years later.)

He then goes on to describe the Indian methods of healing, including not only their rituals, but also their practical medical interventions, such as cutting (with a sharpened bone or shell blade) and simple forms of cauterization by fire, 'which I have tried with good results,' he adds. He continues:

The way we cured was by making the sign of the cross over them, and blowing on them, and reciting a Pater Noster and an Ave Maria; and then we would pray as best

we could to God our Lord to give them health and inspire them to give us good treatment. And God our Lord, and His mercy, willed that as soon as we had done this, all those for whom we had prayed, told the others that they were well and healthy...

So the themes of the odyssey of Cabeza de Vaca are laid out. The poor Karankawas on the Isle of Misfortune give us the signs by which we are meant to read the inner map of the tale – the journey that Cabeza de Vaca made to encounter and understand what it is like to be the Other. Such stories of healing happen too often in his accounts for us to disbelieve them – indeed, as we shall see, they are attested independently by four or five widely separated testimonies recounted by Indians to other Spanish expeditions over the next twenty years. No question, then, that these things happened. As for their meaning, this no doubt lies in the realms of the psychology of healing – and of belief. As far as we know, during his years on or near the Texas coast, Cabeza de Vaca remained a Christian – at least, that is how he presents the story. As far as the Indians were concerned, of course, to separate the world of spirits and the world of perceptible reality was not a meaningful division. The hidden world for them – as it still is for many surviving Native American peoples – is palpable and always liable to break in on the present. For them, the spiritual life *is* life, and everything in the waking world is conditioned by it. To them, it was quite natural that a receptive person such as Cabeza de Vaca might be able to heal, and hence they asked him to do so.

At first, the Spaniard says he does not know how, and uses his Christian techniques of prayer in a true believer's way. It was the beginning of a long, strange and fruitful intermingling of Christian and indigenous religion in these parts. The tale, then, is extraordinary, but neither unnatural nor unbelievable. And it is noteworthy that, at the very end of his account, recollecting these events in the tranquillity of Spain, Cabeza de Vaca – as if in rebuke to those who wrote about Indian 'idolatry' – says simply, that 'in all the thousands of leagues I travelled, I never saw idolatry: for there is none among the Indians'. It is one of the most astonishing statements made by a European in the entire Age of Discovery.

Cabeza de Vaca could now speak the Karankawas' language and began to reconcile himself to a life among the Indians, far away from the Christian world. In the early days he was kept as a slave, working for his hosts. In the spring, he collected birds' eggs on the shore; sometimes he crossed to the mainland to kill a few deer or buffalo, saving the skins for clothing. Eventually, though, he could face their cruel existence no longer, and used his knowledge of their contacts to leave the island and move into the interior where the people treated him more kindly. For the next few years he lived among semi-nomadic Coahuiltecan Indians, trading for them, bartering seashells and coral with the people of the coast.

THESE SUMMER JOURNEYS, he says, took him up to *In the Interior*
100–150 miles into the interior, on ancient trails which
led as far north as Austin, an old Indian crossing place on the Colorado river.
During all this time he worked and lived as an Indian, but studiously avoids all
mention in his book of any relationships with native women. Of course, he would
not have been the first European to marry an Indian: the conquistador Guerrero,
for example, married a Mayan woman in the Yucatan and never rejoined the
Spaniards, even when he had the chance. But what is unique about Cabeza de
Vaca is that he wrote an account of his life with the Indians.

Cabeza de Vaca's journeys into the interior must have led him up past
Houston towards San Antonio and along the San Antonio river where, in the
eighteenth century, the Spanish would later build a string of missions in picturesque locations along the valley. This was the Indian culture that he came to know
the best.

His text mentions many peoples in this hinterland: the main grouping being
the Coahuiltecans, and these he knew well enough to distinguish ten separate
tribes among them. These people lived widely scattered between the coast of
Texas, the Brazos river and the Rio Grande, ranging far inland in the summer in
search of the cacti and fruit that were abundant around the river valleys of the
interior. They lived at the most basic level of subsistence, engaged in communal
hunts for reptiles and insects, and occasionally larger animals; they were incredibly
hardy and, despite the rigours of the climate, went completely naked.

Cabeza de Vaca describes many of their customs, including their use of the
mesquite bean and their preparation of hallucinogens with the peyote mushroom
in their ceremonies. They were archaic, semi-nomadic clans, a patriarchal culture,
which knew little of agriculture and pottery, and which had only simple tools and
cooking implements. When they travelled, they carried their huts on their backs,
rolled up as mats.

Like the Karankawas the Coahuiltecans disappeared as a group before the end
of the eighteenth century, and they are often said to be gone now. But on our
journey northwards from Galveston to the San Antonio river, we made contact
with scattered Indian groups who still claim to represent the Coahuiltecan nation.
One evening we came down to the San Juan mission at a lovely spot in the river
valley. There a ceremony of reburial was being prepared for the bones of the long
dead Coahuiltecan Indian workforce of the mission. That night, as the sun set, the
communal meal was cooking and the fires were lit in the 'sweat lodges' where the
men would chant all night. In the tepee an altar of ash was carefully marked out
beside the carefully wrapped bones. Fragile links were still maintained with the
ancestors Cabeza de Vaca came to know so well.

The Walk to the Pacific AFTER FIVE YEARS OF TRAVELLING, criss-crossing old Texas routes, living with his Coahuiltecan friends, Cabeza de Vaca had probably given up hope of returning to his world. He had learned what it was like to be the Other. Then, amazingly, one spring day, he learned that three other survivors of the tempest were alive and living a short way down the coast. They met: Dorantes; the doctor's son, Castillo; and Estevanico, a resourceful black man – a Moor from Morocco. Each in his way had something special; Estevanico, in particular, even before the expedition, was already the Other. A black person in Spanish society knew how to be that.

This meeting must have been disturbing for Cabeza de Vaca, who had survived alone, cut off from all outside contact, from all that had been familiar in his active life and own thoughts. Maybe he had ceased to think in Spanish. (When de Soto's expedition met Ortiz, a fifth survivor of this expedition, some five years later, they say it took him some days to be able to speak again, that at first he had larded his words with Indian words; he had literally 'forgotten how to speak'.) Perhaps Cabeza de Vaca and his friends experienced the same problem, but once reunited, they decided to make a break for 'home': to escape to Mexico.

They planned to head for Panuco, a place that they knew was to the south on the coast of the Gulf of Mexico (it had been founded by Cortes in 1526). So they parted with their Indian friends and began the long walk south along the Texas shore. Their route has been the subject of controversy for over a century now, especially among Texas nationalists (who would like as much of it as possible to be in Texas). But the path taken by this first exploration of the interior of what would become the United States, and the first crossing to the Pacific, has recently become clearer. When we set out in their footsteps, we hoped to clarify it further.

They walked parallel to the coast, skirting the lagoons of Matagorda Bay and Corpus Christi, where they saw immense stands of prickly pear, high as a horse. Then they cut inland down to the Rio Grande. The crossing place, says Cabeza de Vaca, was where the river was 'as wide as the bridge of the Guadalquivir at Seville' (nearly 700 feet in their day). So Cabeza de Vaca and his friends crossed the Rio Grande not, as has been claimed, where it is a small stream in upper Texas, but low down its course, not far from the sea.

After the Rio Grande they walked across the river plain on the old Indian trail which leads through Cerralvo, where a century later their feats of healing were still remembered by local people. Then, as Cabeza de Vaca describes, a great massif of mountains began to appear in front of them. This was the Sierra Madre, which rises as dramatic jagged-toothed peaks to 12,000 feet, right out of the plain of Monterrey. In the still blue air of the early morning, it is a tremendous sight,

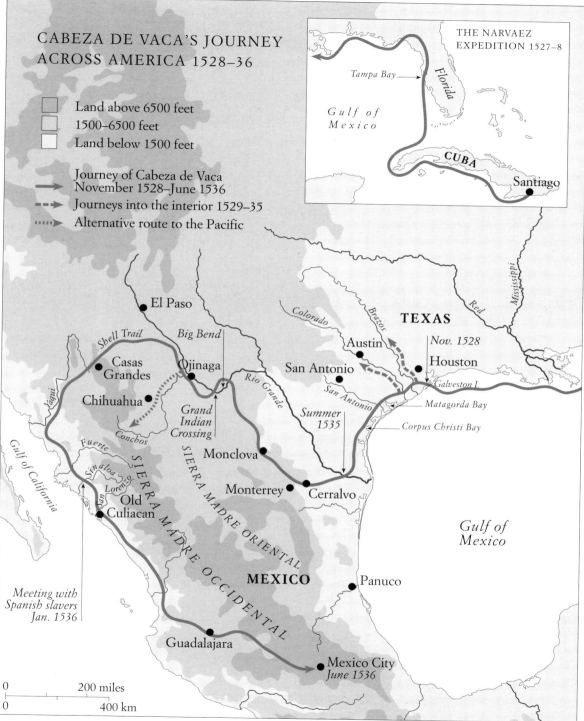

CABEZA DE VACA'S JOURNEY ACROSS AMERICA 1528–36

Land above 6500 feet
1500–6500 feet
Land below 1500 feet

Journey of Cabeza de Vaca
November 1528–June 1536
Journeys into the interior 1529–35
Alternative route to the Pacific

THE NARVAEZ
EXPEDITION 1527–8

Tampa Bay

Florida

*Gulf of
Mexico*

CUBA

Santiago

El Paso

Colorado

Brazos

TEXAS

Red

Mississippi

Shell Trail

Big Bend

Austin

Nov. 1528

Houston

Casas
Grandes

Ojinaga

San Antonio

Galveston I.

Chihuahua

Rio Grande

San Antonio

Matagorda Bay

Conchos

*Grand
Indian
Crossing*

*Summer
1535*

Corpus Christi Bay

Yaqui

Fuerte

Monclova

Sinaloa

SIERRA MADRE ORIENTAL

Lorenzo

Monterrey

Cerralvo

Gulf of California

San Juan

Old
Culiacan

SIERRA MADRE OCCIDENTAL

*Gulf of
Mexico*

*Meeting with
Spanish slavers
Jan. 1536*

MEXICO

Panuco

Guadalajara

Mexico City
June 1536

0   200 miles
0   400 km

▲ The saw-toothed ranges of the Sierra Madre, the landscape through which Cabeza de Vaca and his friends walked in the summer of 1535.

presenting a great wall to anyone coming from Texas and the American south-east into the mountainous uplands of northern Mexico.

You cannot go straight ahead here, but must either turn south to the sea, or north into the interior. The obvious thing to do was to go along the coast, but local Indians told Cabeza de Vaca that under no circumstances should he do this. The tribes between them and the nearest Spanish territories were so hostile to whites that it was virtually certain they would be killed. That news was enough for the little group, and they turned northwards in the lea of the mountains. They would try to cross to the Pacific and make their way back to Mexico City. Although they did not know it, it was a journey of over 2000 miles.

THEIR ROUTE HAS LONG BEEN A MYSTERY, but the sight- *'Find the Mountain of Iron'*
ing at Cerralvo means Cabeza de Vaca and his friends
were now inside Mexico and must have made their way across to Big Bend inside
the wild and beautiful desert scapes of northern Mexico. And day after day they
found themselves with crowds of natives who wanted to travel with these
strangers, who possessed such powerful *mana*, who spoke native Indian languages,
who endured every hardship, and who seemed to be able to perform magical feats
of healing.

For the next stage of the journey, Cabeza de Vaca again gives clues which can
be very precisely picked up on the ground and, as we followed him through northern Mexico, we became all the more excited as we came closer to his footsteps.

Moving along the mountain chain north of Monterrey, they came to a village
where they saw worked copper bells. The source of the metal, they were told, was
further north – and, although it is often claimed that the nearest source is New
Mexico, we discovered from local mining engineers that copper is indeed to be
found not far away. Then, says Cabeza de Vaca:

*The next day, we crossed a mountain [sierra] seven leagues long, the stones of
which were iron slag; and in the evening we reached many houses situated along a
very beautiful stream. The people of the houses came to meet us on the trail with
their children on their backs...*

*They gave us many little bags of margaxita and of alcohol molido which they
used to paint their faces. They gave us many beads and robes of cattle [buffalo hide
robes] and loaded all who were with us with everything they owned.*

*They ate cactus [probably nopal] and nuts from pine trees. In that land there
are small pine trees and their cones are the size of small eggs; but the pine nuts are
better [to taste] than those of Castile, for they have very thin shells, and when they
are still green they grind them and make balls of them and eat them in that way;
and if they are dry they grind them together with the shells and eat them in the
form of a powder...*

It was Don Olsen, back in Austin, who gave me the clues for this part of the trail.
An astronomer and physicist by profession, Don is obsessed by the Cabeza de
Vaca tale, and he has carefully scrutinized the primary sources, discovering, for
example, the fascinating fact that, although all modern editions of Cabeza de Vaca
print *margarita* (that is, mica or pearl), the 1555 edition actually clearly reads
margaxita, which is not the same thing at all, but *iron pyrites* (fool's gold). Olsen
set me the following riddle, rather like Perseus's directions from the nymphs in the
Greek myth:

Cabeza de Vaca crosses the great river, and turns inland at the mountains. So head north-west. Walk along the seven-league mountain. At the end of that sierra, you should find the mountain where the stones are iron slag, by the banks of the 'very beautiful stream'. Then there are three very important clues in Cabeza de Vaca's text: Find a pine tree fruit with a paper-thin shell. Find the stone which shines like fool's gold. Find me the source of the black powder on the eyelids of the Indian women. All in the same place: find it – and you have the route he took up to the junction of the rivers and on to the setting sun.

We made our way by truck from Monterrey, through the delightful little Spanish mining town of Mina. Soon the Sierra Gloria rose on our left – a great whaleback, twenty miles long. This is the seven-league mountain they walked in a single day. It is a scrubby desert area, dotted with thorns and cacti, burning hot for a walker even late in the year, though the Spaniards would have found sources of water along its base.

Early that evening, we reached the northern part of the sierra and turned into a side ravine looking for the pinyon pines, which we had heard used to exist around Monclova, though they were only identified and scientifically labelled in the 1970s. A local guide took us into the lonely ravine, El Chilpitin, inside the Sierra Gloria. In the last hour of daylight, we made our way up a wonderful hidden valley (the haunt of monarch butterflies on their October migration).

Where the track stopped, local goat-herders pointed us on – they knew the pines and still chewed them in season. We scrambled down a scrubby hillside scattered with hard-shell pines and nopal cactus. Soft-shell pines no longer exist in open country or along major routes, we were told, only in secluded canyons.

We climbed down into a deeply etched stream-bed, under a cliff of pebbles, washed clean by winter torrents. Finally, we found the pinyon pine trees, growing in the torrent bed, their branches shining bright green in the golden evening light. They were out of season, but the last cones were still hanging, their kernels dried but edible – shells and all. We had found them. As we drove out of the ravine across the scrub towards Monclova, our guide pointed to a dome-shaped massif rising black on the horizon, blocking out the lights of Monclova: 'That's Mercado – the Mountain of Iron,' he said.

Soon after dawn, we climbed up into the mountain which rears 3000 feet above the plain. Spanish colonists were vying for mining concessions here as early as the late sixteenth century. According to engineers at the mine, there is copper close by (probably the source of the metal the Indians smelted to make the bell that the Spaniards saw). On the slopes, among the heaps of iron slag, we saw the gleam of iron pyrites – fool's gold – which Cabeza de Vaca had carefully described.

But what was the powdered 'alcohol' – *alcohol molido* – which the Indian women used on their eyelids? The mystery has never been solved. Alcohol is an Arabic word which crops up in Spanish and English dictionaries of the period as kohl, a black powder 'such as women use on their eyes'. In a dictionary of 1617, it is identified with stibnite (antimony ore) or possibly lead sulphide. But only a short way from the mountain, on a hill called Real Viejo, we found a lump of manganese ore, its friable surface blackening the hands. This can be found as a very soft sooty powder and, surely, must be what Cabeza de Vaca meant. He saw it only in its powdered form, which he naturally assumed was *alcohol molido,* antimony or lead sulphide, of the kind he had seen on the eyes of Spanish ladies. The mystery was solved.

With Don Olsen's guidance, we had clinched Cabeza de Vaca's route, which has been sought for so long. He came along the Sierra Gloria, through Monclova, and stopped at the beautiful river there, now sullied by an industrial pall. We had, beyond any reasonable doubt, found the route that Cabeza de Vaca and his friends had taken.

Through the Northern Desert: the Great Comanche Trail

THE FINDS AT MONCLOVA gave us the next stage of the journey. He was walking north-west on the ancient trail towards Big Bend (see map, p. 241). So, far from going through the middle of Texas, he kept to the Mexican side on old Indian trails running south of the Rio Grande. Things were starting to fall into place.

The main route comes up from the region of Monclova, south of Big Bend, through the little town of San Carlos, and on to the junction of the Rio Grande and Conchos rivers at Ojinaga (where again, as we shall see, we know for certain Cabeza de Vaca and his friends came). This track is clearly marked on several US army maps from the nineteenth century, and from archaeological investigation it is certainly prehistoric.

So, too, is the very interesting trail down into Mexico which crosses the Rio Grande near Lajitas. US military maps from the 1850s mark it as the 'Indian Trail', or the 'Great Comanche Trail', and the place where it fords the Rio Grande is the 'Grand Indian Crossing'. It seemed to us as we followed in his footsteps that Cabeza de Vaca was most likely travelling on well-established routes. This one in particular seemed to fit his story well, and we decided to explore it from the US side down to San Carlos, where we planned to pick up a truck through to Ojinaga.

Cabeza de Vaca seems to have crossed and recrossed a large river in the Big Bend region. This was probably the Rio Grande, in which case he came down the 'Great Comanche Trail'. The only way to track him comfortably now was on horseback, so we stripped our gear down to a light kit; we took three packhorses,

▲ The Rio Grande at Big Bend, with Texas on the right.

▸▸ We forded the river near the place marked on nineteenth-century maps as the Grand Indian Crossing on the Great Comanche Trail. This route, which was perhaps the one used by Cabeza de Vaca in 1535, has probably been in existence for thousands of years.

sleeping bags, some food and a calor-gas stove, and set off. This ride turned out to be one of the most evocative and thrilling of all our journeys.

Soon after dawn we saddled up, and pushed our horses chest-deep through the Rio Grande and up the sandy ridge the other side into Mexico. The Grand Indian Crossing was an idyllic, silent spot, framed by orange bluffs. With us came archaeologist Bob Malouf, wearing a wide cowboy hat and speaking in a warm Texan burr. Bob is an expert on the prehistoric populations of this vast borderland, and he has made a special study of its ancient trails, many of which go back thousands of years into prehistory.

During those days on horseback, we saw something of the landscape that Cabeza de Vaca would have seen: dramatically eroded gullies, rosy in the dawn, terracotta and burned ochre in the heat of day, lighting up into soft reds, purples and pinks towards sunset. We rode under huge cliffs, past ancient waterholes. These trails were used not only in the nineteenth-century Indian wars, and by the

conquistadors, but back in prehistory – and Cabeza de Vaca's Indian guides would have known them well.

Their food, Cabeza de Vaca says, was austere in the extreme – some of the nomadic peoples in this wild region ate insects when there was nothing else, and Bob Malouf has confirmed that from examination of human faeces on prehistoric campsites on the trail! Along the route we saw natural waterholes, still brimful of water in the winter. Always close by we would find cave sites with pictographs, some of very great antiquity, as we could see from the build-up of rubbish from the ancient middens, sometimes ten or fifteen feet deep, on the hillside below the cave mouth.

In one place, the red-daubed images of people and animals were as clear as the day they were painted. It was a remarkable insight into the native peoples who once lived here – into the world which the four conquistadors were the first out-siders to see. So, too, was the evocative landscape itself – especially at sunset, with the peach glow of weathered cliffs, the jumbles of black boulders strewn over orange screes of sand, and the great brown sierras stretching into the distance.

And silence, except for the coyotes. The clarity of the daubed pictographs, in which one could see the artists' fingermarks, left us with the eerie feeling that the ancient inhabitants were not long gone.

Another point for us to reflect upon in the light of Cabeza de Vaca's text was the shamanistic civilization of the Americas. We had felt this in the Peruvian Andes, in the Ecuadorian Amazon, and now, here again, in the pictographs. The Indian peoples' identification with the life-force of animals and the animal world, their use of peyote, was surely common to the cultures of the early Americas. Cabeza de Vaca reflected on some of these questions, but as usual left a lot unsaid.

At the heart of the American experience, before the arrival of the Christian whites, was this shamanistic religion which, ultimately, must have a deep ancestry in Asia. The deliberate seeking of hallucinogenic experience is likely to be as old as *Homo sapiens*: one of the characteristic human experiences. Among the Coahuiltecans, Cabeza de Vaca says, it was the mesquite bean that was 'most highly prized', and used in all their festivals and dances – as it was in all these cultures. On these lovely and now abandoned cave walls, in the flickering firelight, we could still feel the deep culture of the Americas.

Our first night's camp was at a spectacular location, a terrace high over a wide plain, with a magnificent view looking towards the sunrise – the direction from which Cabeza de Vaca had come, over the mountain ranges towards Monclova where one could clearly make out the great cutting made by the Santa Elena river. Behind the campsite rose steep brown cliffs, below which there was a lovely spring, which had been dammed to form a pool under a huge spreading cotton-wood tree, shining emerald green in the last light.

On the flat terrace where we laid our sleeping bags were two rough stone houses, a store and a cattle byre. All now abandoned, they had been lived in until twenty years ago by a farming family, which then moved away to the nearest town. Close by was a large rubble corral, and two groups of grinding holes in the bedrock. These were prehistoric. The site had been inhabited, thought Bob Malouf, on and off for an unbelievable 5000 or 6000 years.

The flat area in front of the houses was bolstered by a rubble terrace wall; and there we slept on layers of ash and debris from middens going back into pre-history. And as a final touch to complete this evocative historical landscape, a hundred yards to the west of the terrace, there was a steep pyramidal mountain with a *capilla* on top – a tiny square shrine of a kind that has been traditional in native worship for thousands of years – an ancestor of the huge pyramids of classical Meso-American civilization.

It was wonderful to sleep under the stars in a place where people had lived for so long in the history of the Americas. Simple semi-nomadic herders, the kind of people Cabeza de Vaca met and travelled with on his epic journey. And proof, if proof were needed, that the Great Comanche Trail, described by the US intelligence officers in the last phase of its life in the 1850s, was the ancient route between Mexico and the plains of Texas. For all we know, it was trodden by the first migrants into the southern continent over 12,000 years ago.

TWO DAYS LATER WE HEADED NORTH-WEST from San Carlos on a dirt track through dry scrubby mountains.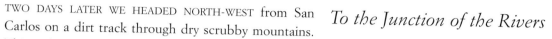

To the Junction of the Rivers

This is the ancient route from the sea through the Monclova region; it came over a place that is still called El Puerto (The Gate), where there is a spectacular view to the Peguis Range and the plain of the Conchos river. The Conchos flows down into the Rio Grande at Ojinaga, a pleasant border town on the Mexican side which the Spanish viceroy dignified with a fortress in the eighteenth century.

Here at Ojinaga, we have the second definite sighting of Cabeza de Vaca since he left Texas. In December 1582, the expedition led by the conquistador Espejo came through here seeking the legendary Seven Cities of Cibola, the mysterious 'towns of gold'. Here they found instead, clustered at the meeting of the rivers, five poor pueblos (the same number that Cabeza de Vaca mentions). The Indians spoke to Espejo in sign-language and mentioned four people who had come through thirty years before – three Spanish and a black man. And once again the same haunting tale: they had healed the sick and even raised the dead.

Today, the junction is a quiet place shrouded in trees between high levees, but the river has shifted its course over time, and the sixteenth-century junction was by the old town – a mixture of mud-brick and concrete houses with corrugated roofs, and an old church with a pillared porch which still stands on a steep little hill. Local legend says Cabeza de Vaca set up a wooden cross on a nearby hill, and local people still point out the spot. Whatever, this is the one place where we know for sure Cabeza de Vaca stood. There are still healers (*curanderos*) here who mix Spanish and Indian rituals just as they have since his time. One of them told me that Cabeza de Vaca and his friends were the first *curanderos*, mingling Christian and native ideas, making that first bridge with the Other.

The Indians here said that Cabeza de Vaca and his friends had raised the dead. And the local *curandera* at the village – a powerful and charismatic woman – told me, tears running down her cheeks at the memory, that her own career as a shaman had begun in the same way: 'I was still a child – everyone else thought the person was dead, and she certainly seemed so. But I had a sudden overwhelming feeling that she was not and I spoke out – consumed by these powerful feelings.'

The point, as Cabeza de Vaca insists, is that there is nothing unnatural or unholy in what they do, or what they believe. Such things are within the realm of

▸ Cabeza de Vaca depicted
as a healer on a mural in
the town hall at Ojinaga.
It commemorates his stay at
the junction of the rivers
in the summer of 1535.

natural human experience. He learned this when dealing with it face to face. In a sense, one could say that the people who inhabit this wide borderland are still his people today. Neither North Americans nor Mexicans, they live in between the two cultures, and between the two thought-worlds, one of which draws on the possessive individualistic world of Europe and the US, one which reaches back into the most ancient experience of the native peoples of America. And this meeting began when Cabeza de Vaca walked along this fissure, this fault line, in this vast zone of contact, all those years ago.

BUT WHERE FROM HERE? The uncertainty over this stage of *The Journey to the Southern Sea*
Cabeza de Vaca's route, it has to be said, is all of his mak-
ing. In his book he says that he and his friends followed 'up the river for seventeen
days'. Then, after those seventeen days, they crossed the river and travelled for
another seventeen days in the direction of the setting sun. But was this in the same
direction as the opening leg up the river, or in a different one? And when he says
they marched 'up the river' before they turned off, which river was it? It has
always been assumed that he meant the Rio Grande, but clearly it could have been
the Conchos. In the sixteenth century, Espejo tells us that the Rio Grande at this
point was about half the size of the Guadalquivir river at Seville (say 350 feet), but
the Conchos was more than twice the size (1300 feet).

So, by 'follow the river' one might deduce that he meant the bigger of the two,
the Conchos. Unfortunately, there can be no certainty. The text may be garbled
here, the details misremembered (it is, after all, a miracle that Cabeza de Vaca
remembered as much as he did after so long, especially as he had no writing implements with which to record his experiences). At any rate, both routes eventually
lead towards the Pacific. One goes straight up the Conchos, exactly on the line of
the setting sun; one goes up the Rio Grande towards El Paso, then cuts westwards
through a natural gap north of Sierra de Alcaparra, coming out in the northern
Chihuahua plain at Rancheria Lucero, which would fit well with his 'seventeen
days march up river' before he turned towards the setting sun.

Suffice it to say that Cabeza de Vaca and his men walked on across northern
Mexico, and were received everywhere as healers. By now they had become as
natives, 'so inured to suffering,' says our hero, 'that we felt no fatigue'.

To cross this little-known part of Mexico is to pass through a succession of
divine landscapes. We left the Junta, westwards up the Conchos valley, through
cottonwood, willow and walnut, as far as the junction with the Arroyo Frio, at the
point where the Conchos comes in from the south. From here (if this is the way he
came), Cabeza de Vaca must have taken native trails, escorted by native traders
across the Mexican basin, through northern Chihuahua, till he came to the foot of
the Sierra Madre Occidental. This he would have climbed to gain access to the
'high plain between two great ranges of mountains', today known as the Babicora
Plains. It is high tableland, fringed by mountains, covered in oak, juniper and agave
on its lower levels, and crowned on its heights with pine forests which, in December
when we came through, were snow-streaked under a pale blue winter sky.

FROM THESE PLAINS, Cabeza de Vaca was following a *On the Shell Trail*
well-established ancient route down to the Pacific: the
Shell Trail. Since prehistory, shells from the Pacific – along with turquoise, parrot

feathers and other coveted ornaments – had been traded between the pueblos of New Mexico and Arizona, and the civilizations of Central America. (Cabeza de Vaca himself mentions the trade in feathers, red and white spondylus shells and 'coral from the Southern Sea'.)

Only a couple of generations or so before Cabeza de Vaca's day, the huge town at Casas Grandes was the great staging post for the shell trade, and archaeologists discovered a ton and a half of shells still piled in its warehouses. The town's massive mud-brick structures still stand twenty feet high in places and are among the most spectacular remains in these borderlands. The soft brown curves of the walls, cut by deep sharp shadows of corners and doorways, lend a hauntingly abstract quality to the scene. In the wintry dawn light it is a place of luminous beauty.

By the time of Cabeza de Vaca, Casas Grandes was largely in ruins, with perhaps only a small village surviving on the site. Certainly, he makes no mention of it – unless it is one of the villages with 'well-built houses' which he describes in this region. One would think he passed south of Casas Grandes itself, his local guides passing him on down the last 300 miles of the Shell Trail to the Gulf of California. For although the town was abandoned in the fifteenth century, the route was still there – through the beautiful uplands 'that lie between great mountains', said Cabeza de Vaca – and down into the splendid valleys rimmed by fine ranges, which abound in walnuts, pine trees, wild grapes, deer, stags, hares and rabbits.

Here, south of the Babicora Plains, comes our third definite sighting of Cabeza de Vaca since the crossing of the Rio Grande, and one that has been curiously ignored in much of the modern literature about his journey. In 1565, a Spanish expedition, led by the conquistador Ibarra, moved up into the north of Mexico and cut across the old Shell Trail. Somewhere near here, they met a group of 300 natives who told them excitedly about Cabeza de Vaca's visit and recalled an incident in which 'Don Alvar' had helped them to recover a number of their people from their enemies. They were sun-worshippers, they told Ibarra, but they went on:

These men [Cabeza de Vaca] had ordered the clouds to rain on their lands; they had healed the sick and raised the dead... They [the natives] insisted and importuned us [that is, Ibarra] to touch and bless them which was the ceremony employed by Alvar Nunez Cabeza de Vaca.

Again, there is the stress on healing – a constant now in the Cabeza de Vaca story. Wherever he went, hundreds of Indian people followed him, and whenever he and his friends performed prayers or healed people, whole communities passed the word on. He had such a fantastic impact that, in accounts written as late as the early seventeenth century, in places as far apart as Monterrey and eastern Texas,

these healing exploits were recalled – in the latter case, well beyond the region where they were actually performed.

Below Casas Grandes, there is a succession of beautiful landscapes with cottonwood trees, and great stands of pines and oaks. We climbed out of the plain southwards over a 7000-foot pass, travelling among brown hills. The winding road ascended through pines, where snow lay on hillsides among the trees and seamed deep in the gullies. Then we emerged into an upland plain, just under 7000 feet high: wide grasslands, yellow-brown now after the hot summer, a few old pines still left dotted about singly on the bare shoulders of the hills.

How did they feel by then? I imagine them sunburned, bearded, half naked and painfully thin. Cabeza de Vaca and his friends had mastered six languages, rapidly picking up sufficient of others to make do; where they could they wrapped themselves in skins against the cold. They had no footwear, of course (they had long since left all European comforts behind).

Travelling in their footsteps by bus, truck, train, horse, and sometimes on foot, it was easy for us. But at times, when we slept out under the stars, or walked on one day through the plain beyond Peguis Canyon, we had a glimmer of what his journey must have been like. Of course, the modern reader is struck by their physical and mental toughness and resilience, their ability to accept total deprivation – 'inured to suffering', they became 'naked unaccommodated men', as Shakespeare was to put it a couple of generations later. (Shakespeare, of course, was also concerned – as many Spanish writers were – with what it is to be human.) But the fact of their survival, perhaps, has more to it than that.

During those five years around the Texas coast, my guess is that Cabeza de Vaca abandoned hope of ever seeing Europe again. Lost in a vast unmapped continent he accepted his lot, composed himself, and remade himself as a simple human being. Only when he met his friends in the last year on the coast was his desire to escape back to his world rekindled. In the meantime, he learned to exist in the Indian way; he made the crossover, thinking, speaking and living as they did. In that time, he discovered what it felt like to be the Other.

THE WEATHER WAS AUTUMNAL throughout their journey in the highlands – but it must have felt like winter in the

To the Sea

mountains. He and his friends crossed to the north of Copper Canyon, through Tres Rios, one would think, and down to the Pacific at the Yaqui river – over 300 miles, and still a hard journey through mountainous forested lands. On this walk to the sea, he gives us many details of the culture of the native peoples: their permanent houses of earth and adobe, their fine textiles, and their agriculture (they cultivated maize and beans). The people here gave Cabeza de Vaca shells,

◄◄ Casas Grandes (opposite, above), the spectacular remains of the largest Native American city in the Mexican borderland. When Cabeza de Vaca and his friends walked the Shell Trail in the winter of 1535, Casas Grandes was abandoned.

The landscape west of Peguis Canyon (below). 'We were always sure that by going towards the setting sun we would find our way.'

◄ Travelling with the Tarahumara, 'the people who walk straight'.

beads, and turquoises traded from the north, and five worked emeralds made into ceremonial arrow-points used in dances. As always, he took a special interest in the women:

The women were more modestly dressed than in any other part of the Indies that we had seen. They wear cotton shifts that reach to their knees and over them a blouse with half sleeves, and skirts of dressed deerskin that touch the ground. And they soap them with a kind of root that makes them very clean and they are very well kept; they are open in front and tied with thongs; and they wear shoes.

Why Cabeza de Vaca thought to give this detailed account of women's clothes, this far on, is not clear. Maybe he wanted his audience to understand that Indian society, although not Christian, was capable of the moral *and* physical cleanliness his readers would have associated with proper values. These interesting observations are, incidentally, a very good description of the women of one major Indian grouping which survives today – the Tarahumara – not only in the detail of their clothes, but also in their insistence on physical cleanliness. To meet them we turned off his route and made a detour to the south where, from the eighteenth century onwards, the Native American survivors took refuge in the immense fissured landscape around Copper Canyon. And, at the beginning of the third millennium, they still are there.

The Tarahumara are the second largest surviving native society in the Americas: 50,000 or 60,000 strong. Some of them still live in caves in the interior and have never had contact with the outside world. On the penultimate stage of our journey we crossed a corner of their territory. We travelled with Tarahumara men and women, and the women told us much the same story that had been told to Cabeza de Vaca. Scrupulous about washing their dresses at night (they carried spares with them), they still wash their clothes using a root, which makes a kind of soap, just as Cabeza de Vaca described.

We moved through their country on foot, with mules taking our gear. It is a harsh landscape, with less than twenty inches of rain each year, so, technically, a desert. Again, there were ancient habitation spots with pictographs. I remember one place in particular. Just as night was coming on, we made a descent of 2000 feet on a narrow steep trail, into a tremendous canyon. We came down through huge pines to a terrace above the river bed, with cliffs towering 500 feet the other side and the river flowing at their base. We camped in front of a cave, the smoke from our fire curling up and around its mouth. It was a chilly upland winter night, but warm inside the cave. Outside, beneath the cold, star-spangled night sky, lay the powerful magic of nature, which city dwellers have long forgotten.

The Tarahumara's name for themselves – Rurimari – does not mean, as is usually translated, 'runners' or 'ones who run fast', but 'those who walk well' – or 'correctly'. This has a moral connotation. To walk well means to walk well in all aspects of life – to be fully conscious, aware of the consequences of one's actions and fully responsible for what one does. Needless to say, as with many Native American societies, most of our categories are simply meaningless to them and many of theirs untranslatable for us. For the Tarahumara, people who leave for the city are 'the mistaken ones', because to join Western consumer society is stupid, is to wander around in a daze, to not understand, to be fixated with owning things, possessing things and naming things, to be obsessed with sex – in short, to not be master of one's own destiny. And who would argue with that?

Meeting by the River

CABEZA DE VACA'S AMAZING ODYSSEY reached its climax early in 1536. He and his friends had come down from the mountains to the Pacific plain in December. Throughout Christmas, they waited on the Yaqui river for the winter floodwater to subside. They then travelled south, keeping on average about thirty miles from the sea. But this route along the coast had already been explored by Spanish expeditions from Mexico, and soon Cabeza de Vaca and his friends began to see disturbing signs of the presence of Europeans. There was evidence of destruction and depopulation; the local inhabitants were terrified. Cabeza de Vaca and his companions were about to encounter their old selves.

By the time they reached the beautiful landscape of the Fuerte river, they were in an empty countryside. The presence of Spanish slavers was soon made known to them. At the end of January or early February, they reached the Sinaloa river and, hearing that an armed Spanish group was nearby, they diverted inland to find them. Soon after dawn, four grandly attired conquistadors saw a strange group of people – a cadaverous weather-beaten, bearded man with a European cast of face, surrounded by a large crowd of Indians. The meeting is one of the most memorable in the Spanish literature of the conquest, indeed in all literature.

At dawn we came upon four Christians on horseback. Seeing my strange attire and that I was in the company of Indians they were greatly startled. They stared at me for quite a while, so great was their surprise that they could not find words to ask me anything. I spoke first and told them to take me to their leader...

So the slave-hunters, far from their own kind, in a wild and unknown country, were suddenly confronted by a bearded, half-naked Spaniard, accompanied by an African and eleven Indians, who announced they were survivors of a shipwreck

▲ Our Tarahumara guide at our camp on the Shell Trail.
The Tarahumara are survivors of a much larger population which
once inhabited the plains northwards to Casas Grandes.

eight years before, and nearly 2000 miles away. Remarkably, we have a short account from Father Antonio Tello of the other side, which, however brief, records the exact place: 'Cabeza de Vaca, Estevanico and eleven Indians met Captain Lazaro de Cardenas and three mounted men at Los Ojuelos, a day's journey from Tzinaba on the Petatlan river' (perhaps today's Sinaloa river).

Cabeza de Vaca hastened back to Dorantes and Castillo, and the several hundred Indians who had been travelling with them. Then, on the banks of the river, they met Diego de Alcarez, the leader of the Spanish slaving expedition. After an embarrassed pause, Cabeza de Vaca asked him for a certified statement of the year, month and day when they met, and the condition in which he had come, 'with which request they complied'. Was he trying to keep a grip on reality (rather like Hamlet faced by the ghost: 'my tables, my tables: let me set it down')?

Cabeza de Vaca was also concerned about his legal rights. There are hints in his narrative that he feared the slavers would kill him, as he immediately took up the Indian cause and tried to persuade the Spaniards to stop oppressing the

natives. It was a nerve-racking moment. The danger in which they found themselves comes out in the remarkable conversation which follows. Reading between the lines, one detects a simmering unpleasantness: there were 'many and great altercations with the Christians', as Cabeza de Vaca discovered to his horror that they planned to enslave the hundreds of native people who had travelled with him, and whom the slave-hunters simply demanded like chattels.

▲ The Fuerte river on the Pacific coast, where Cabeza de Vaca first saw signs of the Spanish presence. 'It made us extremely sad to see how fertile the land was, and very beautiful, and full of springs and rivers, and to see every place deserted and burned…'

As tension grew, the Spanish told the Indians that the four castaways were nobodies, men of their race 'who had been lost for a long time, who were unlucky and cowardly people, and that *they* were the masters, whom the Indians must serve and obey'. The Indians, however, 'refused to believe' that Cabeza de Vaca and his friends were the same race, the same creation, as the slave-hunters. Cabeza de Vaca continues the story in one of the great passages in American literature:

They [the Indians] said the Christians lied. For we had come from the sunrise, the others from where the sun set. We cured the sick, the others killed the healthy;

*we went naked, while the others went in fine clothes on horseback with weapons.
And also that we asked for nothing and gave away all that we were given; while
the others seemed to have no other aim than to steal what they could and never
give anything to anybody. This was the reply given by the Indians to the Christians.*

It is another of those electrifying moments in history, where an ancient text flashes
its meaning across time, where people who have no voice speak. Several fascinating observations lie just beneath the surface of the text. First, Cabeza de Vaca calls
the Indians 'they' and calls himself and his companions 'we', whereas the slavers
are 'the others' or 'the Christians', but not 'the Spanish'. What is the meaning of
this? He is reporting the speech as that of the Indians, but while his narrative
affects simplicity, he is almost using the techniques of a novelist at this point.

He perhaps chose his words carefully. Cabeza de Vaca was not, of course,
denying that he was a Spaniard and a Christian but, in that wonderfully mysterious moment, all conventional categories of the Age of Conquest are subverted and
seem to slip. Even though he took pains elsewhere in his book to emphasize that
he had not lost his Christian faith, was he saying he was not now quite the same as
the Christians? Was he being ironical? Or was he asking his audience to see the
Christians as a stranger might?

Perhaps, in the end, at this moment, he felt neither one nor the other. In fact,
says Cabeza de Vaca, 'we *never* made the Indians believe we were the same race as
the Christians'. It is a truly fantastic moment – a moment of extreme danger that
he feared might end in the death of himself and his friends. But, for some reason,
the slavers did not kill him, and Cabeza de Vaca survived.

After extracting a promise from Alcarez that the Indians would not be
molested, Cabeza de Vaca persuaded his Indian companions to go back to their
homes. Alcarez later broke his word.

The sadness of parting with his Indian friends, some of whom had been
with him for a long time, must have made it a harrowing moment. But Cabeza
de Vaca and his friends had now decided to re-enter their own world, to step
back over the line from the Other to the world of the selves they had been eight
years before.

They knew that a good thirty leagues away – a hundred miles or so – there was
a Spanish town, San Miguel Culiacan, which had been founded by Nuno de
Guzman a few years before on the Pacific Coast at the mouth of the San Lorenzo
river. They decided to go there. Meanwhile, news of their incredible survival had
spread like wildfire among the Spanish settlers on the coast and, when he heard
the news, the mayor of Culiacan rushed out and met them with food and clothes
'in a peaceful settled valley eight leagues before the town'.

In his book, Cabeza de Vaca names this kind man as Melchior Diaz, 'who gave thanks to God for the wonders they had performed'. How typical of Cabeza de Vaca that he remembered the man who showed him kindness, and forgot to mention the significant date and details that he had required Alcarez to write down. (He also forgot his only possession – the one thing he would have liked to keep as a souvenir of his adventures – the five emerald arrowheads.)

'So for about 2000 leagues travelled [6000–7000 miles – the total of all the land and sea journeys from Cuba through to Florida and onwards – the actual walk was 2500 miles] on land, by sea in barges, besides ten more months after our rescue,' he concluded, 'we never stopped walking across the land, *but nowhere did we find sacrifices or idolatry.*'

Cabeza de Vaca's extraordinary summing up, as we have already mentioned, is as much to say that nowhere was the Native American religion idolatrous. This is as clear a pointer to his view of the common core of religious experience as one could wish for. He concludes with a remarkable guess: 'During all that time we crossed from one ocean to the other, from what we carefully calculated the maximum width here is about 200 leagues' (620 miles is an incredibly close estimate, it is actually about 650 miles from coast to coast as the crow flies).

The travellers stayed all February, March and April in Culiacan, gingerly, one imagines, feeling themselves for signs of life flooding back, although it appears that throughout that time, they still wore their Indian rags and chose to sleep on the ground. Then, on 15 May, they left for Compostela, where '…the governor received us well and gave us clothing from his own supplies, which I could not wear for many days, nor could we sleep except on the floor…' Finally, in June, they reached Mexico City, where they were received by the viceroy himself, none other than Hernan Cortes. To him, they told the whole story. Perhaps it was there that Cabeza de Vaca had the idea of writing it down.

Cabeza de Vaca sailed from Veracruz in 1537, wintered in Cuba, and finally landed in Lisbon in August 1538, from where he made his way back to Spain. His story was first published in 1542 in an error-strewn edition, not controlled by him. (By then, he had returned to the New World.) The revised edition came out in 1555, but very few copies survived. Today, it is a bestseller.

Meanings: Shipwrecks and Sea Changes

CABEZA DE VACA'S STORY is not a tale of the fall of civilizations, like those of Cortes and Pizarro. Nor is it an epic of exploration like Orellana's. It is a small story of four people in a vast continent, in a century in which millions died. A small story but, of course, it is also a big story. Its meanings have been scrutinized ever since. Not only has the riddle of Cabeza de Vaca's route generated a literature

▲ A myth in the making: Cabeza de Vaca as a heroic pioneer,
from a now destroyed painting by the American artist
Frederic Remington.

all of its own, but his tale has spawned novels, fictions and films.

The moment when Cabeza de Vaca stares at the Spaniards and sees himself as he was eight years before – his Spanish conquistador self – the moment when he defends Indian rights by putting his own life on the line – moments that come on the heels of the many extraordinary tales of healing – in these incidents this amazing story transcends its time. Like all the best fiction, it is a maturation story, a story of spiritual growth and change. The significance for us is that we can read it not just as a tale of growth in the self of one man, but as a change in civilization, too. As we understand it now, unevolved, intolerant societies (or people) see the Other as threatening, alien, different. To see the Other as a reflection of one's own self, to take responsibility for the Other, and feel for him or her, this moment of fellow feeling is what the French philosopher Emmanuel Levinas describes as 'the birth of morality in history'. For Cabeza de Vaca, that moment arrived on Galveston Island, that first winter on a storm-lashed shore when, half dead and hopeless, his friends drowned, the Karankawas felt for him and wept for him.

The tragedies of the sixteenth century are all the more poignant now as we experience their effects unfolding around us, as we stand on the graveyard of the Karankawas, a people who no longer exist, as we rebury the bones of the Coahuiltecans, or as we bed down with the Tarahumaras in their caves. The journey of Cabeza de Vaca has taken on an additional power because of what has happened since, because only now can we see the long-term effects of the conquistadors' actions working themselves out all over the globe. His tale now strikes us as particularly eloquent because, as an inner journey, it is one that we all must make, whether as people, or as societies, if we are to consider ourselves to be truly civilized human beings.

Aftermath: Paraguay and Death

IS THAT HOW IT APPEARED TO CABEZA DE VACA? His later life constitutes a strange and problematical aftermath. His story, as we have seen, was published, but it was never widely read. It was quoted by some as a kind of adventure in the mould of *Robinson Crusoe*, and by others as an intelligence volume that gave information about the New World, the

interior of North America, and especially 'Florida'. It was read by Las Casas, by Garcilaso Inca, by Oviedo (who interviewed him), and by the historian Gomara, Cortes's secretary. Hernando de Soto talked with Cabeza de Vaca about Florida before his own ill-fated *entrada* – his three-year invasion which ended up devastating the native populations of the American south-east through disease and war. And de Soto's submission to the Spanish crown used Cabeza de Vaca's intelligence on the nature of the land to be conquered to help him get his licence to conquer and rob lands half the size of Europe.

Cabeza de Vaca gave de Soto curiously contradictory information, but would not travel with him – although two of his cousins went against his advice. That said, he didn't buck the trend – he never questioned the right of Europeans to rule the New World. What he wanted was for that rule to be benevolent.

The extraordinary thing is that after all he had gone through – like Orellana – he couldn't wait to get back. He lived in Spain during 1537/40, planning a new expedition, hoping to get the governorship of a large tract of the New World, to rule in his way. In March 1540, he finally got a licence from King Charles V for another American adventure. This time, as de Soto had frozen him out of North America, he went south, to Paraguay.

In November 1540, he sailed with three ships to the River Plate, with the important rank of *adelantado* or governor. By then, colonization there had degenerated into a scramble for loot and opportunistic exploitation, with violent confrontations between settlers and natives. To the Spanish crown, Cabeza de Vaca must have seemed the right kind of person to send, but the vested interests and powers ranged against him were very great, and not surprisingly the suitability of his own personality soon became an issue.

Powerful family interests in Paraguay tried to block him before he sailed, and to strip him of his title. When he set off, he was already encumbered with great debts. Now aged nearly fifty, he had gone beyond his means in every way – financial, physical, maybe even psychological.

The voyage took four months. He landed in Paraguay on 29 March 1541 and marched overland 500 miles to Ascuncion. This journey was remarkable in itself – he was the first to see spectacular landscapes, including the waterfalls on the Iguaçu river. There, he learned of the murder of his predecessor as governor.

Once installed, Cabeza de Vaca attempted to correct abuses against the Indians, to pull the settlers back into line, to restore order and to gather the taxes due to the Spanish crown. All this – and especially his stance against slavery – drew the enmity of colonists, who rapidly organized against him.

Eye-witness accounts of this time suggest Cabeza de Vaca was simply the wrong person in the wrong place, that the abilities which had seen him through

his epic journey were not those needed to handle an awkward administrative conundrum in Paraguay. Moreover – and perhaps this is surprising – he showed himself to be still susceptible to the myths of wealth which drove so many of his contemporaries. Seduced by legends of gold and lost treasure, he led an expedition into the unknown which caused resentment and wrecked his health. In 1544, he was deposed in a settler rebellion, taken prisoner and eventually shipped back to Spain in August 1545. He returned home humiliated.

But the catalogue of disasters did not end there. Early in 1546, he was rocked by accusations of robbery and misappropriation by his enemies, who even cited a long series of abuses against both the Spanish and the natives. Worse, he was now collapsing under the debts run up to equip his expedition. A Spaniard who had met him in Ascuncion says he 'owned not a real's worth in those realms'. And Cabeza de Vaca confessed that 'he was poor and lost and bankrupt, he and his relatives alike'.

His enemies now closed in with a series of lawsuits. In March 1546, an imprisonment order was issued against him by the Council of the Indies. Although he was able to get bail to live in lodgings in Madrid, the litigation dogged him for five years, during which he found his freedom curtailed and spent all his time desperately and obsessively gathering documents to plead his case, while dwelling overmuch on what he had suffered. During this time, those who met him say he was 'impoverished and prematurely aged'; and those who saw him in court affirmed that he cut a sad picture: 'weary and poverty-stricken, he continues his suits against his rivals and it is very pitiful to hear him and to learn what he suffered in the Indies'.

Finally, in March 1551 in Valladolid, the Council of Indies announced sentence. Cabeza de Vaca was stripped of his titles, barred on pain of death from returning to the Indies, and condemned to exile and forced labour in Algeria. His suitors in Paraguay could now demand compensation. The reasons why this came about are still not clear: his legal representatives were never allowed to see the documents which contained the allegations against him, and none of these appears to have survived.

Cabeza de Vaca appealed against the verdict, pointing out that he was bankrupt. His sentence of exile was eventually lifted, but the ban on going back to the New World remained. It was evidently during this time that Cabeza de Vaca felt impelled to write his own story of the case: to revise his earlier account of his adventures and to add the story of his disastrous time in Paraguay. His writings, which were published in 1555 in Valladolid, where he was living in poverty, now became his last chance to justify himself in the eyes of posterity.

Cabeza de Vaca had been trapped in a web of deceit and manipulation by

people who hated him. Perhaps what he had learned about life in his eight years in the wilderness had not best qualified him to rule in the Wild West of Ascuncion. The misfortunes he had experienced, the self-knowledge which had come from plumbing the depths of despair, the isolation and physical hardship he had suffered, and the inner discoveries he had made and articulated in his book, all this no doubt sat uneasily with the outward desires of his time.

His career ruined, his health – so robust in the years he had spent among the Indians – now failed him, too. In September 1556, in view of his serious illness, the king responded to his petition and granted him a small pension to alleviate his poverty and enable him to seek medical attention. At some point in the next two or three years, he died in that town, 'a very poor gentleman'.

Last Thoughts in Valladolid

I AM WRITING THIS IN A ROOM over the courtyard of San Gregorio Valladolid – where the great debate on the human rights of indigenous peoples took place – and looking over the rooftops of the old town where Cabeza de Vaca lived out his last years, and where he died. There are no comfortable conclusions to the amazing odyssey of Cabeza de Vaca. And many questions still remain to be answered, not least the reasons for his ruin, which may lie hidden in his personality, but may be still retrievable from the masses of legal papers which remain to be sifted in the Archive of the Indies.

His chief memorial, though, lies in his little book. As it stands now, it is a fragmentary discourse, a memory of eight years in a few pages (127 pages in the paperback on my table as I write). A tiny text compared, say, with Cieza de Leon or others of his time. Perhaps his publisher would not bear the cost of a longer work, and cut him down; perhaps this was all Cabeza de Vaca committed to writing.

But, as we see it now, it is one of those texts which opens up many intriguing lines of thought, which retains significance, and grows in the minds of succeeding generations. Significantly, perhaps, it has found its audience in our own time.

When he died in poverty, Cabeza de Vaca could never have imagined that his account would one day be viewed as one of the key narratives in the discovery of the New World, and not only as a key ethnographic text, but, more than that, as an inner journey, a spiritual odyssey, which, in modern times, has found its place among the most famous works of travel and in the literature of spiritual growth.

The book has also proved to be one of a small cluster of historical texts which confront that great modern philosophical issue, which is still so pertinent in our own time of disorientation, possessiveness and hatred which is manifested in so many parts of our world, from Chechnya and Kosovo, Rwanda and Sierra Leone, to Palestine and Kashmir: the Encounter with the Other.

EPILOGUE: 'ALL THE WORLD IS HUMAN'

THE FIRE IS BURNING LOW. Outside the tent, a heavenly canopy of stars arches over the Plain of Ghosts, deep in the jungles of Vilcabamba. The rain has cleared the sky, and the Southern Cross is visible now with its two companions, which the Incas called 'the llama's eyes'. And what shooting stars! Our journey is over. We have taken rafts down the Amazon, trekked with pack animals through the forests of Ecuador, spent searingly cold nights on the glaciers of the high Andes, seen molten desert sunsets on the Great Comanche Trail. We travelled looking for traces of this momentous encounter of two worlds, 'the greatest event in history', as Adam Smith and Karl Marx called it (echoing the words of contemporaries, who even then knew they were living through events that were without parallel).

This book has focused on just four stories out of so many that took place in those years between Tierra del Fuego and the deserts of New Mexico. It was the most astonishing age of expansion in human history, which in a few years across the Americas and the Pacific opened up 'a world greater than that which was already known', as Cieza de Leon put it.

I say again that I stood looking at it, and I thought that never on this earth would there be discovered other lands such as these. But of all these wonders that I then beheld, today all is overthrown and lost, and nothing is left standing.

•

BERNAL DIAZ DEL CASTILLO,
The Conquest of New Spain, c. 1565

One World: One Humankind

WE ARE STILL LIVING WITH THE CONSEQUENCES. The conquest opened up the world, marking the beginnings of a globalization which was not only commercial, but also ideological and philosophical; a remaking of mental horizons no less than a redrawing of physical geography. For the first time in history, we find people speaking of one world, whose peoples are seen as subject to the same natural laws, the same process of history. And in that light the Spanish conquest of the Americas raised a profound moral dilemma for the conquistadors, for the imperial government of Spain and for European people in general. Was the conquest of the New World in any sense just?

◀◀ Paradise lost: the Fall of the New World has become an object lesson in our attempts to understand the modern devastation of the natural world and the extinction of traditional cultures.

Did the Indians possess human rights? Should they be converted to Christianity – and if so, how were they to be converted? Could conversion be forcible. By war? And how could such a war be just? Did their practice of human sacrifice and cannibalism show they were morally degenerate, or unevolved? Or were the Indians no less fully human? In grappling with these questions, sixteenth-century people made the first moves towards evolving a conception of universal rights.

Already in 1511, in a sermon in Hispaniola, the Dominican friar Antonio de Montesinos asked his congregation of colonists: 'Are these Indians not men? Do they not have rational souls? Are you not obliged to love them as yourselves?' Others argued quite the opposite, that the Indians were 'natural slaves' and that just war could be waged against the natives by more evolved civilizations which had a duty to bring enlightenment to such barbarous peoples who practised idolatry and human sacrifice.

Throughout the 1530s, '40s and '50s, political theorists and theologians bombarded the Spanish king with advice on his colonial policy. The administration of the overseas empire, especially in the hands of ruthless opportunists such as the Pizarro clan, became the subject of a bitter propaganda war between those who justified the Europeans taking power over the New World and those who strove to protect native rights. In a series of public lectures the theologian Francisco de Vitoria focused the debate on two simple questions: did the Native Americans have genuine political societies with legitimate rulers? Did they possess private property before the Spanish came? To both questions he answered yes.

The Native Americans – whether the tribal societies discovered in the Caribbean and Brazil, or the sophisticated polities discovered in Mexico and Peru – possessed real authority in their public and private affairs, and hence the Spanish had no right to overthrow the native rulers or take away native people's property. From this simple philosophical premise it followed naturally that they were humans no less than Europeans, and had the same rights.

Vitoria also denied the Spanish right to make war on the native peoples in order to force them to accept Christianity. In this case, he said, all human beings possessed an equal right and ability to establish and maintain their own political societies, whether they were Christian or not.

Ranged alongside Vitoria was the Dominican Bartolome de Las Casas, whose most famous work was *A Short Account of the Destruction of the Indies*, written in 1542 and dedicated to the future King Philip II. Las Casas's book was intended to tell the Spanish crown what was really happening in the Americas, and in its first-hand reporting it has all the power of modern accounts of the tragedies in Rwanda or Cambodia. In response to polemics like this, the Spanish crown attempted to frame imperial laws to restrain powerful settlers, such as the Pizarros, who were a law unto themselves. But, of course, such laws were simply not enforceable. The clock could not be turned back. In Peru the colonists revolted. In Mexico the viceroy persuaded the king's agent to postpone promulgation of the new laws until there had been more discussion. Everywhere there was opposition from local officials, landowners and clergy. People had staked all, and made fortunes, and were not willing to give them up. It was in this volatile situation that the king's closest advisers, the Council of Fourteen, met in Valladolid to debate the key issues. It was a moment unparalleled in history.

KING CHARLES V now did something without precedent in the annals of imperialism. He ordered that all Spanish conquests in the Americas be stopped with effect from 16 April 1550 until the matter had been thoroughly discussed by the best theologians, canon lawyers and jurists. So it came about that the two great adversaries, Las Casas and the philosopher Sepulveda vied – though not face to face – from mid-August 1550 in a month of debate in Valladolid in the presence of the Council of Fourteen. But behind the mounds of evidence hovered one simple question: what is it to be human?

What Is Human?

Las Casas, now seventy-six years old, had seen at first hand the horrors of genocide in the New World. His opponent, Juan Gines de Sepulveda, was a great theologian and humanist but he had never been to the New World. For Sepulveda, the essential qualities of Spanish civilization were 'prudence, intelligence, magnanimity, moderation, humanity' – and the Christian religion. The native societies he saw as devoid of civilization and hence virtually devoid of humanity. As he said to the king's council:

Do not fool yourselves into thinking the Indians lived in an idyllic world before the Spanish came. On the contrary, they waged continuous ferocious wars against each other and practised cannibalism on the vanquished. All in all is there any more convincing proof of the superiority of some human beings to others, in intelligence, spirit and valour, and the fact that such people are slaves by nature? It is true that some display a certain talent for craftsmanship, but this is not proof of human intelligence, for we know that animals, birds and spiders do kinds of work that no human industry can completely imitate...

Such to conclude is the character and customs of these inferior beings – barbarous, uncivilized and inhumane, and they were like this before the coming of the Spaniards. And this is not to speak of their impious religion and the wicked sacrifices in which they worshipped the devil as their God, in the belief that they could offer him no finer tribute than human hearts... How can there be any doubt that these peoples, so uncivilized, so barbarous, tainted by so many vices and

▶ 'This was not a victory, nor a defeat,' says the modern monument on the site of the final battle for Mexico City in 1521. 'It was the sorrowful birth of the mestizo nation which is the Mexico of today.' Painting of a mestizo (mixed race) marriage in eighteenth-century Mexico.

De Efpañol y Meftif

corruptions, have been justly conquered by a nation that is most humane and excels in every kind of virtue?

LAS CASAS SUBMITTED A GIGANTIC DOSSIER which he had ### 'Humankind Is One'
gathered like a journalist from decades of working in
the Americas – a scathing rebuttal of Sepulveda's idea that those who acted in King Charles's name were humane, noble people. His fundamental argument, though, was the conviction that the world is indeed one, that human beings are the same, and all have the possibility of self-fulfilment and of achieving goodness: 'No nation that exists, no matter how rude, uncivilized and barbarous, savage or brutal, cannot be persuaded into a good way of life – provided that the method used is that proper and natural to men – namely love, gentleness and kindness.'

Then came his finest hour:

For all the peoples of the world are human beings. And the definition of humans, collectively and severally, is one: that they are rational beings. All possess understanding and volition, being formed in the image and likeness of God; all have the natural capacity or faculties to understand and master the knowledge that they do not have – all take pleasure in goodness and all abhor evil. All men are alike in what concerns their creation. And no one is born enlightened. From this it follows that all of us must be guided and aided at first by those who were born before us. And the savage peoples of the earth may be compared to uncultivated soil that readily brings forth weeds and useless thorns, but has within itself such natural virtue that by labour and cultivation it may be made to yield sound and beneficial fruits. Thus all humankind is one.

It was a noble declaration. But although Las Casas won the debate, the realities of power overruled the voices of morality, and of Christian conscience. In the end, the ban on further conquests was lifted. As we know all too well from our own experience of the world, an ethical foreign policy will always give way to realpolitik.

WHILE THE CONQUERORS DEBATED the justice of their ### *Visions of the Vanquished*
deeds among themselves, the vanquished were rapidly
coming to terms with what, to them, was a world newly remade. 'We thought we were the whole world,' said the Inca Titu Cusi, 'for till then we knew of no other.' For Titu Cusi and the other Indian commentators we have followed in this story, the encounter of the two worlds had turned their own upside down. Some products of the encounter, such as the historian Garcilaso Inca, embraced the Spanish

civilizing project. Others, such as Waman Poma, became disillusioned by the injustices of Spanish rule and wrote in a very different vein, well aware of the debate within Spanish culture on human rights:

'We did not know of the rest of the world till you conquered us,' wrote Waman Poma to the king of Spain. 'But *plainly it is our rights which have been violated... Peru belongs to us, not the Spanish, just as Africa should be for the Africans and Asia for the Asians.*'

Like Las Casas, Waman Poma directly addressed the king of Spain, in his astonishing 1200-page work of history, anthropology and social commentary – perhaps the greatest of the surviving sixteenth-century visions of the vanquished:

Although the Incas may have begun as barbarians, and though their dynasty was derived from a woman, Mama Huaco Coya, their dynasty developed over a very long period of time... Our Indians should not be thought of as a backward people who yielded easily to superior force. Just imagine, Your Majesty, being an Indian in your own country and being loaded up as if you were a horse, or driven along with blows from a stick. Imagine being called a dirty dog or a pig. Imagine having your women and your property taken away from you without a shred of legality. What would you and your Spanish compatriots do in such circumstances? My own belief is that you would eat your tormentors alive and thoroughly enjoy the experience... To conclude, it is not the Spanish administrators and employers who are the rightful owners of Peru. According to the laws of both God and man, we Indians are the proprietors. With the exception of Your Majesty alone, the Spanish are only foreign settlers. It is our country because God has given it to us. We are the true masters.

On 1 January 1613, when Waman Poma was about eighty years old, he set out for Lima with his precious completed manuscript, 'accompanied by my son, my horse Guiado, and my two dogs Amigo and Lautaro, walking through the mountains in deep snow and intense cold', still hoping that somehow his manuscript would reach the king himself. In an astonishingly prophetic summary, Waman Poma gives us his conception of the world imagined anew: a future world as a commonwealth of nations in which, just as the Inca had ruled the Land of the Four Quarters, the king of Spain would be a kind of international Inca: a fountain of justice, titular administrator of the earth, whose Four Quarters are now America, Europe, Africa and Asia, each under its own rulers with the king of Spain *primus inter pares*. In this way the Pachacuti, the world turned upside down, might after all be righted.

Needless to say, King Philip III never read it.

LOOKING BACK OVER HIS LIFETIME from the perspective of the 1570s in Mexico, the great upholder of Aztec culture Bernardino de Sahagun saw a different historical trajectory in the fall of the Americas, though one that now seems no less prophetic than Waman Poma's. 'When the Spaniards came to this land which would be called the New World,' wrote Sahagun, 'it was full of innumerable people.' Now, however, devastated by disease 'from the Canaries to Mexico all the nations are gone...' Reflecting on the tragedy, Father Sahagun recalled the prophecy of a Dominican, that in the end no Indians would survive, 'that the colonists would multiply and people the New World so that when generations of Indians have gone, the land will be entirely repopulated by newcomers.'

Now as we approach the 500th anniversary of the conquest, the prophesy has almost come about. Now only a few of the native peoples of the New World have not encountered the white man; only a few still exist in their primal state, ignorant of the worlds of New York and London. And only a few more, such as we met in our journey, like the Huarani or the Tarahumaras, knowing something of this outside world, still refuse contact, and reject the gifts brought by Cortes, Pizarro and those who came after them.

'The End of the Nations'

▲ An Indian Everyman – one face to stand for the vanished millions. 'All humankind is one,' said Bartolome de Las Casas.

'The Last Conquistador'

IT WAS AFTER THE JOURNEY WAS OVER that I met Stuart. Descended on his mother's side from a conquistador, he has the dark eyes, high brow and aristocratic bearing of a Spanish *hidalgo*. In bleak wintry weather we walked round the old streets of Trujillo. We stood outside the grand house of the Pizarros, all new money, with sculpted Incas on its façade, chains round their necks, and the striking faces of the Pizarro brothers, and of Dona Francisca, Francisco's half-Inca daughter. We shivered with the ghosts in the empty Orellana house and saw the crumbling fortress of Cortes's Medellin squat on its hill. Stuart's ancestor was one of them, Mansio Serra de Leguizamon.

Mansio went to Peru in his teens, saw Atahuallpa dead, and fought against Manco's generals in the battles around Lima. With his Toledo sword he killed Incas in the barbican at Sacsahuaman and went with Gonzalo Pizarro to Vilcambamba. His adventures did not stop there. Mansio survived imprisonment and torture in the civil wars; he took an Inca princess as his lover, but left her for the gambling tables of Lima. And in a last flicker of glory, he returned as an old man to Vilcabamba with the viceroy, and saw the last Inca refuge destroyed. On his deathbed in Cuzco on 18 September 1589, at the age of seventy-eight, Mansio addressed this remarkable testament to King Philip II (in Stuart's translation):

For the peace of my soul and before I start this will, I declare that for many years now I have desired to speak to the Catholic majesty of King Philip our lord, knowing how Catholic and most Christian he is, because I took part in the name of the Crown in the discovery, conquest and settlement of these kingdoms when we deprived those who were the lords, the Incas, who had ruled them as their own. And it should be known to His Most Catholic Majesty that we found those realms in such good order that there was not a thief or a vicious man, nor an adulteress, nor were there fallen women admitted among them, nor were they an immoral people, being content and honest in their labour. All things from the smallest to the greatest had their place and order. And that the Incas were feared, obeyed and respected by their subjects as being very capable and skilful in their rule, as were their governors.

I wish Your Majesty to understand the motive that moves me to make this statement is the peace of my conscience and because of the guilt I share. For we have destroyed by our evil behaviour such a government as was enjoyed by these natives. They were so free of crime and greed, both men and women, that they could leave gold or silver worth a hundred thousand pesos in their open house... So that when they discovered that we were thieves and men who sought to force their wives and daughters to commit sin with them, they despised us. But now things have come to such a pass in offence of God, owing to the bad example we have set them in all things, that these natives from doing no evil have turned into people who can do no good, something which must touch Your Majesty's conscience as it does mine, as one of the first conquistadors and discoverers, and something that demands to be remedied.

I inform Your Majesty that there is no more I can do to alleviate these injustices other than by my words, in which I beg God to pardon me, for I am moved to say this, seeing that I am the last to die of the conquistadors...

FURTHER READING

THE CONQUEST OF THE NEW WORLD is a vast field of study in many different disciplines: this short bibliography is designed only to help the interested reader into the subject, with an emphasis on narrative history and readability.

First, a broad-sweep narrative: Ronald Wright *Stolen Continents* (1992, reissue 2000) is a *tour de force* to add to his wonderful travel book *Time among the Maya* (1990); and a broad view on long-term aspects of the encounter: Alfred Crosby *The Colombian Exchange: Biological and Cultural Consequences of 1492* (1972) and *Ecological Imperialism* (1986). On the impact of New World plants and animals: R. Sokolov *Why We Eat What We Eat* (1991); H. Hobhouse *Seeds of Change* (1986). On the impact of disease: Noble David Cook *Born to Die* (1998). Useful summaries of sources, and where to look: R. Schlesinger *In the Wake of Columbus* (1996) and *Keys to the Encounter: A Library of Congress Resource Guide for the Study of the Age of Discovery* (1992). For broad orientations: J. H. Elliott *The Old World and the New* (1983 reprint) and *Spain and Its World 1500–1700* (1989). On ways of seeing: F. Chiapelli (ed.) *First Image of America* (1976). On the idea of the Other: T. Todorov *The Conquest of America: The Question of the Other* (1984); S. Greenblatt *Marvellous Possessions* (1991); Anthony Pagden *The Fall of Natural Man* (1982) and *European Encounters with the New World* (1993). Other books on European conceptions of the New World and its peoples are listed in Schlesinger, above.

A very useful anthology of texts: B. Keen (ed.) *Latin American Civilization* (1996). On maps, physical and mental: *Cartografia Historica del Encuentro de Dos Mundos* (1992); on Mexico: Barbara Mundy *The Mapping of New Spain* (1996). Lastly a wonderful art book: Jay A. Levenson (ed.) *Circa 1492: Art in the Age of Exploration* (1991).

CHAPTERS 1 AND 2: MEXICO
Overviews
Hugh Thomas *The Conquest of Mexico* (1993) is the most recent and authoritative; S. Gruzinski *The Conquest of Mexico* (1993) looks at the representation of these events. On Aztecs: Richard F. Townsend *The Aztecs* (1992). For a moving view of Aztec society and thoroughly recommended: Inga Clendinnen *Aztecs* (1991);

I found her 'Fierce and Unnatural Cruelty' in S. Greenblatt (ed.) *New World Encounters* (1993) the most useful short discussion of the conquest of Mexico, and I have gratefully used her ideas, especially in Chapter 2. On changing perceptions of the Aztecs: B. Keen *The Aztec Image in Western Thought* (1971). On the thorny question of whether they thought the Spaniards gods: D. Carrasco *Quetzalcoatl and the Irony of Empire* (1992 edn). On the journey: following Cortes's route I found most thoughtful Jorge G. Lacroix *The Itinerary of Hernan Cortes* (1973). For a wonderful fund of pictures: *Mexico: Splendors of Thirty Centuries*, introduction by Octavio Paz (1990), and S. Gruzinski *Painting the Conquest* (1992). For an excellent guide book: J. Collis and D. M. Jones *Blue Guide Mexico* (1997).

Texts

As always, it is best to read the first-hand sources, which are unusually rich: *Cortes' Letters from Mexico*, trans. and ed. by A. Pagden (1992); Bernal Diaz *Conquest of New Spain*, trans. J. M. Cohen (1963); *The Conquistadors*, trans. and ed. Patricia de Fuentes (1993 reprint), contains several shorter texts, namely Juan Diaz, Andres de Tapia, Francisco de Aguilar and the Anonymous Conquistador, plus letters of Alvarado and the *Chronicle of Garcia del Pilar*; Cortes's chaplain's account, F. Lopez de Gomara *Cortes: The Life of the Conqueror*, trans. L. B. Simpson (1964).

From the other side, Bernadino de Sahagun's monumental *History of New Spain*, ed. Arthur Anderson and Charles Dibble (13 vols); vol. 12 is the tale of the conquest told by Aztec eye-witnesses and, one hopes, will be made available in a cheap popular edition. Excerpts are in M. Leon-Portilla *The Broken Spears* (1962), which also includes the annals of Tlatilulco, and the great laments – on which see too *Flower and Song: Poems of the Aztec Peoples*, trans. E. Kissam and M. Schmidt (1977). Sahagun's problematic reworking of Book 12, *Conquest of New Spain: 1585 revision,* ed. H. F. Cline and S. L. Cline (1989); L. N. D'Olwer *Fra Bernadino de Sahagun* (1987) is a monument to the compiler of one of the world's greatest works of historical literature.

Modern Mexican literature has also mined a very rich seam on the conquest; for introductions: Octavio Paz *The Labyrinth of Solitude* (1985); Carlos Fuentes *A New Time for Mexico* (1997 edn). And lastly, for a useful look at the Malinche myth: S. M. Cypess *La Malinche in Mexican Literature* (1991).

CHAPTERS 3 AND 4: PERU

Texts

Key contemporary narratives, including those of Francisco de Xerez, M. de Astete on the journey to Pachacamac, Hernando Pizarro, and the record of the share-out of Atahuallpa's gold, are in *Reports on the Discovery of Peru*, trans. C. Markham (1872); Pedro Pizarro's *Relation of the Discovery of Peru* (1571), trans. and ed. P. Ainsworth Means (1921). Sarmiento de Gamboa (the conquistador who met Queen Elizabeth I, see page 183) *History of the Incas*, trans. C. Markham (1907); Augustin Zarate, *Discovery and Conquest of Peru* (1968), trans. J. M. Cohen; Garcilaso de la Vega Inca *Royal Commentaries of the Incas* (1609), trans. H. V. Livermore (1966); Bernabe Cobo *History of the Inca Empire* (1653), trans. and ed. R. Hamilton (1979); Cobo's *Inca Religion and Customs*, trans. and ed. R. Hamilton (1990); Juan de Betanzos *Narrative of the Incas* (1557), trans. R. Hamilton and D. Buchanan (1996). Pedro de Cieza de Leon's wonderful *Chronicle of Peru*: part 1, 1553, trans. by C. Markham, in *Hakluyt Society* 33 (1864); and part 2, 1554, *Hakluyt Society* 68 (1883); these are now trans. H. de Onis and ed. V. von Hagen (1976); for later parts, the reader must still rely on Markham's *The War of Las Salinas*, *Hakluyt Society* 54 (1923); *The War of Chupas*, 42 (1918); and *The War of Quito*, 31 (1913). For part 3 on the conquest, more recently discovered, trans. Noble David Cook (1999).

Sources from part-Inca writers include Santa Cruz Pachacuti's *Relacion de Antiguedades* (1993) and Titu Cusi's *Instruccion* (1992), ed. L. R. de Hurtado; for partial translations see *New Iberian World: A Documentary History of the Discovery and Settlement of Latin America*, vol. IV, ed. J. H. Parry and R. C. Keith; and also R. Wright *Stolen Continents* (1992).

Waman Poma's text is ed. John V. Murra, Rolena Adorno and Jorge Urioste (3 vols, 1987); there is also an edited trans. by C. Dilke, *Letter to a King* (1978); the facsimile first published in 1936 is still available in print. On Waman Poma's work: Rolena Adorno *Chronista y Principe*, 2nd edn (1989) and *Guaman Poma: Writing and Resistance in Colonial Peru* (1986).

Modern studies are led by John Hemming's *The Conquest of the Incas* (1993 edn), a massive study of the events, with a rich bibliography; Rafael Varon's uncovering of the tentacles of the Pizarro mafia in *Francisco Pizarro and His Brothers* (1997); Maria Rostworowski *History of the Inca Realm* (1999). On surviving cults: Michael Sallnow *Pilgrims of the Andes* (1987); on rulership: Susan Niles *The Shape of Inca History* (1999). On sacred landscapes: the classic study is Tom Zuidema *The Ceque System of Cusco* (1964); see also Brian S. Bauer *The Sacred Landscape of the Inca* (1998) and J. Reinhard's short but rich *The Sacred Center* (1991). A still useful text on the quipu is L. L. Locke *The Ancient Quipu* (1923); on the roads: John Hyslop *The Inca Road System* (1984); on Inca architecture: a wonderful book of photos and plans, John Hemming and Edward Rannay *Monuments of the Incas* (1982), should be republished. Studies of individuals: on Francisco Pizarro, the work of the leading authority, Jose Antonio Busto *Francisco Pizarro* (revised 1987) is as yet untranslated, as is his invaluable biographical dictionary of the conquistadors of Peru (1986, 1987). Other biographies: on Sarmiento de Gamboa, Stephen Clissold *Conquistador* (1954); on Mansio Serra de Leguizamon, Stuart Stirling *The Last Conquistador* (1999), to which I am indebted for the translation on page 274.

CHAPTER 5: AMAZONIA/ORELLANA
Texts
All the Orellana documents, including the letter of Pizarro, relevant excerpts from Oviedo, statements from participants and the Carvajal Diary, plus the story of Orellana's later expedition with testimonies (and even oddities such as extracts from *The Deeds of the Pizarros*, a trilogy by the seventeenth-century dramatist Tirso de Molina!), are in a most judicious and valuable book: J. Toribio Medin *The Discovery of the Amazon* (1935, pbk reprint 1988); it does not, however, include the remarkable account drawn from eye-witnesses by Cieza de Leon in *The War of Chupas*, trans. C. Markham, *Hakluyt Society* 42 (1918). A convenient collection of narratives is J. M. Cohen *Journeys down the Amazon* (1975); John Hemming *The Search for El Dorado* (1978), with a valuable bibliography, is especially good on the expeditions into Venezuela and Colombia which preceded the Pizarro–Orellana expedition.

The important and massive collection by Gonzalo de Oviedo, *A General and Natural History of the Indies* (1535–47), has yet to be translated into English; for a recent text see J. Perez de Tudela (ed., 1959).

On Orellana: a short account is B. Bernhard *Pizarro, Orellana and the Exploration of the Amazon* (1991). George Miller's *Orellana* (1954) is a wonderful imagining of the story closely based on the sources and conditions. On a later conquistador of the Amazon: Stephen Minto, *Aguirre* (1993).

On the wider history of Amazonia, and the destruction of its peoples, there are two brilliant distillations of a vast body of source material: John Hemming *Red Gold: The Conquest of the Brazilian Indians* (1978) and *Amazon Frontier: The Defeat of the Brazilian Indians* (1987).

Particularly useful on our journey: M. Cabodeville, *Coca la region y sus historias* (1996), and *Culturas de ayer y hoy en el Rio Napo* (with English text) (1998). On the Lake of Gold in Colombia (Lake Guatavita – the source of the legend) see Warwick Bray *The Gold of El Dorado* (1978). In modern literature: V. S. Naipaul *The Loss of El Dorado: A History* (1969). Among many films conflating the tales of Orellana and Aguirre, unmissable for its atmosphere is Werner Herzog's *Aguirre: The Wrath of God* (1972).

CHAPTER 6: CABEZA DE VACA

Texts

There are several translations, usually of the 1555 version: try *Castaways*, trans. and ed. Enrique Pupo-Walker (1993); a new and authoritative edition of the 1542 version is promised under the editorship of Roleno Adorno. For a fictionalized biography, Morris Bishop *The Odyssey of Cabeza de Vaca* (1933). On Estevanico, John Upton Terrel *Estevanico the Black* (1968). On the journey and the archaeology of the Native American peoples encountered by the Spanish in Florida and the south-east, valuable information has been amassed by scholars of the later de Soto expedition: C. Hudson *Knights of the Sun* (1997); P. Galloway *The Hernando de Soto Expedition* (1997); J. T. Milanich and C. Hudson *Hernando de Soto and the Indians of Florida* (1993); L. Clayton, V. J. Knight and E. Moore *The De Soto Chronicles* (2 vols 1993). On the native societies of the Texas coast there is a truly vast amount of specialist work, so I will confine myself to what is relevant to the journey: the standard work is John R. Swanton *The Indians of the Southeastern United States* (1969 reprint). Donald Chipman 'In Search of Cabeza de Vaca's Route Across Texas', in *The Southwestern Historical Quarterly* 91, pages 127–48 (1987) is valuable; Alex Krieger's summary of his important but unpublished thesis is 'The Travels of Alvar Nunez Cabeza de Vaca', in *Homenaje a Pablo Martinez del Rio* (1984). On the Spanish impact: A. F. Ramenovsky *Vectors of Death: The Archaeology of European Contact* (1987); R. S. Weddle 'Spanish Exploration on the Texas Coast 1519–1800', in *The Bulletin of the Texas Archaeological Society* 63, pages 99–122.

EPILOGUE

On Las Casas and the issue of human rights and the conquest: a useful starting point is B. de Las Casas *A Short Account of Destruction of the Indies* (1542); on Vitoria: *Principles of Political and International Law in the Work of Francisco de Vitoria*, extracts trans. A. T. Serra (1946). Lewis Hanke *Aristotle and the American Indians* (1959), *The Spanish Struggle for Justice in the Conquest of America* (1949) and *All Mankind Is One* (1974); 'Bartolome de Las Casas' in J. Friede and B. Keen (eds) *History* (1971).

A Note on the Translations

A special acknowledgement is due to the translations used in my text. Quotations from the Florentine Codex are based on Anderson and Dibble; from Cortes's letters on Anthony Pagden; from Woman Poma on Christopher Dilke; from Cieza de Leon on Clements Markham and Noble David Cook; and from Cabeza de Vaca on Enrique Pupo-Walker. To all, my grateful thanks.

ACKNOWLEDGEMENTS

This book is the product of making a series of films for PBS in the USA and the BBC in the UK, so a lot more debts have been incurred than may first meet the eye. Film-making is a team effort, and this is never more apparent than when one is struggling up a glacier at 17,000 feet, rafting down the Amazon, or marooned on a forced march through the Peruvian jungle. The end result is the work not only of the film crew, but of the helpers on the ground, the back-up at base and everyone at home.

I would first like to thank David Wallace, who directed the films with his customary skill, touch and care; producer Rebecca Dobbs, who never lost her nerve (even when she had lost us!); Sally Thomas, Barbara Bouman, Kevin Rowan, John Cranmer and Chloe Sayer for their help starting us off. Once again Peter Harvey shot the films (and after all these years it is still a delight to view his rushes); the sound was by Judy Headman, Chris Duncan-Brown and Neil Lacock. Howard Davidson composed the memorable music used in the films. Chris Lysaght did the Herculean labour of assembling the films, and Gerry Branigan had the difficult task of taking over halfway through – and did a wonderful job. Thanks too to Lawrence Rees for his judicious and always helpful criticism.

Films rely on their local fixers, and we were very lucky to work with some of the best. Starting with Peru, Deborah McLauchlan organized our long shoots there with fantastic good humour, stamina and conscientiousness. On the road, my special thanks to Don Juvenal Cobos and all the Cobos family at Huancacalle for the trek to Espiritu Pampa, and to Raoul and Porphyrio our cooks and helpers; to Carlos Infante for his great company during the days in the forest, and for his expert translation in Quechua; Barry Walker for setting up things in Cuzco; Vince Lee for trekking advice; Pepe Valdivia our driver; Engineer Abraham Mayta Salcedo for his memories of Pumamarca; Jorge Flores Ochoa, who was most generous with his time and unrivalled knowledge in Cuzco; Julia and Teo Chambi; Don Miguel H. Milla; Peter Frost; Wolfgang Schuler; Gonzalo Pizarro; Wendy Weeks and her family for memorable days at L'Albergo in Ollantaytambo – one of the most delightful places in which one could hope to stay; Hieronimo and friends from Mawallani who helped us up to Qoyllur Riti with such good grace; Juan de Dios Garcia; Arturo Cervantes for showing us the modern traditions of

Pachacamac; thanks too to the staff of the Miramar Ischia, which became our home from home in Lima; to INC Peru, and to Peruvian Railways who were most kind in giving us special facilities. Among scholars, I am especially grateful to Efrain Trellis, Rafael Varon and Professor Maria Rostworoswki; to Ricardo Espinosa for sharing his great knowledge of Inca roads; to Juan Ossio for our memorable meeting in Copenhagen with the Waman Poma manuscript; and to Dr John Hemming for talking things over at the very start.

In Mexico my thanks to Wiggie and Chris Andrews and their family, and to Michel Antochiw in the Yucatan; Ray Sinatra and Anders Ehrnberg for their heroic efforts on our second shoot – unfazed by storms that wrecked our gear, flooded our tents and marooned our back-up vehicle, and unstinting in their energy, commitment and good humour. Thanks too to Eduardo Matos Moctezuma; Felipe Solis; INAH; the Museum of the City of Mexico; the Veracruz Film Board; Virginia Sinatra; Anastacio Ek; Dr Arellano Pina; Juan Alvarado at Villa Rica; Armando Chan; Olivia Priego; Geney Torruco; and to Felix Alvarado of the Mexico City Condores, who piloted us over the city; Admiral Miguel Carlos Carranza Castillo; Marta Turok; Margo Glantz; Soledad Ruiz; Amaro Izaguere and Luisa Cordova Colorado at Xico; our driver Arturo Espinosa; and the poet Natalio Hernandez for all his help and time, and for his moving readings of his own poems, and of the ancient Nahuatl laments.

In Ecuador Stephanie Stevens looked after us at the Café Cultura, our home from home in Quito, and facilitated our expeditions; Gyneer Coronel and his team made our time on the Coca and Napo rivers unforgettable; Alberto Vazquez-Figueroa, Ivan Cruz and Michel de Cabodeville gave us most valuable help and advice; John Collee for taking time out to be our doctor on the Coca and Napo, and for his always delightful company; Enrique Mora and Ariruma Kowi in Quito; Martin Burgoyne for a great tip; Luis Garcia in Coca; Nelson Tapui and family; Father Joaquin Garcia in Iquitos; Edith Huani Inuma, Luisa, Julio Chang and family and all at Francisco Orellana, that loveliest of places. In Brazil, Bob Nadkarni, Terese Aubreton, Manoel Moura Tukano and Dr Joao Ferraz from the National Institute of Amazon Research.

In the USA my thanks first to our colleague Leo Eaton for a very inspiring reconnaissance trip into the hidden Texas; to Nadia Voukitchevitch, who fixed for us in Florida; Captain Ken Nelson and his crew, and the US Coastguards; Chief Sonnie Billie for a memorable night recounting Seminole traditions: and Swamp Owl for taking me into the swamp. In Galveston Bob Moore and friends from the University of Texas; Sammy Ray for showing me how one might survive on oysters and 'swamp potatoes'; and Wendy Wilson for looking after us so well; at San Juan Father Balty, Ted Herrera, Isaac Cardenas and Ramon Vasquez. In Texas I must give special thanks to Don and Marilyn Olson and their team at the University of Austin who inspired and directed our journey into Northern Mexico, based on their detailed research with which they were unstintingly generous. Don also very kindly procured for me a copy of Alex Krieger's thesis on Cabeza de Vaca's route: for all, my grateful thanks. Connie Todd at Southwest Texas State University gave us access to the precious text of the 1555 edition; Ezequiel Aguero and Brooks Anderson took us to the 'mountain of iron' at Monclova; in Big Bend Lico and Linda Walker organized our trek into the desert of North Mexico and were terrific companions on it; Bob Malouf, University of Alpine, Texas, came along and his presence made our ride to San Carlos on the Great Comanche Trail all the more illuminating; Enrique Madrid for sharing his knowledge and wisdom; Bryant Holman for his great help and enthusiasm around La Junta (and onwards); the community and Mayor Victor Sotelas of Ojinaga; and our very helpful and knowledgeable driver Bacho Lopez; Skip McWilliams for our wonderful time in Copper Canyon; and the Tarahumara community, who allowed us to share their world for a short while, even though we no longer know how to 'walk straight'.

In Copenhagen my thanks to the staff of the Royal Library for allowing access to the Waman Poma manuscript. In Spain, Anthony Garton for advice and introductions; Carmen de Salas for giving up her house in Trujillo as a film crew base; Condesa Aline de Quintimilla for loaning us Pascualete for a day; and Suzy Polart, Trujillo's walking library on Francisco Pizarro! My thanks also to Stuart Stirling for a memorable trip to Estremadura, and for introducing me to his ancestor Mansio Serra de Leguizamon (see page 273).

My thanks also to Chris Weller, Sheila Ableman, Shirley Patton, Martha Caute, Barbara Nash, Linda Blakemore, Deirdre O'Day and Miriam Hyman for getting this book together in record time; to Lavinia Trevor and to Jim Cochrane; and to Kevin Sim for the gift of more than Miller's gripping book on Orellana.

At PBS Kathy Quattrone set the ball rolling; John Wilson and Sandy Heberer ran with it; Leo Eaton and Wendy Wolf were rocks, as usual; Frances Lee and the staff of Canning House library were unfailingly helpful; and David Drew gave generously of his expert advice and offered that special gift – the loan of books.

Last of all, my family have put up with my long absences with great forbearance and loving kindness: I cannot find words to express my debt to them. But perhaps I might end with a belated thanks to Professor George Huxley, who twenty years ago steered me towards the Las Casas–Sepulveda debate while I was contemplating a programme about Troy: 'You should do this one day, it would make great TV!' I hope it has done; it was certainly thrilling to make, and I hope some of that excitement has come over in these pages.

INDEX

Page numbers in italics refer to the photographs

PICTURE CREDITS

BBC Worldwide would like to thank the following for providing photographs and for permission to reproduce copyright material. While every effort has been made to trace and acknowledge copyright holders, we would like to apologize should there be any errors or omissions.

Page 1: Biblioteca Medicea-Laurenziana, Florence/Bridgeman Art Library; 2 Musée des Beaux Arts, Marseilles/Giraudon/Bridgeman Art Library; 3 MayaVision; 6 Biblioteca Nacional, Madrid/Bridgeman Art Library; 7 MayaVision; 8 The Art Archive; 9 Mary Evans Picture Library; 10 MayaVision; 14 Museum für Voelkerkunde,Vienna © Erich Lessing/Art Resource, New York; 18 Staatliche Kupferstichkabinett, Dresden/AKG London; 19 The British Library/The Art Archive; 23 MayaVision; 27 (above) Academia de San Fernando, Madrid/AKG London; 27 (below) Museo de America, Madrid/Bridgeman Art Library; 30 MayaVision; 31 Biblioteca Nacional, Madrid/Bridgeman Art Library; 32 & 35 Biblioteca Medicea-Laurenziana, Florence/Bridgeman Art Library; 39 Museo degli Argenti, Florence/Bridgeman Art Library; 42 Biblioteca Nazionale, Florence/SCALA; 43 National Museum of Anthropology, Mexico/Werner Forman Archive; 46 Biblioteca Medicea-Laurenziana, Florence/Bridgeman Art Library; 47 Museo de America, Madrid/AKG London; 50 & 51 MayaVision; 54 Museo de America, Madrid/AKG London; 55 Museo de America, Madrid/ Bridgeman Art Library; 58–9 Schalkwijk/Art Resource, New York; 66 Biblioteca Medicea-Laurenziana, Florence/The Art Archive; 67 British Embassy, Mexico City/Bridgeman Art Library; 70 Biblioteca Nacional, Madrid/Giraudon/Art Resource; 71 South African National Gallery, Capetown/Bridgeman Art Library; 74 The Art Archive; 75 Museo de America, Madrid/Bridgeman Art Library; 78 National Museum of Anthropology, Mexico City/Werner Forman Archive; 81 Biblioteca Medicea-Laurenziana, Florence/AKG London; 83 AKG London; 87 The Art Archive/Mireille Vautier; 90 MayaVision; 91 The Art Archive/Private Collection; 94 Bibliothèque Nationale, Paris; 95 MayaVision; 98 The Art Archive/Private Collection; 103 Biblioteca Medicea-Laurenziana, Florence/Bridgeman Art Library; 102 Museo Nacional de Historia, Castillo de Chapultepec, Mexico City/Giraudon/Art Resource; 104 MayaVision; 106 The Art Archive; 110 The Hispanic Society of America, New York; 111 AKG London; 115 Museo de la Casa de la Moneda, Potosi © Gilles Mermet/AKG; 118 South American Pictures © Kathy Jarvis; 130–1 MayaVision; 134 Pedro de Osma Museum, Lima/The Art Archive; 135 Christie's Images/Bridgeman Art Library; 139 (above) MayaVision; 139 (below) & 142 Bruning Museum, Lambayeque, Peru/The Art Archive; 144 MayaVision; 146 Robert Harding Picture Library © Christopher Rennie; 147 The British Library/AKG London; 150–1 MayaVision; 154 Photosearchers Inc., New York © François Gohier; 156 from: Felipe Guaman Pomo de Ayala Nueva Corónica y Buen Gobierno Institut d'Ethnographie, Musée de l'Homme, Palais de Chaillot, Paris, p.398; 158–9 © Loren McIntyre; 162 Photosearchers Inc., New York © N.H. (Dan) Cheatham; 163,166, 170–1, 174, 175, 178, 182, 183 MayaVision; 186 Museo de America, Madrid/Bridgeman Art Library; 190 The Art Archive; 191 South American Pictures © Tony Morrison; 194 Staatliche Kupferstichkabinett, Dresden/AKG; 198 MayaVision; 199 Towner Art Gallery, Eastbourne/ Bridgeman Art Library; 202, 203, 205, 207, MayaVision; 215 Bridgeman Art Library/Private Collection; 219 MayaVision; 222–3 Magnum © Bruno Barbey; 226 MayaVision; 227 National Museet, Copenhagen/Bridgeman Art Library; 230 AKG London; 233 arxiu fotogràfic, Institut Amattler d'Art Hispanic, Barcelona; 234 MayaVision; 242 Bruce Coleman Inc., New York © M.P.L. Fogden; 246 Bruce Coleman Inc., New York © Drew Thate; 247, 250, 254, 255, 258, 259, MayaVision; 262 © The British Library; 266 Musée des Beaux Arts, Marseilles/Giraudon/Bridgeman Art Library; 270 Museo de America, Madrid © Joseph Martin/AKG London; 273 AKG London.

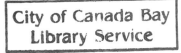